Best Blackjack

Frank Scoblete

Bonus Books, Inc., Chicago

06 05 04 03 02   5   4

Library of Congress Cataloging-in-Publication Data

Scoblete, Frank.
      Best blackjack / Frank Scoblete.
          p.   cm.
      Includes index.
      ISBN 1-56625-057-9 (paper)
      1. Blackjack (Game)   I. Title.
    GV1295.B55S36   1996
    795.4'2—dc20   96-10964

Bonus Books, Inc.
160 East Illinois Street
Chicago, Illinois 60611

Composition by Focus Graphics, St. Louis, Missouri

Printed in the United States of America

This book is dedicated to

Larry Gelbart,
for his encouragement

and
to my good friends

Barry Kissane and Catherine Poe

Contents

"They laugh that win!"

—William Shakespeare, *Othello*

Author's Apologia

The first draft of this book was grammatically and politically correct. I was using the construction "he/she" like there was no tomorrow—in honor of my good friend and feminist writer, Catherine Poe, who was one of the first writers in the country to use the construction. Then I reread the manuscript. It sounded awkward and silly—sorry, Cathy—so I dumped it. Then I went to "their" but my wife, the beautiful A.P., said: "You can't use a singular construction with a plural pronoun." Then I changed all the constructions to plurals. That sounded as dumb as "he/she." So I have reverted to the generic "he" when talking about dealers and players in the singular. Whenever possible, I've kept the plurals and when dealers in the anecdotes are women I've kept them women, even if I don't name them. Fully half of the dealers and players in blackjack are women.

I also have another reason for using the generic "he"—and that is my upbringing. It took me many years to learn how to get a sentence down on a page, a sentence that made sense. My first and toughest teacher was Sister Patricia Michael of the Sisters of Charity and she was quite put out of charity whenever I used "improper English." She pounded this into our heads: "Whenever you talk about 'man'—it means man and woman. Thus, use 'he.' For 'H' represents heaven and 'E' represents earth and man's body came from the dirt of earth and his soul is made in the image of God who is in heaven." It took me a long time to learn that lesson but, having learned it, it's hard to give it up. So my women readers—indulge me.

Acknowledgements

This book was a labor of love, as blackjack is my favorite game and is undoubtably the game that I play the most. To realize this book I had the help of a host of players, researchers and sources. Many people did not want public recognition of their efforts—so I thank them now, generically.

For the rest, thank you blackjack players and experts: Bill and Billie, Gene and Jennifer, K.F., C.K., C.F., Jack Harkness, Ray Scott, David D., Brian, Phil, John F. and Lorraine Julian, Mr. Yueh, Alan Tinker, Gerard E., Dr. James Wallace and Michelle Finbar-Wallace.

Thanks also to my intrepid researchers: Howard T. Mann, Alene Paone (my beautiful A.P.—"the artist's wife"), and Dr. James Schneider, my computer expert.

To Linda Gerard and to June!

Thanks to: Albert Ross, Walter Null, and William Decker, my agents. And to Annette St. John and Dave Satkowski.

Also to Rudi Schiffer, the publisher of *Good Times Magazine* and the host of *The Good Times' Hour*—thanks for your loyalty and enthusiastic support and for giving me a great forum in print and on the air in Memphis.

To Howard Schwartz at the *Gambler's Book Club* in Las Vegas—for everything as always. And to all the people at Paone Press: Don, Peg, Gloria, John, Al, David, Abigail, Greg and Mike.

I would also like to thank all the great blackjack experts and players, both quick and dead, whose works, insights, and adventures have inspired me. They are truly giants. I stand on their shoulders to view the blackjack kingdom.

And, as always, a special thanks to the Captain, who started me thinking about gambling in a serious way. For everything, Captain, here's looking at you, kid!

Prologue

Like Gaul, this book can be divided into three parts. For beginners, there are complete sections on how the game is played and the basic strategies to employ for single- or multiple-deck games. Once you've conquered that, your second step is card counting. Finally, for those of you who know the basic strategies and count cards, there is a wealth of information concerning aspects of blackjack play not usually found in most books—some tricks that can make the casinos give you treats, interviews with the great players and the like.

The fact of the matter is that there is so much blackjack information out there in the world of print that players often don't know what is important. They try to learn *everything* right away. They confuse knowing everything about blackjack with being able to know how to beat the game. Is there some BIG secret in the blackjack world that I will reveal in this book? Yes. I'll reveal it right now. This is 90 percent of the game. Learn this secret and you'll be a winning player. Here it is: play good games, count cards accurately, and get as much money as you can afford to (and as the casino will let you) onto the table when the game favors you (i.e., bet bigger!). That's the BIG secret. All other considerations are secondary such as strategy changes, arcane questions about the effects of certain card removals, types of shuffles, new options of play and so on. Except for the BIG secret (play good games, count accurately and get the money out when the game favors you) everything else about blackjack (that is 99 percent of all the written information) deals with stuff that isn't all that important to winning money at this game.

Best Blackjack will explain how to get the money out and which games to play. It will give you a great card-counting system (easy to use and accurate) that will allow you to find those times when you should get the money on the table. *Best Blackjack* will also show you how to get the money on the table without drawing too much attention to yourself—something you must learn to do if you want a long blackjack-playing career.

And like Caesar, if you conquer all the material relating to basic strategies, card counting, and the tricks of the trade, you are on your way to becoming a king or queen of the blackjack tables. However, to become such a monarch, you must not only conquer the technicalities of expert blackjack play; you must conquer yourself. This last is the most difficult thing a player has to do. To play winning blackjack requires a certain amount of control over yourself as well as control over the games you choose to play. To be a success at blackjack requires the mastering of the externals of the game (strategies, counting systems, game evaluation, etc.) and the internals of the game (your emotions and emotional expectations). But isn't that true of any successful enterprise?

Wherever possible, I have used the voices of blackjack experts to speak to my readers. I have spoken to dozens of gifted card counters. Some of these experts are recreational players who play blackjack for the fun, the challenge and the profit. Others are professionals whose incomes are wholly or in part derived from playing this game. I have asked them to share their ideas and experiences with me. I have also spoken to recreational players who don't count cards but play basic strategies, thereby cutting the casino edge to less than .60 percent.

As I have done with all my books, I have tried to give blackjack a human face. Thus, wherever possible, I've let the people speak—both good players and bad—so that you can make the acquaintance of the citizens of this blackjack kingdom. But my intentions for you are greater than just citizenry. I want you to rule in the blackjack kingdom. To do that you must play the *best* blackjack.

Chapter One
The Truth about Blackjack

In my book, *Guerrilla Gambling: How to Beat the Casinos at Their Own Games* (Bonus Books), I wrote an introduction to the blackjack section which, having reread it, says quite a bit of what I want to say as far as preliminary remarks go. So I'm lifting some of it for part of my introduction here. Since I wrote it to begin with, I don't feel any qualms about adding or subtracting a thing or two here or there. So here goes.

Without question, the most popular casino game is blackjack. It is also the most written about, debated, and analyzed game offered by the casinos. It has the greatest number of experts playing it—and an even greater number of idiots. It is a game made for the computer buffs and mathematicians because, unlike most casino games, blackjack is dynamic—the true odds of the game are constantly shifting from moment to moment and from hand to hand.

At any given moment, the player may have an edge; the next moment, the casino will have it. Because of this dynamism, proper blackjack play, that is basic strategy and card counting, can theoretically result in a slight overall, long-run advantage for the player. It is the possibility of gaining this slight advantage that has caused a cottage industry of books, newsletters, and scholarly conferences to spring up in the past 30 years. It has also caused quite a few people, who have no business playing the game, to saunter to tables and face casino edges in the double digits owing to their poor and uninformed play.

Unlike casino games such as craps and roulette, which are independent trial games, where past events have no influence over future events; blackjack is a dependent trial game because what just happened (ie., what cards were played) will influence what is about to happen (what cards are left to be played). For this reason, expert players can take advantage of such knowledge to gain a theoretical edge over the game. How does that work? Here's an example: if all four aces have been played in a single-deck game (an honest game, of course), there won't be any blackjacks on the next round. You can bet your life on it!

Blackjack Myths

Unfortunately, there are quite a few myths about blackjack that should be laid to rest before venturing any further. These myths have been promulgated by both the casinos and some writers of gaming books.

Myth # 1: All blackjack players have an edge over the casino and can win in the long run.

Sorry. Most blackjack players are so poorly prepared for their *sorties* into casinoland that blackjack makes more money for the casinos than any other table game. Stupid players think that they can beat the game because they have heard or read somewhere that brilliant players have done so. So they play and lose, lose, lose. Brilliant players, on the other hand, never tire of warning neophytes to be careful and not expect too much too soon, that blackjack is a roller coaster. Indeed, blackjack is a roller coaster even if you have an edge because during any stretch of time (a session, a day, a week, a month or more) luck can be the key variable in determining your fate at the tables. What's more, in an informal survey I took for this book during my last six months of play, I found that most players had not read a single book on the subject of blackjack. How can they hope to win when they don't really know how to play?

Myth #2: If a player learns the proper basic strategy for playing the hands, he will win in the long run. (Note: Basic strategies have been developed by computers for the playing of each hand you receive against the dealer's up card. These basic strategies are considered the optimal way to play each hand in the long run.)

Not so. The basic strategy for both single- and multiple-deck blackjack games cannot give you an edge over the casino (except in rare single-deck games with extraordinary rules where the player might have a .10 percent edge off the top). At best, you can play even or almost even in a single-deck game, and face a .35 percent to .61 percent house edge in multiple-deck games, depending on the number of decks and the rules. Basic strategy is the best way to play, except for card counting, but it can't give you a long-range advantage over the casinos. Basic strategy can only make you a tough player, a good player, and a non-sucker. A good basic-strategy player can even get the best of it, if he includes comps in his figuring, but it's unlikely playing basic strategy alone will give him an edge.

Myth #3: Card counting guarantees that in the long run I will be a winner at blackjack and make a fortune in the bargain.

This is the myth that causes the most misery for unwary and uninformed would-be card counters. Card counting can give you a theoretical edge over *certain* blackjack games in the long run. However, card counting cannot give you an edge over *every* blackjack game. So many other factors have to be considered *in addition to the skill of the player* when establishing the beatability of a blackjack game. These I shall go into later on in the book but suffice it to say that just because you learn how to count cards, and can do so proficiently, is not a guarantee that you will beat all of the casinos all of the time in the long run. Indeed, more card counters have gone broke faster than have basic-strategy players because card counting calls for tremendous escalation of bets in certain situations and this causes wild swings in a player's bankroll. An under-financed card counter is courting economic disaster.

As far as getting rich from playing blackjack is concerned, this is another myth that has been propounded over and over by some of my fellow gambling writers and particularly by systems sellers. You've seen the advertisements in newspapers and magazines: "Win $1000 a Day or More Playing Blackjack!" "How to Win Thousands an Hour at Blackjack!" "Secret to Winning Millions at Blackjack Revealed!" "You Can Become Rich Playing Blackjack!" These advertisements are bogus for several reasons, not the least of which is that casinos *won't let you get rich playing blackjack!*

Truthfully, I know of no one who has *gotten* rich from playing blackjack. I know individuals who have won large sums of money over their blackjack playing careers—especially people involved in team play (see chapter 15). These individuals, however, started with large sums of money. A great card counter wins in proportion to the bets he can afford to make over an extended period of time, and the fluctuation he is willing to experience in his bankroll without getting a heart attack. There are no five-dollar blackjack bettors who become million-aires solely from playing blackjack. In fact, there are very few blackjack professionals who actually make good livings from playing. For most experts, writing about playing is more profitable than actually playing. This is as true for me as for anyone else. Writing this book, though nowhere near as exciting as, say, doubling on an 11 versus a dealer's 10 in a high count, is nevertheless a more economically rewarding experience because over time this book will keep paying me royalties. I can only win money at blackjack when I'm playing blackjack.

Why can't you take your skill and go into those casinos and make thousands a day—as some of the systems sellers claim?

First, most of the casinos tend to look with disfavor on card counters and will readily ban anyone who is the least threat, be it real or imagined, to the casino's bankroll. Second, anyone betting big money is watched closely and, if he is considered a good player, the casinos will take measures against him. Even in states where the banning of card counters is illegal, such as New Jersey, the casinos simply use more decks, cut more cards out of play, stop mid-shoe entry, and limit the kinds of bets that can be made in games where mid-shoe entry is allowed. When all else fails—the casinos simply shuffle the cards when they think an individual player is betting big enough and is expert enough to take advantage of a given situation to the casino's detriment. Casinos in Atlantic City, a town that offers mediocre games at best, are occasionally so paranoid about card counters that they go to incredible lengths in their attempts to protect their games, including the arrest and prosecution of some card counters as "undesirables" (see chapter 16). Big money brings big scrutiny and the longer you play big money, the more you'll win and the greater your chances for detection and counter attack.

So card counting is not an absolute road to riches. But it is the road to winning. It is the necessary technique for players who wish to spend a significant amount of time at the blackjack tables with some confidence that they can take the laurels of victory from the casino in the long run.

How much can you actually win over the course of time? According to blackjack author Stanford Wong in a letter written for the November 1995 issue of *Blackjack Confidential Magazine,* in a blackjack-playing career spanning 16 years, he won a total of $300,000. That's an average of $18,750 per year. Not bad for a hobby, but not great for a profession. However, I'm sure Mr. Wong had many other sources of income when he was winning that $300,000. So, if you have a regular job and you want to add some nice spending money to it, then blackjack could be just the right bet.

And the good news is this. If you know the right games to play and the right techniques to employ while playing them, you can (and probably will) win at blackjack in the long run. You won't be able to quit work or lounge around a pool all day in friendly casinoland but you will be able to get the edge. With this edge you should be able to win in the long run if you satisfy two conditions. The first is that you must have a big enough bankroll to sustain long losing periods. The second is that you must play perfectly. Unlike most other casino games, the mathematics of blackjack will favor the card counter who plays good games and has enough money to weather the inevitable storms of bad luck. But it only favors you a little. The slightest mistake here or there is usually enough to reduce your edge over the casino to nil.

A word of caution is also advised here. Many people, especially those who are somewhat dissatisfied with their jobs or lot in life, also the young (particularly young men) look to blackjack as a glamorous way to chuck it all and start anew. They envision themselves as going to Las Vegas, making their fortune at the tables, and living the good life—perhaps being served grapes at pool side by buxom belles in skimpy outfits (as a male I regrettably write the male version of fantasies most of the time—so if you are a woman reading this, just substitute the woman's fantasy version of the good life). It isn't that way at all. The more you play in the casinos, the more you realize it isn't all that glamorous a lifestyle. As recreation, it is fun and exciting. As a job, frankly, it stinks. Playing every day for a living is dull and boring. It is also nerve-wracking.

P.K., a professional player of some stature in the eyes of other professionals, told me this:

> Being a professional player was exciting when I was young and before the casinos got to know me. Now, it's causing me ulcers. I don't live the good life and I barely make ends meet. I dropped out of high school and came to Vegas after a stint in the military. I was going to be rich playing blackjack. It never happened. The total amount of money I've made at blackjack is impressive—if you don't have to live on it. The total amount of money a mailman makes in twenty years is impressive, too. Except you have to live on that money so it isn't sitting there in one lump so it can impress everyone. If I had to do it all over again, I would have had a regular career and played blackjack on the side for a little extra cash and a lot of extra excitement.

Most professional blackjack players scratch out a living in the shadows. Since they can't bet big for fear of being banned, they bet small. I know one blackjack player who was so good, he was only allowed to play in the casinos with the worst games! No other casino would let him in. That's the equivalent of a Michael Jordan being asked to wear 20-pound ankle weights when he was playing. No matter how good a player is, he can't overcome the disadvantage of such a handicap—in the professional card counter's case the handicap is being asked to leave good games or having to keep bets at the lower range in order to be allowed to play.

My advice to you is to do as I do and as I say. Enjoy the challenge and thrill of playing the best blackjack, enjoy the possibility of extra money, but don't quit your day job. As recreation and as a challenge, as a sport, or hobby, blackjack is a fun thing. As a career, it leaves a lot to be desired.

Why Best Blackjack?

If you are already successfully counting cards and you're a winning player, you'll probably only read this book for its color and its insider tips. There are no earth-shaking mathematical revelations contained herein, although there are some interesting deviations to be found. I know some tricks that I'll share with you and these can help even the best players become better.

I don't intend to fill the pages of *Best Blackjack* with charts and arcane discussions of situations that rarely occur at the tables. There are several great blackjack newsletters and books that really handle the "how many angels can dance on the head of a double down" situation for those who wish to pursue the outer limits of the blackjack universe. *Best Blackjack* is a reader-friendly book. In chapter 23, I'll make some recommendations for further reading if you are so inclined.

If you have never played blackjack before or if you have been playing the "I have my own strategy" strategy or if you have been dissatisfied with the one or few blackjack books you have read in the past, this book is especially for you.

If you master the concepts in *Best Blackjack*, you will be a winning blackjack player. Can you master them? Absolutely. I did. I'm not a genius. I'm not a mathematician and I have a lousy memory. But I've been playing winning blackjack for years and years and years.

To become a winning player only takes effort and desire and the knowledge of which games to play (and how to play them) and which games to avoid. To win in the long run at blackjack, you must learn basic strategy and then how to count cards. That's a given. That's the BIG secret that I revealed in the prologue. But there is also a lot to learn besides that, including what things not to bother with. It is in the "besides that" area that I think this book will set itself apart from the other blackjack books that have been written thus far. There are a lot of little secrets to attach to the BIG secret that will go a long way to making you a great player.

Chapter Two
How the Game is Played

Blackjack Layout

The traditional blackjack table has six or seven spots for players to place their wagers. This particular diagram shows a six-spot table. On rare occasions, you can find blackjack layouts that contain only five betting spots.

DEALER

Blackjack pays 3 to 2
Dealer must draw to 16, and stand on all 17's

PAYS 2 TO 1

INSURANCE

PAYS 2 TO 1

Soft Hands and Hard Hands

Blackjack appears to be a simple game and, indeed, its structure is quite easy to follow. All the cards have their face value. An eight equals an eight, a two equals a two, and so forth. All picture cards equal 10 as does, naturally, a 10. An ace equals either an 11 or a one. It is up to the player to decide how he is using the ace. Hands with an ace as one of the first two cards are called *soft hands*. Hands without an ace as one of the first two cards are called *hard hands*.

Objective

The objective of a blackjack game is to beat the dealer. Do not be fooled by casino brochures, usually found in your hotel room, that say that the object of the game is to get as close to 21 as you can without going over (busting).

Here are two examples of the kind of "misinformation" that casinos dispense in the guise of helping novice blackjack players. The first comes from Atlantic City's Claridge Casino Hotel's *Gaming Guide;* the second comes from Mississippi's Isle of Capri Casino's gaming guide, *How to Play the Isle.*

According to the Claridge's guide: "In Blackjack, the object is to draw cards that total 21, or closer to 21 than the Dealer's cards." The brochure then goes on to discuss the value of the cards and the various options the player has including hitting, "until you total 21 or come as close to 21 as possible. But, if you go over 21, you 'bust' and automatically lose your bet." It is not until the third to last paragraph that the brochure informs the would-be player that the dealer can "bust" and "you win even money" if he does so.

The Claridge brochure is not terribly misleading, just somewhat hazy on the real details of blackjack's objective. How close to 21 must a player get? Could a player opt not to take any cards, even though his hand is quite far away from the magical 21? The Claridge leaves the novice with the "sense" that one should at least *try* to get close to 21.

The Isle of Capri's guide goes all out to obfuscate the objective while being objectively truthful. After telling us how popular blackjack is, the brochure states: "The object of this game is to have your cards total 21 or as close to 21 as possible without exceeding it." Then the brochure discusses procedures before coming to this lazy, hazy sentence: "Once you have your two cards and *feel* [italics mine] you need additional cards to beat the dealer, you gesture for additional cards (called 'hits') until you decide to stand." In a single sentence, the brochure tells us that it is possible to beat a dealer who busts, without actually using that "bust" word: "If a dealer's point total exceeds 21, all players win who have a total of 21 or less."

Now, the Isle of Capri is not lying in its brochure so much as planting a seed in the minds of the reader that 21 is a laudable goal and one that should be attempted. In truth, this is not always the case. So let me repeat: *The objective of a blackjack game is to beat the dealer.* This can be done in one of two ways. You can beat the dealer because you have a better hand that is 21 or under, or you can beat the dealer because *he* has gone over 21 and *busted.* On many hands you will not even attempt to get "close to 21"—in fact, you'll often stand on hands that are as far away from 21 as you can get!

If either the player or the dealer has an ace and a 10-value card as his first two cards, this is called a blackjack or *natural* and is usually paid off at three to two for the player. If the dealer has a blackjack and the player has a blackjack, the hand is a standoff or *push* and nobody wins. In fact, any time the dealer and the player have the same valued hand it is a *push.* Never play in a blackjack game where the dealer wins the pushes, unless it is a face-up or double exposure game, the strategy for which is quite different than for regular blackjack.

Procedure

Blackjack tables generally seat six or seven players. Each player places a bet in the betting area in front of him. After the shuffle the dealer will ask a player to cut the deck. After the player has done so, the dealer will take the top card and place it in the discard rack. This card is called the *burn card* and the procedure itself is called *burning a card.* Some casinos have slightly different rules concerning cutting cards and burning cards. In many games using the shuffle machines, the players will not cut the cards. In some casinos, the player may ask to see what the burn card is. In others, this is not allowed. In some casinos, the ones that are paranoid about card counters, the dealer will burn several cards and sometimes even burn cards during the actual rounds of play.

When the shuffle and burning of cards is completed, the dealer deals each player two cards. In single-deck games, the cards are dealt face down to the players from a hand-held deck. In multiple-deck games, the cards are usually dealt face up from a shoe, which is a box that contains cards. The dealer also deals himself two cards, one face up and one face down. All your playing decisions will be based on the face-up card of the dealer.

Once the player is dealt his first two cards, he must decide whether to ask the dealer to *hit* him, that is, give him another card; or, he must indicate that he is content with his first two cards and will *stand*. In games where players get to hold their cards (usually single- and double-deck), you indicate you want another card by lightly scratching your cards along the felt. When you wish to stand, you slip your cards face down under your chips. In games where the cards are dealt face up (usually shoe games of four, six and eight decks) you must use hand signals to indicate your desire because you aren't allowed to touch the cards. If you want to hit a hand, you point or tap the table. If you wish to stand, you wave your hand palm down over the cards to let the dealer know "no cards."

The player can also decide to do any of the following with his first two cards:

Splitting Pairs

If he has a pair of the same number, the player can *split* them and make each card the first card of a new hand. The dealer will then deal him a second card on the first hand and the player will play out that hand. When he is finished, the dealer will deal him a second card on the second hand and the player will play out that one. In hand-held games, the player will place his cards down and put up the extra money for the split. In games where the cards are dealt face up, the player will put out the extra money and say "split them." The dealer will then split the cards.

Doubling Down

The player can *double down* on his first two cards (when allowed). This means that the player is placing a bet equal to or less than his initial bet and will now receive only one card. In hand-held games, the player will put his hand down face up and place a bet equal to or less than his original bet and say, "Double" or "Double for less." In games dealt face up, the player will put a bet that is equal to or less than his original and also say, "Double" or "Double for less."

Surrender

In some casinos, the player can *surrender* his hand. That means he gives up playing the hand in exchange for losing only half his bet. In hand-held games, you turn over your cards and say, "Surrender." In face-up games, you simply say: "Surrender." Surrender is a good option when used properly. There are two types of surrender, late surrender and early surrender (see chapter four).

Insurance

The player can *insure* his hand against a dealer's face-up ace. He would put out a bet that can be as much as half his original bet in the area of the layout marked *insurance*. The insurance bet pays two to one. This bet is a side bet where the player who is insuring is wagering that the dealer indeed has a blackjack—thus, the dealer has a 10 in the hole with the ace on top. This is a very poor bet and should never be made, unless the player is counting cards and has a reasonable assurance that the 10 is underneath.

If the player should bust his hand (go over 21), the dealer will immediately remove both the player's bet and his cards. If the dealer should subsequently bust, the player who has busted first still loses. This is the casino's biggest edge—the player must play his hand first and if he busts, regardless of what the dealer eventually does, the player loses.

Once all the players have played their hands, the dealer plays his. However, the dealer does not have any individual discretion in the playing of the hands but must play according to a prearranged set of rules. These rules are usually posted at the table for everyone to see and there is very little variation from casino to casino. The dealer must hit all hands that total 16 or less, and stand on all hands that total 17 or more. The only area where casinos differ in the application of these rules concerns the soft hand of 17 (ace + six). Some casinos have their dealers stand on soft 17. Some casinos have their dealers hit a soft 17. It is to the player's advantage if the casino's rule is to stand on a soft 17.

When the dealer has finished playing his hand, he pays off the winners and takes the bets from the losers who didn't bust beforehand.

Simple? Quite. Yet, there are many rules variations within the structure of blackjack that can make the game more or less favorable for the players. These I shall discuss in chapter four.

Chapter Three
Basic Strategy

Knowing how the game of blackjack is played is not the same as knowing how to play the game. For every set of rules, there are distinct computer-tested basic strategies designed to optimize one's chances of winning. This does not mean that you have to memorize dozens of basic strategies since the overwhelming majority of decisions that you will have to make are the same in all strategies. However, basic strategy has two major categories—single-deck and multiple-deck—and if you intend to play blackjack, you must decide which strategy to memorize. Those of you who decide to play single- *and* multiple-deck games should seriously consider first mastering one and then mastering the other.

The best way to decide which one to memorize (or which to memorize first) is to check out the casinos in which you intend to play. If you are going to be a regular in Atlantic City, then you should memorize the multiple-deck basic strategy since all the blackjack games in Atlantic City are of this variety. If you are going to play in Las Vegas or Mississippi, you should memorize the single-deck strategy first because Las Vegas and Mississippi have quite a number of casinos offering single-deck games. Would it hurt a Las Vegas player to use a single-deck strategy against a multiple-deck game or vice versa? Only marginally, since the strategies usually differ most on hands that don't occur with great regularity. But if you want to be the best player that you can be, you should know both strategies. In the war against the casinos, it's best to be fully armed.

At first it might seem a daunting task, memorizing the several pages of material that are coming up, but don't let that stop you. In fact, if you spread your learning out over several weeks, doing a little at a time, you will readily assimilate the basic strategy you've selected. Once you've learned it thoroughly, every so often review it. After awhile, especially if you play once a month or more, you'll discover that basic strategy has become a solid part of your memory and will need very little refresher work to stay fixed.

A friendly caution is hereby given—don't play blackjack without learning a basic strategy because players who trust their own instincts and ideas are giving the casino a monumental edge. You are better off skipping the game of blackjack altogether and playing one of the other, less complex casino games, than playing improperly at blackjack. The casinos make a fortune from poor blackjack players. Do not join their company.

Since there are more multiple-deck games in the world than single-deck games, I have decided to give the multiple-deck basic strategy first. The left hand column will contain the player's hand; the right hand column will contain the decision you should make based on the dealer's up card. How many cards compose a given hand is essentially irrelevant except for splitting or doubling down purposes. For example, if you have a nine composed of two cards—a four and a five, or a three and a six, etc.—you would double down against any dealer up card of three through six. If you had a nine composed of three cards—say, a four, two and three—you would hit until you had 12 (or more) and then follow the basic strategy for that hand. Thus, if the dealer is showing a six and you have three cards that total nine, you would hit. If you received a four, you would now have 13. The basic strategy calls for standing with a 13 against a dealer's up card of six. Any hand which is 11 or under, no matter how many cards compose it, hit until you reach 12 (or more) and then follow the basic strategy for that hand. You never hit hard hands of 17 or more against anything. Players who hit hard 17 will bust 70 percent of the time.

If you have played blackjack before, but you haven't employed a basic strategy, some of these moves will seem strange. For example, many players blanch at hitting a hand of 12 against the dealer's two or three. Many players cringe when having to split a hand of 8:8 against a dealer's 10. Many of these moves do seem almost suicidal but in fact they are the proper strategies. Remember that millions of hands have been generated by computer to establish these basic strategy rules. And many of these rules are designed *to lose you less* in bad situations [see chapter seven]. Also, keep in mind that all soft hands become hard hands when the ace can no longer be used as an 11.

Basic Strategy for Multiple-Deck Games

Player's Hard Hand	Decision Based on Dealer's Up Card
8	Hit against everything.
9	Double against 3 through 6. Hit against everything else.
10	Double on 2 through 9. Hit on 10 and ace.
11	Double on 2 through 10. Hit on ace.
12	Hit against 2 and 3. Stand against 4, 5, 6. Hit against 7 through ace.
13	Stand against 2 through 6. Hit against all else.
14	Stand against 2 through 6. Hit against all else.
15	Stand against 2 through 6. Hit against all else.
16	Stand against 2 through 6. Hit against all else.

(*If surrender is allowed, you will surrender a hand of 15 against a dealer's 10. You will surrender a 16 against a dealer's 9, 10 or ace.*)

17, 18, 19, 20, 21 . . . . Stand against everything.

Player's Soft Hand   Decision Based on Dealer's Up Card

A:2 .... Double against 5 and 6.
Hit against all else.

A:3 .... Double against 5 and 6.
Hit against all else.

A:4 .... Double against 4, 5, 6.
Hit against all else.

A:5 .... Double against 4, 5, 6.
Hit against all else.

A:6 .... Double against 3, 4, 5, 6.
Hit against all else.

A:7 .... Double against 3, 4, 5, 6.
Stand on 2, 7, 8, ace.
Hit against 9 and 10.

A:8, A:9 .... Stand against everything.

Player's Pair   Decision Based on Dealer's Up Card

A:A .... Split against everything.

2:2 .... Split against 2 through 7.
Hit against all else.

3:3 .... Split against 2 through 7.
Hit against all else.

4:4 .... Split against 5 and 6.*
Hit against all else.

If doubling after splits is allowed, otherwise hit.

5:5 .... Double 2 through 9.
Hit against all else.

6:6 .... Split against 2 through 6.
Hit against all else.

7:7 .... Split against 2 through 7.
Hit against all else.

8:8 .... Split against everything.

(If surrender is allowed, surrender 8:8 against a dealer's 10.)

9:9 .... Split 2 through 6; 8 and 9.
Stand against 7, 10, and ace.

10:10 .... Stand against everything.

If you are playing multiple-deck games, the overwhelming majority of casinos will allow you to double down after splitting pairs. For example, if you have 2:2 and the dealer is showing a five, you would split your twos. Now, the dealer deals you a nine on the first two. You have 11. You would double down your 11 in this situation. The rule of thumb is to treat either half of a split the way you would a regular hand and follow the basic strategy tables as indicated. Some casinos will allow you to resplit pairs up to four times. Thus, if you received a 2:2 and split and received another two, you would resplit and so forth. If the casino has not posted whether or not you can double after splits or resplit pairs, don't hesitate to ask. These options are favorable to the player, and the player should take advantage of them.

Basic Strategy for Single-Deck Games

The single-deck game is the best game for the blackjack player to play, especially if the rules are liberal when it comes to doubling down and splitting. If you have the option of playing single- or multiple-deck games, you would be foolish to choose the latter (all other things such as penetration percentage, rules, etc. being equal). A single deck offers so many more opportunities for the basic-strategy player and the card counter alike.

Player's Hard Hand	Decision Based on Dealer's Up Card
8	Double against a 5 and 6. Hit against all else.
9	Double against 2 through 6. Hit against all else.
10	Double against 2 through 9. Hit against all else.
11	Double against everything.
12	Hit against 2 and 3. Stand against 4, 5, 6. Hit against all else.
13	Stand against 2 through 6. Hit against all else.

14 ....Stand against 2 through 6.
                                      Hit against all else.
15 ....Stand against 2 through 6.
                                      Hit against all else.
16 ....Stand against 2 through 6.
                                      Hit against all else.

(If surrender is allowed, surrender a 15 or 16 against a dealer's 10.)

17, 18, 19, 20, 21 ....Stand against everything.

Player's Soft Hands   Decision Based on Dealer's Up Card

A:2 ....Double against 4, 5, 6.
                                      Hit against all else.
A:3 ....Double against 4, 5, 6.
                                      Hit against all else.
A:4 ....Double against 4, 5, 6.
                                      Hit against all else.
A:5 ....Double against 4, 5, 6.
                                      Hit against all else.
A:6 ....Double against 2 through 6.
                                      Hit against all else.
A:7 ....Double against 3 through 6.
                                      Hit against 9 and 10.
                                      Stand against 2, 7, 8, ace.
A:8 ....Double against a 6.
                                      Stand against all else.
A:9 ....Stand against everything.

Player's Pair   Decision Based on Dealer's Up Card

A:A ....Split against everything.
2:2 ....Split against 3 through 7.
                                      Hit against all else.
3:3 ....Split against 4, 5, 6, 7.
                                      Hit against all else.
4:4 ....Double against 5 and 6.
                                      Hit against all else.

(If doubling after splits allowed, split against 5 or 6.)

5:5 ....Double against 2 through 9.
Hit against all else.

6:6 ....Split against 2 through 6.
Hit against all else.

7:7 ....Split against a 2 through 7.
Hit against 8, 9, ace.
Stand against a 10.

(If surrender is allowed, surrender 7:7 against a dealer's 10.)

8:8 ....Split against everything.

(If surrender is allowed, surrender 8:8 against a dealer's 10.)

9:9 ....Split against 2 through 6; 8, 9.
Stand against 7, 10, ace.

10:10 ....Stand against everything.

Additional Single-Deck Strategies

The single-deck blackjack game is quite different from the multiple-deck game because the composition of a given hand is actually an important factor in your decisions. For example, in a multiple deck any player's hand of 12 is to be treated as equal to any other hand of 12. Not so with a single deck. A 10:2 is to be handled differently than, say, a 5:7 when facing a dealer's up card of 4. In the former situation, you would hit; in the latter situation, you would stand. Now, on the basic strategy for single deck, I have not added any of the refinements that follow because they will not drastically alter your long-run expectations. However, if you want to get an extra edge, I recommend you incorporate the following variations of play into your single-deck strategy:

1. Hit 10:2 against a dealer's four. Stand on all other hard 12s against a dealer's four.

2. Hit 10:3 and 9:4 against a dealer's two. Stand on all other hard 13s against a dealer's two.

3. Stand on any three or four card total of 16 against a dealer's 10.

4. Stand on a 9:7 against a dealer's 10. If surrender is allowed, however, you would surrender this hand as you would any 16 against a dealer's 10.

5. If you can double after splitting pairs:
   a) split 2:2 against a dealer's two.
   b) split 3:3 against a dealer's two or three.
   c) split 4:4 against a dealer's five or six.

Chapter Four

Blackjack Rules and Their Effect on the Player's Edge

There are good blackjack games and bad blackjack games and you should be able to distinguish between them. Basic-strategy players and card counters alike benefit by liberal rules, and are hurt by tight games with few options for the players. Even if the option is only marginally helpful to a player, it is better to play at a game with this option, all other things being equal. The world of blackjack is an ever-changing landscape and new rules come and go. However, for good or ill, most of the following rules can be found often enough that it is worth knowing their impact on your expectations.

What follows will first be a discussion of the rule or option. If the option has a + + after it, that means it's a good option for the player. If the option has a − − after it, that means it's a bad option for the player.

Doubling on Any First Two Cards: A good rule for the basic-strategy player when used properly. For basic-strategy players, follow the doubling strategies for the single and/or multiple decks. For the card counter, this is an even better rule since a card counter will find many more opportunities upon which to double. If the dealer should have a blackjack, you only lose your initial bet on any double down. + +

Doubling on 9, 10, and 11 only: This is not a good rule for single-deck basic-strategy players since there are times when you will want to double on eight. This rule is primarily aimed, however, against card counters to diminish their opportunities for doubling in advantageous situations. − −

Doubling on 10 and 11 only: Awful rule and any game that stipulates this should be avoided if better games are available. − −

Doubling on 11 only: Yuck. − −

Splitting Aces: Good rule, especially if the casino allows you to resplit aces. When you split aces you can only receive one card on each ace, thus you cannot double down after splitting aces. If the dealer has a blackjack, you only lose your initial bet. + +

Resplitting of Aces: Good for the players. After you split your initial pair of aces, if you should receive another ace on one of your split aces, you can resplit that pair. + +

No Splitting of Aces: Bad for the players. − −

Splitting Pairs: Favorable rule for the player, especially if you can double down after splitting. + +

No Resplitting of Pairs: Bad for the players. − −

No Splitting of Pairs: Bad for the players. − −

Doubling After Splitting Pairs: Good rule for the player. + +

Doubling on Three or More Cards: Favorable rule for the player but you'll rarely find this rule in casinos that offer good penetration in their games. + +

Insurance: If the dealer has an ace as his up card you can insure your hand for up to half its value. Bad rule for basic-strategy players. Never insure anything, even your own blackjack. However, insurance is a wonderful rule for card counters who will know exactly when to take it. Quite often the difference between a winning or losing session for a card counter is proper use of the insurance option. Even in blackjack games of one round before a shuffle, there will be times a card counter benefits from taking insurance. Basic-strategy player: $--$; card counters: $++$

Early Surrender: The player has the option of surrendering his hand when he sees his first two cards. In exchange, he gets back half his bet—even if the dealer has a blackjack. Very good option for basic-strategy player. Great option for card counters. $++$

Late Surrender: Same as above except . . . and this is a BIG except . . . if the dealer has a blackjack, you lose your entire bet. Good option for player. $++$

Six-card Winner: Favorable to the player. It is only slightly more favorable to card counters. You win if you get 21 or less with six cards. $++$

Five-card Charlie: If you receive 21 with five cards, you win a bonus from the casino—usually two to one. This favors the player. $++$

Seven-Seven-Seven 21: In some games, the casino will pay a handsome bonus if you can get three sevens of the same suit. Don't hold your breath waiting for this as it happens rarely. However, some casinos will pay a small bonus if the player gets three sevens of any suit. This is favorable to the player if:

1) You don't deviate from basic strategy when you get two sevens in an attempt to get a third; and

2) You don't have to put up a side bet to get the payoff. $++$

Six-Seven-Eight Suited: Favorable to the players if you don't change your basic strategy in an attempt to suit up, except in the case of a six-seven suited (13) against the dealer's two. $++$

Over-Under 13: You make a side bet that the next hand dealt you will be either over 13 or under 13 on the first two cards. Aces count as one for this and the dealer takes all hands of 13. Very unfavorable rule for basic-strategy players. Marginally helpful rule for certain card counters. Value: −6.56 percent for the over and −10.06 percent for the under. (See chapter 13 for complete discussion of the Over–Under 13 option.) − −

Dealer Hits A:6 (Soft 17): Bad rule for all players. Often helps the dealer improve an otherwise bad hand for the house. − −

Red or Black: This is a bet where the player guesses what the color of the dealer's face-up card will be. At first this would seem like an even game off the top but the house stipulates that if the two of the color you chose shows up, your bet is a push. This gives the house an advantage over the basic-strategy player. Color counters can get a strong edge. (See chapter 12 for a more complete discussion of this option.) Basic-strategy players: − −; color counters: + +

Dealer Wins Pushes: All ties go to the dealer. The most devastating rule against the players. − −

Blackjack Pays 1 to 1 (2 for 1): Bad rule for the players. − −

Blackjack Pays 2 to 1 (3 for 1): Great rule for the players but you'll be hard-pressed to find it on any of today's games except during special promotions. + +

No Doubling: Bad rule for the players. − −

No Hole Card Blackjack: You won't find this option in America. However, if you travel to foreign casinos, you'll run into it. Dealer doesn't take a hole card until all the players have played their hands. Bad rule for the player because the casino will take all double downs, splits and resplits if the dealer gets a blackjack. − −

Blackjack Jackpot: A large progressive jackpot that climbs as play continues. This option is starting to catch on. You win it if on the first hand out of the shoe, you receive an ace and jack of a specified suit. Good for players as long as you don't play an otherwise inferior game in order to go for the bonus. + +

Progressive Blackjack: For a side bet, the casino will give you the opportunity to win a large progressive jackpot. Generally, you have to get four cards of the same suit or some such hand to win. − −

Number of Decks: The greatest single variable in determining the viability of a given game is the number of decks. As a general rule of thumb, the fewer the decks, the better it is for the players—if the rules are similar. The single-deck game offers opportunities for card counters, basic-strategy players and the relatively unknowledgeable alike. A single-deck game can range from a +.15 percent in favor of a player to a −.10 percent (sometimes more) against the player, depending on the rules. Multiple-deck games tend to have somewhat more liberal rules because of the advantage to the casino of using more decks. Thus, a double-deck game with good rules will have approximately a .31 to .35 percent advantage in favor of the house; a four-deck game will have approximately a .41 to .52 advantage in favor of the house; a six-deck game will have approximately a .58 percent advantage for the house; and an eight-deck game will have approximately a .61 percent advantage in favor of the house. The assumption on all these house edges is that the player is playing perfect basic strategy. For the non-basic-strategy player, the house edge can be as much as eight percent or more depending on how foolishly a person plays.

Penetration: How many cards a dealer deals is called penetration. If a game deals all the cards out, that's 100 percent penetration. For the basic-strategy player, the depth of penetration is of little significance. However, for the card counter the depth of penetration is another key variable in determining whether to play a given game. The more penetration, the better the game. The minimum necessary for a decent game is 75 percent in multiple-deck games and 66 percent in single-deck games.

Face-up or Double Exposure Blackjack: More casinos are starting to offer this game, even though it never really caught on in Las Vegas. Generally, dealt from a shoe of six to eight decks, this game is a radically different one from regular blackjack since *both* the dealer's cards are dealt face up. The basic-strategy charts for it are also quite different.

Chapter 11 will contain basic-strategy and card-counting information for this game. Card counters: + +; Double Exposure basic-strategy players: − −

Multiple Action Blackjack

In Multiple Action blackjack, a player must play a minimum of two hands. Note that all the options are on the layout. When a player wants to double, split, or take insurance, he puts his money on that portion of the layout. This alerts the dealer as to his intentions.

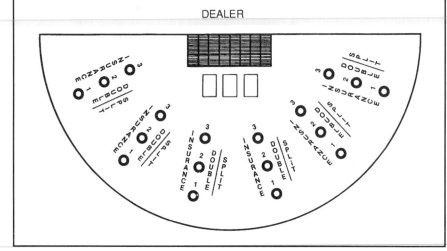

Multiple Action Blackjack: This game is getting tremendous publicity in Las Vegas, Atlantic City and I even found it in Mississippi. The player plays three hands against the dealer's face-up card. The rub is this—the dealer gives himself three different hole cards, one for each hand the player has played. (The dealer keeps the same face-up card for all three of his hands.) The dealer plays each hand separately. The player has played *all his hands*, however, before the dealer does anything. Should the player bust on any one of his hands, he loses all three hands. This game has the exact same expectation as regular blackjack if all the hands are played according to basic strategy against the dealer's up card. The problem occurs when players are so afraid of busting that they stay on hands they shouldn't. The casino eats these people alive. For card counters, this is a good option because they can get more money into play without suspicion. Bet two hands at the table minimum until the count goes up and then go to three hands with twice as much on each for each point in the true count over two in multiple-deck games. For basic-strategy players—beware! Play just as you would normally against the dealer's up card or you are asking for "multiple" losses over the long haul. Card counters: $++$; basic-strategy players: $--$

Chapter Five

Card Counting: Getting the Edge on the Casinos

The game of blackjack has always been a big money-maker for the casinos. Today, according to published casino reports, blackjack wins approximately $15 for every $100 cashed in by the players at the tables. For the players that means on average they lose $15 for every $100 they buy in for. Wow! Blackjack is a gold mine for the casinos. And remember something about this $15 figure: it has been over 30 years since card counting was discovered and over 40 years since the appearance of a basic strategy that reduced the casino's edge to between approximately one-half percent to zero percent. So how come the casinos are still winning such big bucks at the blackjack tables? Simple. The payers (this must be a Freudian slip of the word-processor key—I meant to open the sentence with "players" but I'm leaving it because "payers" is actually more appropriate) are not playing the best blackjack. The "payers" are playing the worst blackjack because they are playing self-styled strategies that give the casino such a magnificent win percentage on them. It makes you wonder why the casinos even worry about card counters when so many of the players are so bad.

And it doesn't have to be this way at all because card counting is not difficult to learn. In fact, I think learning the theory of card counting is much easier than memorizing basic strategy. By the end of this chapter, you will know *how* to count cards. Whether you will be actually able to *do* it is an entirely different matter. The actual counting of cards in a casino—with lights flashing, people talking, slot machines jingling and clanging, waitresses asking you if you want something to drink, while music blares in the background—is not that easy.

The difference between a card counter starting out and a basic-strategy player starting out is this—the basic-strategy player must put in quite a bit of time memorizing at home because he plays by rote, but once he has mastered the strategy, he can play it mechanically; the card counter, on the other hand, cannot master the art at home. He must go to a casino and see if he can concentrate amid the din and distractions and be able to do in a casino what he did so well at home.

Big Cards — Little Cards

The theory of card counting is quite simple: big cards favor the players, small cards favor the dealer. This is a fact backed up by tens of millions of computer simulations over four decades of blackjack study. Thus, as the game is progressing, if the deck contains more big cards (10s and aces) because more little cards have been played, it will be to the player's advantage. Whereas if the deck contains more little cards (twos through sixes), it will favor the dealer. Of course, having a deck favor you is not the same as a guaranteed win, nor is having an unfavorable deck a guaranteed loss. However, in the long-run analysis of blackjack, the player will win more hands when the decks contain high cards than he will lose, and he will lose more hands when the decks contain low cards than he will win.

Card-counting systems take advantage of this fact in four ways:

1. All card-counting systems keep track of the relationship of small cards to big cards in the remaining deck.

2. When the cards remaining in the deck favor the player, the player will bet larger sums of money. When the cards remaining in the deck favor the casino, the player will bet smaller amounts or the minimum amount allowed.

3. Certain changes to basic strategy are made based on the "count" that increase a player's advantage or decrease his disadvantage when playing certain hands.

4. The use of the insurance option now becomes viable at certain times.

If you have decided to learn how to count cards, you have another big decision to make. What card-counting system will you use? There are literally dozens of different counting systems on the market, some selling for upwards of $500. To make matters worse, most of the traditional card-counting systems are good! There are card-counting systems that keep track of every card in the deck; there are systems that are four level systems—that is, cards are assigned a value of +1 to +4 (and −1 to −4); there are three and two-level systems. Some are so difficult and so elaborate that only a genius could play them. Some are so simple that mere mortals (you and I) can play them.

You are lucky for, unlike me, you don't have to attempt to play a representative sampling of all these systems before deciding which to choose. I did. I've played three-level counts, two-level counts and one-level counts with side counts of aces and fives. They all work.

Unfortunately, for me, they all work about as well as the simplest and easiest to learn and use—a one-level count, called the Hi-Lo count, that only follows certain cards. Recent research, and blackjack is a well-researched game, has shown that there isn't much difference in performance between a good one-level count and a good multi-level count. The only real difference is the level of difficulty in learning and executing the multi-level as opposed to the single-level counts. So why bother wasting time learning a more difficult count when its advantage over a simpler count is minuscule? Also, what little advantage the multi-level counts give over the one-level counts is usually more than eliminated by the very real likelihood that you will make mistakes due to fatigue.

So the count we'll deal with will be the Hi-Lo.

Card Values in the Hi-Lo Counting System

2 = +1	7 = 0	10 = −1
3 = +1	8 = 0	jack = −1
4 = +1	9 = 0	queen = −1
5 = +1		king = −1
6 = +1		ace = −1

As you are playing, if more small cards are coming out of the deck, you have what is called a *positive count* or *high count*. If more large cards are coming out of the deck, you have what is called a *negative count* or *low count*. After a round of play, if the count is positive, the next round should theoretically favor the player because a greater proportion of the large cards remain in the deck to be played. If the count is negative after a round of play, the next round favors the casino because a greater proportion of the small cards remain to be played.

Why do the large cards favor the player and small cards favor the house?

1.   **Large cards make a blackjack more likely.** Although the player and the dealer have an *equal* chance of getting a blackjack, the player is paid off at three to two. For example, if the player wagers five dollars, he is paid $7.50. Thus, if a player gets one blackjack in one round of play and the dealer gets one blackjack in another round of play, the player comes out ahead, assuming his bets were the same in both rounds. The converse is also true. With small cards remaining in the deck, a blackjack is less likely.

2.   **The dealer will bust his bust hands.** Although the dealer will get slightly better hands in a positive count (as will the player), when the dealer has a bust hand (12 to 16), he is more likely to actually bust. The dealer must hit his bust hands, the player doesn't. In a negative count, the dealer will hit his bust hand and is more likely to make a good hand because small cards are more likely to come out.

I want to reinforce what I said earlier. The fact that something is *more likely* to happen doesn't *guarantee* it *will* happen every time. When you count cards, you will have very high positive counts where the dealer will draw to his bust hands and still get small cards. You will have negative counts where blackjacks appear—one after another. Over time, over the long run [whatever that is—(see chapter 18)], what is more likely to happen will happen more often than what is less likely to happen. But sometimes that long run is a long time coming—especially when you are losing hand after hand.

That's why many counters prefer to use guerrilla tactics against blackjack, rather than play a traditional game that demands countless hours in order to get into the long run (see chapter 14).

Now, that you know the values of the cards, you have to hit upon a workable method for counting them. You have to keep a *running count* of the cards as they come out of the deck.

In games where every player has his cards dealt face up (usually multiple-deck shoe games), you can wait until every player receives his hand and then count as the dealer hits them or passes them by. For example, if the player in the first baseman's seat (the seat closest to the dealer's left) has a 10 and a two, the count is neutral. If he hits his 12 and gets a six, the count is now +1. Now, you would move on to the next player. He has two 10 cards. The count is now −1. Thus, you would follow the dealer around the board. This is only one method of counting in a face-up game.

You could, for example, scan the table and cancel out conflicting pairs when every player has two cards. The beautiful A.P. counts this way. Thus, a player with two 10s and a player with two fives cancel each other out immediately and the count is neutral. You will have to practice at home to decide what counting procedure is best for you.

In single-deck games and double-deck hand-held games, the cards are usually dealt face down. Thus, you have to wait until the player busts or the dealer turns the player's cards over at the end of the round to count them.

To become proficient, you have to put the practice in. Card counting is, as you have just seen, easy to understand, hard to actually do at first. However, once you master card counting, you never forget how to do it. Like riding a bike, counting cards and playing basic strategy can become second nature.

What should also become second nature are the variations in basic strategy required based on the count. There are literally hundreds of variations both for single and multiple-deck games. However, much like the numerous card-counting systems, memorizing hundreds of strategy variations will not yield you much value for your time. You are better off simply memorizing the few strategy variations for certain hands that occur with some regularity and in count ranges that you are more often likely to have. Thus, the following variations should be incorporated into your arsenal.

Variations in Single-Deck Basic Strategy

All strategy variations in single-deck games are based on the running count.

Running Count	**Variation in Strategy**
−1 or less	Hit 13 against the dealer's 2 or 3.
+1 or more	Stand on 12 against the dealer's 2 or 3.
	Stand on 10:2 against dealer's 2, 3, or 4.
	Insure all hands against a dealer's ace.
	Double on 10 against a dealer's ace.
+2 or more	Stand on all 16s against a dealer's 10.
	Double A:8 against a dealer's 5.

These few variations in strategy will help you considerably in playing certain hands. Remember that at a +1 or more, you insure all your hands against the dealer's ace—even the hands 11 or 10 which you are doubling down. The correct use of the insurance option in a single-deck game is probably the key variation to employ and often makes the difference between a winning or losing session.

Variations in Multiple-Deck Basic Strategy

Counting into a multiple-deck game is slightly more complicated than counting into a single-deck game because you have to keep track of two different counts—the *running count* and the *true count* (sometimes called *the count per deck*). The running count is the count you keep as the game is progressing. Thus, if the following cards appear: 4, 8, 6, ace, 10, 5, 3, 2, 7, 4—you have a running count of +4 (4 = +1; 8 = 0; 6 = +1; ace = −1; 10 = −1; 5 = +1; 3 = +1; 2 = +1; 7 = 0; 4 = +1). But what if this were the first round of play in an eight-deck game—would you have an edge over the casino? No.

To establish whether a count actually means you have an edge over the casino (or whether the casino has an edge over you), you must divide the number of decks remaining to be played into your running count—this is your *true count* because it gives you a true indication of what is actually happening with the remaining cards.

Say you have a running count of +8 with four decks remaining to be played in an eight-deck game, your true count would be +2. You divided the decks remaining to be played, four, into your running count +8, which gave you a true count of +2.

Now, exactly what does this mean in terms of an actual edge? As a general rule of thumb, any positive true count equals a .50 percentage point in favor of the player. Thus, a true count of +2 equals one percent in favor of the player. However, the casino has approximately .50 percent on the player in a multiple-deck game so the above situation would give the player a .50 percent edge over the casino.

With four decks remaining to be played in an eight-deck game, you ask yourself the question: Is a .50 percent edge worth very much? The answer is somewhat ambiguous. If you were playing millions of hands just like this—four decks remaining to be played with a .50 percent edge, then, yes, that .50 percent is a viable edge. But if you are playing only 100 hands in this situation, you probably wouldn't notice anything at all—you'd win some and lose some. That's because in a multiple-deck game with four decks remaining and a .50 percent edge, many of the cards can be clumped behind the shuffle point (the shuffle point is the area of the shoe where the dealer places the plastic card that indicates how many cards have been cut out of play).

For a true count to be significant in a multiple-deck game, it should give you an edge of at least one percent or more. Thus, your true count should be approximately +3 before you consider any severe escalation of bets. In fact, many blackjack pros don't even bother playing the first two decks of an eight-deck shoe but prefer to count *outside* (that is, behind the players) until the true count is +3 or more. If the count reaches this with six or fewer decks remaining, the player jumps in and begins to place bets. This guerrilla technique of jumping in on positive decks only is often called Wonging because it is named after Stanford Wong, the pseudonym used by a very popular and astute blackjack author who originated the idea. Wonging is an excellent, though tedious, way to beat the six- and eight-deck games.

There is no magic formula for estimating decks other than practice. You have to get a visual feel for what composes one deck, two decks, three decks, etc. The best way to do this is to buy enough decks so that you can practice estimating at home before you try to do so in a casino. Getting a reasonably accurate true count is a necessary skill if you wish to have a chance against the multiple-deck games.

In a single-deck game, you do not need to be able to get a true count in order to know whether you or the casino has the edge. Any negative count favors the casino and any positive count favors the player. You can, if you want, get a true count for a single-deck game as well. This can be done by dividing the fraction of the decks remaining to be played into the running count—thus, a running count of +3 with a half deck remaining would be a true count of +6 because .50 divided into three equals six. However, in a multiple-deck game, the true count is the basis of all decisions and must be ascertained at all times.

True Count	Variation in Strategy
−2 or less	Smallest bet possible or sit out and don't play.
−1 or less	Hit 13 against the dealer's 2 or 3.
+2 or more	Stand on 12 against a dealer's 2 or 3.
	Double down on 11 against an ace.
	Stand on 16 made with three or more cards against the dealer's 10.
	Double on 8 against a dealer's 6.
+3 or more	Insure every hand against the dealer's ace.
	Double down on 10 against the dealer's ace.
	Double down on 9 against a dealer's 2.
	Double down on 8 against a dealer's 5.

With the above variations in basic strategy and with precise card counting, you can gain an edge over many, if not most, blackjack games. Although a first read through of this material might seem somewhat daunting, in reality the skills necessary to beat casino blackjack are not out of the reach of the average person. A little hard work spread out over time is all that is needed. If you give yourself, say, a month to learn basic strategy perfectly and another month to practice card counting at home, then there is no reason why you shouldn't expect, with a little casino practice, to become a winner.

Indices to the Right of Me,
Indices to the Left of Me

Variations in strategies are often called indices in the blackjack world. Although I have only given you a dozen or so strategy changes (the most important ones and the ones that appear most frequently), there are literally hundreds of them in the blackjack literature. Here's where a mountain a minutiae distracts from what is important. What is better to do: only play basic strategy in high and low counts but in high counts get the money on the table, or—learn all the variations in strategy so that when the count calls for it you can change accordingly but *not* increase your bets in high counts or decrease your bets in low counts? The answer is obvious—it is better to play basic strategy and vary your bets than to vary your strategy and flat bet. Learning hundreds of indices might make people at a blackjack convention feel awe for you but I doubt that it will significantly increase your ability to win money at the game, even if you do vary your bets. Trying to keep hundreds of obscure hands in your head, so that for the once-every-ten years they come up in the real world you'll know what to do, is going to cause you to tire much more quickly. You'll probably not be able to play as long or with as much precision. The few tenths of a percent that you add to your advantage by knowing a host of indices will be reduced by the probability of making counting mistakes due to loss of concentration as you root around trying to dislodge at what indices you double when you have 3:2 against a dealer's four in a game where the dealer hits a soft 17.

The number of hours it takes to memorize several hundred variations in basic strategy would be better put to use working a second job to get the money to be able to increase your bet when the count calls for it. Then it would be time well spent. I'm not alone in this way of thinking. David D., a longtime blackjack pro, concurs: "You should know the important indices, especially for insurance, standing on 16, hitting or not hitting 12 or 13 against the dealer's two or three. These hands come up frequently enough that they are worth knowing. But the most important thing is to get the money out in high counts. Usually you won't have to make many decisions in high counts. The biggest thing is to be able to keep the pit bosses in a friendly mood as you're varying your bet size. It's better for the pit to be unaware of what you're doing than for you to be aware of what to do in some rare situation. I focus my attention on counting, getting the money out, and making friends in the pit. I play basic strategy with a few changes. I've been doing this for over 20 years."

Still, for those of you who wish to know the hundreds of variations based on the true count that are available to you, chapter 23 will recommend further reading in this arcane vein.

Chapter Six
Blackjack Betting and Money Management

The key to winning money in traditional blackjack play is to bet more when the count favors you, bet less when it doesn't. That's the BIG secret as you know. Theoretically, the best procedure, if you could afford it, would be to bet the table minimum when the house has the edge and bet the table maximum when you have the edge. However, do this in today's casinos and you'll be asked to leave the premises or the dealer will shuffle up on you. (As a lark, a friend of mine once did this very thing at a single-deck game in a casino in Las Vegas. The minimum bet was two dollars, the maximum was $200. On neutral and low counts, he bet that two dollars. As soon as the count went to a +2, he zoomed up to $200. He lasted ten minutes before he was told to get out.) Also, very few people can afford the staggering fluctuations in bankroll that can occur when your bets vary so dramatically. You'll be sky high one moment—

economically and emotionally—and lower than Hades the next. Even if you were allowed to play this way, you would find that you needed an incredible bankroll to sustain a one to 100 betting spread.

Still to win at traditional blackjack, you must escalate your bets in positive counts, otherwise the casino's slight edge will grind you down. The player's edge only comes in high counts and it is the money bet in high counts that nullifies the casino's win rate over you. The average blackjack win rate is as follows: the house wins approximately 48 percent of the time, the player wins approximately 44 percent of the time, and the other eight percent of the time the hands are a tie. A card counter will win more big bets during that 44 percent than he will lose and these wins will also overcome the total losses he encounters in negative decks. More than enough to turn the casino's advantage his way. (Remember, some of that 44 percent are double downs and splits which will increase his overall winnings, since all proper double downs and splits either increase wins or decrease losses.)

Most current blackjack authors recommend a betting spread of one unit to four units (some go as high as six units) based on the true count. Thus, in a neutral or negative deck, you would bet your minimum of one unit. If the true count was +1 in a single deck or +3 in a multiple deck, you would bet two units. If the count was respectively +2 or +4, you would bet three units; if the count was +3 or +5, you would bet four units. The total bankroll for a traditional card counter should be somewhere between 800 and 1,000 units. Such a bankroll should help you weather the sometimes rather long but inevitable losing streaks. An under-financed card counter will invariably get wiped out because the swings of fortune are so great owing to the escalation of bets in high counts.

Unfortunately, for the card counters, most casino pit people have read most of the same blackjack authors and are on the lookout for the one-to-four-unit spread, especially if the bet is bumped directly from one unit to four units. They are on the lookout for proper use of the insurance option and the surrender option. They are also on the lookout for anyone who varies his strategy with the count. Some of the casino pit people know as much as card counters because many casino people *are* card counters. (Conversely, *most* casino pit people have only a vague awareness of the elements that go into successful blackjack play.)

I spoke to a very astute Las Vegas pit boss whose casino offers good single- and double-deck games with liberal rules. He had this to say about the traditional methods of card counters:

A single card counter can't really hurt the casino's bottom line in any significant way unless he's playing for tens of thousands of dollars over an extended period of time. However, hundreds of card counters can hurt us by taking up the spaces at the table that would otherwise be occupied by inferior players and by winning small amounts consistently. That's why we ban them. We know about every trick they use to fool us because we've read the same books they have. The first thing you look for is bet spread and proper use of insurance—especially in a single-deck game. I mean anyone who insures a stiff hand against the dealer's ace when a big bet is out is probably counting cards. The casinos that are offering the better games usually hire people who are good counters in order to catch good counters.

I remember when I was playing at the Golden Nugget in downtown Las Vegas and the casino pit crew had clipboards with the words COUNTER CATCHERS stenciled on them. They were especially on the lookout for players who bet green ($25) and varied their bets upwards with the count. The red chip players (five dollars) didn't seem to concern them and several counters were varying their bets from five dollars to $30 in gradual stages right under their noses. I would recommend that if you are going to play the traditional blackjack games that you escalate your bets only by doubling the previous bet and preferably only after a win. This tends to resemble what many players do when they feel that they are on a hot streak—they escalate their bets by doubling their previous bets. You can also consider taking insurance when you have the *smallest* possible bet out so that when you take it with a big bet out, it will seem natural. Don't do this too often, however, because your edge is slight at best and you can wipe it out by making too many foolish plays.

The 10 Commandments of Card Counting

1. Thou shalt not let anyone at your table know that you can count cards.

2. Thou shalt not let the pit people know you count cards.

3. Thou shalt not let the pit people know you play basic strategy.

4. Thou shalt not let the pit people know you've read a book on blackjack.

5. Thou shalt look like a gambler and not a card counter when betting.

6. Thou shalt not give advice to others, even if they are playing stupidly, even if they ask you for advice. Just say: "You have to do what you want to do."

7. Thou shalt not look like a card counter—cool and calculating and confident in your abilities—but rather react as a regular player reacts to the ebbs and flows of the game.

8. Thou shalt say, when a discussion of card counting comes up at the table (as it will), that "I don't believe it's possible to remember all the cards. I think it's a lot of baloney."

9. Thou shalt leave the casino when you feel the least bit of heat from the pit (heat being unusual attention by the pit to your play).

10. Thou shalt not covet a gambler's lucky streak, or throw good money after bad, or in any other way lose your composure.

It is quite important to stress once again that while card counting is not illegal, the casinos do not look with favor upon the people who can beat them. The more intelligent pit people and casino owners tolerate card counters as a necessary evil (their opinion) on the road to winning that 15 percent from their blackjack playing public. But many pit people work in casinos where paranoia reigns supreme. As an expert player, you are better off never letting anyone know you know how to beat the casinos. This violates a natural human tendency to want to brag, however slightly, about one's achievements.

There are two reasons you don't want to do this. In a casino, you can bring undo attention upon your playing and betting strategies. You don't want some pit person bird-dogging your every move. You especially don't want to be photographed from the eye in the sky. You also don't want to be shuffled on, harassed or kicked out. It will be obvious to many pit people that you know how to play basic strategy, especially if you've been playing at that table or casino for a prolonged period of time. This is no big deal as many intelligent people stumble upon a basic approximation of basic strategy from years of playing. If you are ever asked whether or not you play basic strategy just say: "Yeah, I got a strategy card from the gift shop."

You also don't want to give advice to other players, even if they ask for it. In any short-run moment, your advice might not be successful. Let us say you have a low count of −3, and the player gets a three against the dealer's up card of two. The call is easy. You hit the hand. So now you tell some player who's asked your advice: "Oh, yeah, hit it." And he does, receiving a 10 for a bust. Now, the dealer turns over his hole card and he has a 10. The dealer has 12. He hits with a four, giving him 16, and then a five, giving him 21. Not only has your advice (the correct advice) lost the hand for the player who asked for your advice, but the other players will more than likely be angry that they lost their hands (or pushed) as well because the dealer hit to 21. Obviously, you know that your advice was good, that the dealer was more than likely to hit and make a hand since little cards were left in the deck. But for that moment, you have to face the scowls or jeers of the other players. Since the hitting and standing decisions of the other players are irrelevant to your overall expectation [yes they are, even if it doesn't *feel* as if they are (see chapter nine)], then you are better off letting people make their own decisions.

The second reason you don't want to brag has nothing to do with the casinos but it does have to do with your self-esteem. When I first started to beat the casinos on a regular basis, I told everyone I knew about this great new development in my life. I'm an exuberant type and I like to share my good fortune with others. So I told people what I was doing. No one believed me. In fact, I was ridiculed. People who had never read a book on gaming, people who had never studied the games themselves, felt free to dismiss me as an idiot. This is the flavor of what I got:

"Oh, yeah, sure, you can beat the casinos." [Sarcastic tone implies I'm a moron.]

"If you can beat the casinos, how come you're not rich?" [Same logic as: "If he's so tall how come he can't touch the sky?"]

"Nobody can beat the casinos." [That means, I'm lying.]

"If people could beat the casinos, there wouldn't be any casinos." [Another logical proposition.]

"I don't know anyone who ever wins every time." [Argument based on their limited experience and a misunderstanding of the facts.]

"Everybody thinks he has a system until he loses." [Scorn for the moron.]

"It's all luck, that's all it is. You've just been lucky." [This is from Mount Olympus as the tone implies omniscience on the part of the speaker.]

And so it went. People were willing to begrudgingly concede that I had been lucky for several years, but they weren't capable of assimilating the fact that skill was involved. I would try to explain to some of them that when I said I could beat the casinos, I wasn't saying that I won every time or that I was getting rich from this activity. But strangely, somehow or other, this was the popular conception. My mouth was saying one thing but people were hearing another. I felt like the prophetess Cassandra of Greek mythology who could accurately predict the future but no one could understand what she was saying. She had been cursed by the god Apollo to utter coherently stated but incoherently received words. That was my lot when it came to explaining to my associates what I was doing.

Their feeling was that if I were truly winning I would be carrying trash-bag loads of money with me all the time. Since I obviously wasn't doing that, then I must be lying or deluded...or both. You'll find this too. Once you say that you have the skill to beat the casinos, you will be looked upon as a liar or an exaggerator or a fool. If you try to explain what it means to have the edge over the casinos, you will not be heard. Ears will shut as tightly as a bank vault. Sadly, many of the very same people who dismissed me way back when are now steady customers in Atlantic City. They lose and lose and lose. I don't say a word. Some of the people, who know I'm a writer, have no idea that I've written about casinos and how to beat them. I'm not telling them either. Many people have made themselves deaf, blind and therefore dumb when it comes to learning the truth about gambling.

So you're better off keeping silent at the table of the casinos and at the table of life or you might not like what you have to swallow. Of course, among my card-counting buddies and the Captain [see my book *Beat the Craps Out of the Casinos: How to Play Craps and Win!* (Bonus Books)], I don't have to practice such restraint since they are perfectly aware of what it means to have an edge over the casinos.

Looking Like a Gambler

The card counter has to mask his play from the eyes of casino personnel if he wants to enjoy a long playing life. Casinos want to cater to gamblers, not winners, because gamblers, by their very nature, are long-term losers. Thus, the successful card counter must try to look like a gambler if at all possible. That means getting the money on the table in such a way that the casino doesn't know you are moving bets up and down based on the count. The question is how do you do this? Here are two experts, both winning players, who have come up with solid ways to get, respectively, a huge betting spread, and the traditional one-to-four spread.

Our first is Brian. He's 42 years old and has been playing blackjack for 20 years, mostly in Las Vegas. Although blackjack is not his main source of income, he plays on average 100 to 130 days per year. He lives in Los Angeles. Here's his advice.

Brian: My current money-management and betting system is radically different from the one-to-four spread. However, if you are going to use the one-to-four spread as your method of betting, then a total bankroll of between 200 and 400 units would be appropriate. I would lean more towards the 400 units so as to give me a satisfactory cushion during the inevitable losing streaks.

But I prefer my way to the traditional way. My total "active" bankroll is 4,000 units with a "reserve" bankroll of another 8,000 units should my "active" bankroll ever get wiped out. (I have yet to even get near to being wiped out.) Whenever my "active" bankroll goes to 6,000 units, I take that excess 1,000 units and invest it in something else. When my bankroll begins to shrink, I bet less. Thus, if I lose, say, 2,000 units, I cut my betting in half.

Here is my current strategy as it applies to blackjack betting. I say "current" because blackjack conditions are fluid and always changing, and your betting strategy often has to change with them.

In single-deck games (figure three rounds of play), I start with two hands of four units each (total is eight units). When the count goes to +1, I go to two hands of eight units each. When the count goes to +2 or higher, I go to two hands of 10 units each. So in neutral to high counts, my spread is 8 units to 20 units, not a very large swing. However, when the count goes down to −1, I reduce my bets to two hands of two units each. When the count goes to −2, I go down to two hands of one unit. When the count goes to −3 or lower, I go down to one hand of one unit. Thus, my effective spread is one-to-20.

I never increase by more than double my previous bet. So after the first round, if the count is +2 or more, I don't jump up from eight units to 20 units. I go from eight to 16, which is just doubling my previous bet on both hands. This is something that a lot of players do and it won't really be noticed. If on the third round of a single-deck game, the count is still +2 or above, then I go to my 20-unit bet.

In double-deck games, I start out with two hands of three units each. When the true count goes to +1, I go to four units on each hand; at true-count plus two, I go to five units on each hand. At +3 or more, I'll go to 10 units on each hand. When I feel I can get away with it, I'll try to go to 12 units per hand if the decks remain positive. That is the one-to-four spread that most casinos are looking for but I'll still do it if I can get away with it.

In double-deck games, when the true count goes to −1, I drop to two units on each hand; at true count of −2, I drop to one unit on each hand; and on −3 or less, I go to one hand of one unit. Again, I have an effective range of one to 20 units.

In four- and six-deck games, I start with two hands of one unit each and as the true count increases, I double my previous bet if I have been winning. So if I won the last hand of one unit and the next hand is a true count of +2, I'll double my one unit to two units. This is what a gambler would do and should not bring any attention on me. [This betting strategy can be used against eight-deck games, too.]

What if, however, the true count is +5 and I had a multi-unit bet up and lost? Would I go back down to one unit? No. It is a natural thing for a gambler to keep betting big once he has escalated his bets after a few wins. So as the count remained positive, I would bet the count for that stretch. So the multiple-deck betting scheme is really this: start escalating after a win as the count goes up. Once you lose, and the count is still up, stay at the previous betting level until you win again. If the count is still up after another win, you can increase your bet. If, on the other hand, the count goes down, drop down in gradual stages. So if you have a 20-unit bet (10 units per hand) and the count is suddenly negative, you would drop to 10 units (five and five). This will happen quite a bit because when the count is positive the high cards will come out—which then lowers the count for the next round, sometimes quite a lot.

You will note that my biggest bet, except for the few times I might daringly go to 12 units per hand, is 20 units, 10 on one hand and 10 on the other hand. This is .01 or .02 percent of my "active" bankroll. You can translate that into money. A person whose unit bet is five dollars would need $20,000 dollars in an "active" blackjack bankroll to play as I have described above.

I realize that most people would not want to have to accumulate a bankroll of $20,000 to play this way. That's no problem. The key to my method of betting is the realization that casino personnel are looking for dramatic escalation of bets *[yes, even one to four is now considered dramatic]*. My betting starts with a multiple-unit bet so that I can go up or down without any single movement being all that dramatic. Since you are never going down or up more than twice or half of the bet you had previously, the casino personnel tend to overlook your betting spread.

My second expert is Phil. He's 34 years old and has been playing blackjack for 11 years. He lives in Las Vegas. He doesn't have the bankroll that Brian has and thus he must be more conservative in his betting strategy. I showed him Brian's remarks.

Phil: For those of you who want to play but don't want to go for that huge one-to-20 spread that Brain currently employs, you can start with any multiple-unit bet and double it in high counts and halve it (or more) in low counts. If you only want to play one hand of four units, you would go to eight units in a positive count and two or one in a low count. You're still getting a very effective one-to-eight spread in such a game. Or you can go from a two unit bet off the top to a four unit bet in high counts and down to a one unit bet in low counts. That's the one-to-four spread. The thing you definitely don't want to do is start with a one unit bet and then jump to four units in a high count. That's too much of a jump, especially if you're playing green or black chips. Red chip bettors can get away with that at most casinos but higher-end players probably can't.

I tend to favor Brian's approach because it gives me the widest possible spread. With such a spread, however, you must be willing to face the inevitable roller-coaster ride. Your bankroll will go up and down quite dramatically [see chapter 21].

Spreads and the Edge

How much of a spread is necessary for a player to get the edge? This is a tough question but a general rule of thumb applies here. Penetration in single-deck games must be at least 66 percent, then with a one-to-three or one-to-four spread you should be able to get a one percent to two percent edge, depending on the rules and your skill level. In multiple-deck games, with a minimum of 75 percent penetration and with a one-to-eight spread, you can get edges of .25 percent to .75 percent. With penetration of 85 to 95 percent and a betting spread of one-to-20, you can get an edge of between .50 and one percent. (Note: I've lumped all multiple-deck games together here. With rules and penetration being equal, the four-deck games will be towards the higher end of expectancy, while the eight-deck games will be towards the lower end.)

Although some authors have claimed that players can get edges of five percent or more, it is not substantiated by the mathematics on real-world games. Theoretically, if you could spread from one unit to 1,000 units, you might be able to get huge edges but no casino will allow that. In addition, very few players would have the bankroll to sustain such enormous fluctuations that would result from such a spread.

For a decent card counter, it is not unreasonable to expect to play single- and double-deck games with upwards of a one to 1.5 percent edge; nor is it unreasonable to expect to get a .50 percent edge on multiple-deck games. If the penetration and the rules are favorable on any of these blackjack games; if your betting spread is large enough; if you play perfectly and count without too many errors, you have mathematically turned the tables on the casinos.

What Your Edge Means

What does it mean to have a one percent edge on a casino? Quite simply it means that for every $100 you bet at the tables, you can expect to win *in the long run* one dollar. This is why it is not that easy to get rich playing blackjack.

Let us assume that the casinos would let you play unhindered. Let us assume that you are spreading from $10 to $100 and that your average bet is $50. Let us also assume that on average you are playing 60 hands an hour (that's one hand a minute) and that you play four hours a day. Let us also pretend that you live in a perfect blackjack world where you make no mistakes in strategy or in counting and that the mathematics of the "long run" work out in a year's time (which they wouldn't necessarily do in the real world). How much can you expect to make if you played five days per week?

With a one percent edge and an average bet of $50, you will make $30 per hour and $120 per day. You will make $600 per week. You will make $31,200 in a year. Not great but not bad.

How much money would you need to start with so that you could be reasonably assured that you wouldn't lose it all in one stretch of horrible luck? Let's be arbitrary and safe. 400 times your average bet would be enough to assure that with perfect play (and this is a best-of-all-possible-worlds scenario I'm writing here) and perfect strategy decisions, you would have enough to last. So you would need $20,000 to begin with. This $20,000 would be over and above what you needed for shelter, food, clothing, entertainment, rainy-day problems or your kids' tuitions. This $20,000 would be strictly gambling money.

Could the above scenario work itself out in real life? Probably not. The blackjack world is not the best of all possible worlds and your play would be severely restricted. To get that one percent edge, you would have to play the better games and get a wide betting spread up there. You would have to avoid heat from casino personnel. You would have to not get bored being in casinos five days a week for every week of a given year. In the real world, you can make thousands of dollars playing blackjack, yes. But at the end of the first year of play, you would only have a slightly greater chance of being substantially ahead as being somewhat behind. You would have to have an awful lot of money sitting in reserve to allow you to live for a year, two years, or three years or more as you wait for your blackjack bankroll to become fruitful and multiply.

Still, as a recreational player, as one who plays blackjack as another might play tennis, in the course of five to 10 years, you can sock away a substantial amount of money from blackjack winnings. That one percent edge, over time, is a strong harbinger that you'll be a winner. For you, it is worth getting a gambling reserve of cash and playing as often as the spirit moves you because, in the end, you'll be able to tell everyone you know that you are a winner—except they won't believe you.

Chapter Seven
Hands that Horrify?
It's Expectation!

As you know, blackjack is a game where the proper standing, hitting, splitting and doubling decisions are necessary in order to cut the house edge down to a minimum. These proper decisions have been arrived at by computer simulations of millions of hands and are called basic strategy. Without perfect play, the house has a rather large edge over the player who states: "I have my own strategy." Some experts calculate this edge as somewhere between two and a half and eight percent, depending on the "I have my own strategy" the player employs. The actual casino win rate is closer to 15 percent. But some of the basic strategies for playing the hands seemingly defy common sense. Indeed, some of the strategies seem downright suicidal.

For example, the dealer is showing a 10. You have two eights. According to basic strategy the proper move is to split them if the game you're playing doesn't allow surrender. It's the worst feeling in the world when you split those eights and get two 10s on them. Now, you have two hands of 18. If the dealer has a nine or 10 under his 10, you've lost two hands instead of one. Note the pained expressions on the faces of players who receive this hand. No one likes to split eights against a 10, despite the fact that it's the right move.

Because of the stomach-churning quality of some of the decisions that you have to make to play perfectly, many blackjack players will deviate from basic strategy on some hands. These hands I call "horrifying hands" because they make you blanch when you get them. Let's listen to some of the players:

"I never split aces against a dealer's up card of 10, nine, eight or seven," says Mildred of Connecticut. "You only get one card on each ace and you could wind up with two small cards. Now you have two rotten hands instead of one rotten hand. I'd rather just stay with my two aces and take a hit."

"Every time I hit my 12 against the dealer's two or three it seems as if I always get a 10," says Johnny of Nevada. "So now I let the dealer take the card. I'd rather see if the dealer busts because I always seem to."

Ella of Mississippi declares: "If I have 16 and the dealer has a seven showing, he only has a pat hand if he has a 10 under there, right? So I don't take a card. There's a better-than-even chance that the dealer will have a non-10 card. Let him bust. It seems stupid for me to hit my 16 against a dealer's seven. It's a losing proposition."

Joe of New Jersey states: "If I've got an 11, I don't double against a dealer's 10. I figure the dealer has a 10 in the hole so I've got to get a 10 to win. I have to get a nine to push. It's not even a 50-50 proposition. I have no idea why the books say you should double on an 11 against the dealer's 10."

Even some gambling writers have deviated from basic strategy on these hands because their "logic" (translate that as their "feelings") tells them that these hands are losers. Thus we have a situation in blackjack that pits one's feelings against the cold simulations of the computer. I understand the feelings, believe me. When I get two eights against a dealer's 10, I'm not jumping for joy thinking "hooray, I get to split them and maybe lose two hands!" But I realize that it's the right play in the long run. In a moment I will explain why these "horrifying hands" must be played according to basic strategy.

But first let's list the top 20 "horrifying hands" in order of their horror with the worst first. These are my opinions based on talking to other blackjack players. I didn't take a formal poll. In fact, you might disagree with the order and might have hands that I didn't include.

Hand	Basic Strategy	Feelings
8:8 vs. dealer's 10	split	stand or hit
8:8 vs. dealer's 9	split	stand or hit
12 vs. dealer's 2	hit	stand
12 vs. dealer's 3	hit	stand
A:A vs. dealer's 10	split	hit
A:A vs. dealer's 9	split	hit
16 vs. dealer's 7	hit	stand
16 vs. dealer's 8	hit	stand
11 vs. dealer's 10	double	hit
10 vs. dealer's 9	double	hit
11 vs. dealer's 9	double	hit
10 vs. dealer's 8	double	hit
9:9 vs. dealer's 8	split	stand
7:7 vs. dealer's 7	split	hit
9:9 vs. dealer's 7	stand	split
2:2 vs. dealer's 7	split	hit
3:3 vs. dealer's 7	split	hit
A:A vs. dealer's 8	split	hit
A:7 vs. dealer's 9	hit	stand
A:7 vs. dealer's 10	hit	stand

For each of the above hands you can understand the "logic" behind doing the wrong thing. This logic essentially involves the perceived risk a person is taking. A pair of aces against a dealer's ten is a losing hand. Why compound the loss by doubling? Hit your A:A and you will lose in the long run on this hand, goes the "logic," but you will only lose the one bet.

Basic strategy tells us something else, however. Split them and it is still a losing hand, but (and this is the big BUT) you will *lose less money* in the *long run* if you split than if you hit. Many of the horrifying hands fall into that category. Basic strategy does not usually make a winning hand from a losing hand. It only allows you to lose less.

This idea of losing less is also misunderstood. You will lose less *money* if you follow basic strategy when you have losing hands and, conversely, you will win more *money* by following basic strategy when you have winning hands. You will not necessarily win or lose more hands. Let me use a somewhat absurd example. Would you rather win one bet of $200 and lose 99 bets of one dollar or win 99 bets of one dollar and lose one bet of $200? Obviously, if you gamble to make money and not to see who can technically win the most decisions, you will opt for winning one hand of $200 and losing 99 hands of one dollar. When the betting sequence is over, you're ahead $101. The hand you were playing lost more decisions but it simultaneously won you more money! Only a fool would choose winning 99 hands and losing $101. Unfortunately just such foolishness is evident every day at the blackjack tables.

This is the difference between playing basic strategy and playing your own strategy. Indeed, you might actually win more hands by playing your own strategy but you will simultaneously lose more money. This is the difference between the *monetary expectation* and the chances of winning. You gamble for the monetary expectation, not the total number of wins.

Let me be even more precise here. Take the hand of 10 versus the dealer's nine. Basic strategy says to double down. In reality, doubling increases your chances of losing more hands but (another big BUT) increases your chances of winning more money.

Let us pretend that you are betting $100. You are now given a 10 versus the dealer's nine. If you go against basic strategy and hit the hand, you will win 56 percent of the time and lose 44 percent of the time for a net gain of $12 on that hand. However, if you double down you will only win 54 percent of the time and you will lose 46 percent of the time. Still, you will have won more actual money because your bet is doubled! In fact, you will have won $16. Basic strategy says to go for the money.

Now, let's take a look at the hand that I consider number one on the horror hit parade—the 8:8 versus a dealer's 10. The proper basic strategy is to split. But is it better to split or to just take a hit? If we hit, according to the computer, we will lose $51 for every $100 bet. However, if we split, we will only lose $44 for every $100 bet. That is a net gain of seven dollars. Thus, it is better to split those eights. It is still a losing hand but you lose less.

This is the key behind basic strategy. Again, the idea is to win more money, not necessarily more hands. So those horrifying hands are still horrible but now you know why you have to do what you have to do.

The Question of Insurance

Another difficulty some people have with basic strategy concerns the use of the insurance bet. Basic strategy says to never insure any hand, even if you have a blackjack. Yet, most players playing a version of the "I have my own strategy" strategy feel quite confident that the best use of the insurance bet is to insure all your blackjacks and 20s against the dealer's ace.

As with most reasoning based on feelings in blackjack, taking insurance when you have a blackjack or a 20 (or any other hand) is a mistake for the basic-strategy player. In a single-deck game, the casino has approximately a 5.88 percent edge on this bet. That's figuring that the deck is neutral. But let us pretend that it's the first round of play and you receive two 10-value cards. Just knowing that the dealer has an ace and you have two 10s should be reason enough not to take insurance—the casino has an even bigger edge than the 5.88 percent because the deck is now depleted of two cards that can help the dealer make his blackjack.

Sometimes in a single-deck game, a non-counting player can, by perusing the board in the first round of play, actually have situations where insurance might be warranted (see chapter 14). In multiple-deck games this won't happen. The insurance bet in four-, six- and eight-deck games is largely a waste of time, even for the card counter who needs true counts of +3 or more to consider insuring his hand. In a multiple-deck game the casino will have upwards of a 7.47 percent edge on the insurance bet, depending on the number of decks. That 7.47 percent translates into a loss of $7.47 for every $100 bet on insurance.

Although the casinos would like you to think differently, the insurance bet is not insurance for the hand that you are playing. It is merely a side bet as to whether or not the dealer has a 10 in the hole with his ace showing. Unless you're counting cards, insurance is another area where a player's feelings are not reflected in the computer's analysis. When basic strategy says never take insurance, there's a legitimate reason for it.

Surrender—Hell!
(Hell, yes, that is.)

There is such a thing as emotional blackjack and, sadly and self-defeatingly, some decisions bring out the macho in people (men and women alike). One such decision concerns whether or not to surrender some hands against some dealer up cards. As you know, basic strategy says to surrender 15 and 16 (including 8:8) against the dealer's 10 in multiple-deck games and 7:7, 8:8, 15s and 16s against the dealer's 10 in single-deck games. These are the right surrender decisions and you should make them.

But many players and dealers feel that it is cowardly to surrender. I remember once at Tropworld in Atlantic City, I had a dealer who was always riding me every time I made a decision to surrender. "Did you come to play or surrender?" he'd ask me. As so often happens with chance, this particular session with this particular dealer saw me getting a lot of hands that called for surrender. I surrendered four 16s in a row at one point against the dealer's 10s! Another time, I had a player tell me that I was a "coward" for surrendering, also an "idiot" because the casinos "put that rule in to trap people." Well, maybe they do and maybe they don't trap people. But a good player follows basic strategy on the surrender option for the same reason he follows it for the "horrifying hands" previously mentioned—you will lose less money in the long run if you do!

So remember, sometimes it's better to surrender and live to fight another day!

Chapter Eight
More Than You'll Ever Need to Know

You're at the local blackjack convention and a man with glowing eyes approaches you. His name is Noah Life. You know he's a blackjack buff, a guy who has memorized every trivial statistic there is to know about the game and he can cite indices as to how many aces can dance on the head of the female dealer he's tried unsuccessfully to pick up who has been dealing for six months in a double-deck game with 71.5 percent penetration when the sun is shining with a 40 percent probability of rain for tomorrow and for 40 days and nights thereafter. Noah knows these things. You also know that Noah loves to ask questions about the game; questions the answers to which he already knows.

"Excuse me, chum," he says. "But in a Northern Nevada single-deck game and a true count of +3 after one round of typical hitting and standing, how much of a betting spread would twice the Kelly Criterion indicate?"

Now, to answer Noah's questions you have to know what a Northern Nevada game is; what a true count of +3 is; know that the number of cards that have come out is irrelevant because he's given you the true count which takes into consideration the number of cards that have come out (that's his red herring to throw you off). Then you have to know what the Kelly Criterion is. It might also be helpful to know what counting system he's using.

This chapter is for those of you who want to wow them at the local blackjack salon. If you have mastered the information already presented about basic strategy, card counting, bet spreads, camouflage and variations based on the count, you are already on your way to being a casino killer. The information in this chapter is not irrelevant to you so much as some of it's an awful lot to learn for a much smaller return on your time, energy and brain cells. But for those of you who wish to know as much as you can, this chapter is for you.

The Kelly Criterion

I've put this first because it is actually something to seriously consider when playing blackjack. The Kelly Criterion is a bet-sizing scheme based on your knowledge of the percentage advantage you have over the house at any given moment. As you know with every point in the true count, you gain .50 percent over the casino. Unfortunately, not all games start out neutral so for some games, you have to have a true count of +3 to actually have an advantage over the casino. Kelly asserts that you should bet your advantage. Thus, in a six-deck game with a true count of +3, you would have approximately a one percent advantage over the house. Therefore, bet one percent of your total gambling bankroll. (Total bankroll = $10,000; one percent = $100.) As your advantage increases, you increase your bet (total bankroll $10,000; two percent = $200); as it decreases you decrease your bet so that when you have no advantage or, if you're at a disadvantage, you bet the table minimum or you stop playing. A system such as this assures that you'll rarely go broke since any decrease in your overall bankroll is reflected in your proportional betting. Thus, after a bad week at the tables, your initial $10,000 bankroll might be $8,000 and a one percent advantage now calls for an $80 bet.

Blackjack buffs talk often in terms of Kelly, as in: "I bet twice Kelly in high counts." That means if this particular individual has a one percent advantage over the house, he'll bet two percent of his bankroll. Is the Kelly Criterion a good way to go? Yes and most blackjack experts use some form of proportional betting to insure against ruination. Here's a simple Kelly betting scale for multiple-deck games. We will assume that you start off the game with a .50 percent edge for the casino against you. We will also assume that you have 1,000 units as your betting bankroll.

True Count	Percent Edge	Conservative Betting	Aggressive Betting	Super Aggressive Betting
−1 or less	−1% or less	sit out	table minimum	table minimum
neutral (0)	−0.5%	table minimum	table minimum	table minimum
+1	even	table minimum	table minimum	table minimum
+2	+0.5%	table minimum	5 units	10 units
+3	+1%	5 units	10 units	20 units
+4	+1.5%	8 units	15 units	30 units
+5	+2%	10 units	20 units	40 units
+6	+2.5	13 units	25 units	50 units
+7 or more	+3 or more	15 units	30 units	60 units

Here's a Kelly betting scale for single-deck games that start off even:

True Count	Percent Edge	Conservative Betting	Aggressive Betting	Super Aggressive Betting
−1 or less	−0.5% or less	sit out	table minimum	table minimum
neutral (0)	−0.0%	table minimum	table minimum	table minimum
+1	+0.5%	table minimum	5 units	10 units
+2	+1%	5 units	10 units	20 units
+3	+1.5%	8 units	15 units	30 units
+4	+2%	10 units	20 units	40 units
+5	+2.5%	13 units	25 units	50 units
+6	+3	15 units	30 units	60 units
+7 or more	+3.5	18 units	35 units	70 units

Betting Efficiency and Playing Efficiency

Professionals often characterize blackjack card-counting systems based on a dual criteria — betting efficiency and playing efficiency. The betting efficiency is how closely the true count measures the real advantage over the house. The ideal betting efficiency is 100 percent. Playing efficiency is how closely a card-counting system relates to changes in playing strategies. The highest realistic expectation for playing efficiency is approximately 70 percent. One can get higher playing efficiencies by using a side count of specific cards in addition to your normal count. The Hi-Lo count which I use and recommend has a betting efficiency of 97 percent and a playing efficiency 51 percent.

Now, let me introduce you to other counting systems, some of them quite difficult to learn and even more difficult to implement flawlessly in casinos. You will note that most don't perform as well as the Hi-Lo in betting efficiency, which to me is the most important criteria since it indicates when to get the money on the table.

Zen Count

Developed by Arnold Snyder, this is a multi-level point count that values cards as follows:

Cards:	2	3	4	5	6	7	8	9	10	A
Value:	+1	+1	+2	+2	+2	+1	0	0	−2	−1

Betting efficiency = 96%   Playing efficiency = 63%

Halves Count

Developed by Stanford Wong, this is a multi-level point count that values cards as follows:

Cards:	2	3	4	5	6	7	8	9	10	A
Value:	+0.5	+1	+1	+1.5	+1	+0.5	0	−0.5	−1	−1

Betting efficiency = 96%   Playing efficiency = 54%

Uston SS Count

Developed by Ken Uston, this is a multi-level unbalanced count because all the values do not add up to zero. It values cards as follows:

Cards:	2	3	4	5	6	7	8	9	10	A
Value:	+2	+2	+2	+2	+2	+1	0	−1	−2	−2

Betting efficiency = 99%   Playing efficiency =56%

Uston Advanced Point Count

Developed by Ken Uston, this is a multi-level point count that values cards as follows:

Cards:	2	3	4	5	6	7	8	9	10	A
Value:	+1	+2	+2	+3	+2	+2	+1	−1	−3	0

Betting efficiency = 90%   Playing efficiency = 69%

Uston Advanced Plus-Minus Count

Developed by Ken Uston, this is a single-level point count that values cards as follows:

Cards:	2	3	4	5	6	7	8	9	10	A
Value:	0	+1	+1	+1	+1	+1	0	0	−1	−1

Betting efficiency = 95%   Playing efficiency = 55%

Uston Ace-Five Count

Developed by Ken Uston, this is a single-level point count that values cards as follows:

Cards:	2	3	4	5	6	7	8	9	10	A
Value:	0	0	0	+1	0	0	0	0	0	−1

Betting efficiency = 54%   Playing efficiency = 5%

The Triple Count

This is a multi-level point count that values cards as follows:

Cards:	2	3	4	5	6	7	8	9	10	A
Value:	+1	+1	+1	+2	+1	+1	0	−1	−3	−2

Betting efficiency = 97%   Playing efficiency = 45%

Thorp Ultimate Count

Developed by Edward O. Thorp, this is a multi-level point count that values cards as follows:

Cards:	2	3	4	5	6	7	8	9	10	A
Value:	+5	+6	+8	+11	+6	+4	0	−3	−7	−9

Betting efficiency = 100%   Playing efficiency = 53%

The Systematic Count

Developed by Lawrence Revere, this is a single-level point count that values cards as follows:

Cards:	2	3	4	5	6	7	8	9	10	A
Value:	+1	+1	+1	+1	+1	+1	0	−1	−1	−1

Betting efficiency = 96%   Playing efficiency =549%

The Revere Advanced Point Count

Developed by Lawrence Revere, this is a multi-level point count that values cards as follows:

Cards:	2	3	4	5	6	7	8	9	10	A
Value:	+2	+2	+3	+4	+2	+1	0	−2	−3	0

Betting efficiency = 92%   Playing efficiency = 66%

The Revere Point Count

Developed by Lawrence Revere, this is a multi-level point count that values cards as follows:

Cards:	2	3	4	5	6	7	8	9	10	A
Value:	+1	+2	+2	+2	+2	+1	0	0	−2	−2

Betting efficiency = 98%   Playing efficiency = 56%

Red-Seven Count

Developed by Arnold Snyder, this is a multi-level unbalanced point count that values cards as follows:

Cards:	2	3	4	5	6	7	8	9	10	A
Value:	+1	+1	+1	+1	+1	0.5*	0	0	−1	−1

Betting efficiency = 98%   Playing efficiency =54%

*The reason this is called the Red-Seven count has to do with the recommendation of the originator that instead of dealing with a fractional 0.5 for the seven, just count either the black sevens or red sevens as +1 and ignore the other color.

Olsen TruCount

Developed by Eddie Olsen, this is a multi-level point count that values cards as follows:

Cards:	2	3	4	5	6	7	8	9	10	A
Value:	+1	+1	+1	+2	+1	+0.5*	0	−0.5*	−2	−1

Betting efficiency = 98%   Playing efficiency = 55%

*As in the Red-Seven count above, the Olsen TruCount recommends counting either the black or red sevens or nines and ignoring the others rather than using a fractional point count.

McGhee Plus-Minus Count

Developed by W.B. McGhee, this is a single-level point count that values cards as follows:

Cards:	2	3	4	5	6	7	8	9	10	A
Value:	+1	+1	+1	+1	+1	+1	−1	−1	−1	+1

Betting efficiency =71%   Playing efficiency = 51%

Hi-Opt I

Developed by Charles Einstein, Lance Humble, and Julian Braun, this is a single-level point count that values cards as follows:

Cards:	2	3	4	5	6	7	8	9	10	A
Value:	0	+1	+1	+1	+1	0	0	0	−1	0

Betting efficiency = 88%   Playing efficiency = 61%

Hi-Opt II

Developed by Lance Humble, this is a multi-level point count that values cards as follows:

Cards:	2	3	4	5	6	7	8	9	10	A
Value:	+1	+1	+2	+2	+1	+1	0	0	−2	0

Betting efficiency = 91%   Playing efficiency = 67%

Full Card Count

This is an unbalanced single-level point count that values cards as follows:

Cards:	2	3	4	5	6	7	8	9	10	A
Value:	+1	+1	+1	+1	+1	+1	+1	+1	−2	+1

Betting efficiency = 72%   Playing efficiency = 61%

Griffin Seven Count

Developed by Peter Griffin, this is a multi-level point count that values cards as follows:

Cards:	2	3	4	5	6	7	8	9	10	A
Value:	+4	+4	+5	+7	+5	+3	0	−2	−5	−6

Betting efficiency = 100%   Playing efficiency = 54%

C-R Point Count

Developed by Carlson R. Chambliss and Thomas C. Roginski, this is a multi-level point count that values cards as follows:

Cards:	2	3	4	5	6	7	8	9	10	A
Value:	+0.5	+1	+1	+1	+1	+0.5	0	0	−1	−1

Betting efficiency = 98%   Playing efficiency = 56%

Canfield Expert Count

Developed by Richard A. Canfield, this is a single-level point count that values cards as follows:

Cards:	2	3	4	5	6	7	8	9	10	A
Value:	0	+1	+1	+1	+1	+1	0	−1	−1	0

Betting efficiency = 87%   Playing efficiency = 62%

Canfield Master Count

Developed by Richard A. Canfield, this is a multi-level point count that values cards as follows:

Cards:	2	3	4	5	6	7	8	9	10	A
Value:	+1	+1	+2	+2	+2	+1	0	−1	−2	0

Betting efficiency = 92%   Playing efficiency = 67%

Now, on to some more things you don't really need to know to be a winning blackjack player but might want to know anyway.

Rules and Locations

In the past various locations were characterized by their rules. You had Las Vegas Strip rules, Las Vegas Downtown rules, Atlantic City rules, European rules and so on. There actually was a time when all casinos in a given venue offered the same rules but that is in the distant past. Today you can find Northern Nevada rules in Strip casinos and Strip rules in the Downtown Las Vegas casinos. But at a cocktail party with Noah Life, you had better know what set of rules is usually associated with what location or you'll find yourself sitting alone in a corner, sipping champagne and wondering what all the fuss is about.

Northern Nevada Rules

1. Any pair may be split.
2. Split aces receive only one card on each.
3. Resplitting of non-ace pairs up to four times.
4. Doubling is permitted on 10 and 11 only.
5. No doubling permitted after splitting pairs.
6. Dealer hits soft 17.
7. No surrender.

Las Vegas Strip Rules

Put on Nat King Cole, open a bottle of champagne, look your beautiful wife (or handsome husband or sensationally significant other) in the eyes and begin a slow and . . . oops, sorry, we're talking blackjack, not sex. . . .

1. Any pair may be split.
2. Split aces receive only one card each.
3. Splitting up to four times is allowed.

4. Doubling is permitted on any first two cards.
5. No doubling after splitting pairs.
6. Dealer stands on all 17s.
7. Insurance is available.
8. Surrender is not available.

Atlantic City Rules

1. Any pair may be split.
2. Split aces receive only one card each.
3. Resplitting of pairs is not permitted.
4. Doubling is permitted on any first two cards except blackjack.
5. Doubling is permitted after splitting, except for aces.
6. The dealer stands on all 17s.
7. Insurance is available.
8. Surrender is available.

European Rules

1. Any pair may be split.
2. Split aces receive only one card each.
3. No resplitting of pairs is permitted.
4. Doubling on 9, 10 and 11 only.
5. Dealer stands on all 17s.
6. Insurance is available.
7. Dealer does not receive a hole card until all players have played their hands.
8. Surrender is not allowed.

As I stated, these sets of rules are no longer really found exclusively in the locations where they were named. It's archaic to characterize them by their location names but some players still like to do this.

Barber Pole Betting

This is sometimes used to camouflage card counting. You size your bet with various denominations of chips (say, ones, fives, 25s, 100s) all in one stack. When the count is low, your stack has more lower level denominations. When the count is high, your stack has more higher level denominations. The height of your stack never changes but the value goes up and down based on the count. Sloppy pit personnel will not then notice your dramatic escalation of bets since it always looks as if your betting the same stack. This is also called rainbow betting. It has a major drawback as many dealers get quite annoyed at this style of betting and will often "color you up" as they pay out your wins. Also, many casinos make their dealers call out "checks play" when you bet a certain amount (usually $100 at a five dollar- or $10-minimum table). This will draw attention to your barber pole and astute pit personnel might just know what you're attempting.

Depth Charging

This is a technique of blackjack play developed by Arnold Snyder that is geared to the single-deck game. The player will always increase his bet as the cards are coming out, whether the count is low or high. However, the player will know all the variations in strategy to be used in all counts and in this way get an extremely small advantage. The card-counting system to be used for this has to be one with a good playing efficiency and side counts of other cards are recommended. Although depth charging gives the player a slight advantage, it is not worth the great effort required to learn all the necessary indices.

Chapter Nine
Any Questions?

The following are the most frequently asked questions:

Does the depth of penetration have anything to do with the accuracy of your count?

Yes. The deeper you go into the deck the more accurate your count is. However, this sharpening of the accuracy is very slight until you get down to the the very end when it soars. For example, in an eight-deck game, when you get down to the last 40 cards, your count is extremely valuable as opposed to the first 40 cards when the same count is merely indicative. In an eight-deck game, many players prefer to either sit out the first two decks or flat bet the minimum, regardless of the count. After two decks, if the count is positive (or, for some, neutral) they will sit down to play.

Are there dealer-biased tables and player-biased tables?

In retrospect, you can plainly see if a table had been dealer-biased, player-biased or neutral because you can add up the money won and lost, the number of players who won or lost, etc. The problem is translating this information so that you can make predictions about the future of the table. Some systems have been sold that claim to do this. The most notable is the TARGET system of Jerry Patterson. This system claims to be able to show you which tables are player friendly based on a number of criteria including whether players are betting multiple chips, whether players have been winning and are happy, whether players have been at the table a long time, and so forth. I've read Patterson's material and I can tell you this—it can't hurt you to play at a table where people have been winning and are friendly and happy in a multiple-deck game. In single-deck, you'd probably rather go head to head with a dealer even if the dealer has blown people away previously—as long as that dealer thoroughly shuffles the cards. TARGET appeals to the emotional side of playing blackjack, just as blaming poor players for bad plays that seemingly affect the outcome of the game appeals to our innate desire to assign a scapegoat to random events. When I enter a casino to play multiple-deck games, here's what I do: I look around for the dealer with the best shuffle point. That's the single, most important thing. If several dealers have good shuffle points, then I check which of these tables will allow me to play two hands, and of these which have the players that seem the happiest and have been winning. The third criteria is simply an emotional one but I am never one to discount the emotional side to any human endeavor. So if it makes you feel better to target tables as I do, by all means do so. I don't buy the idea that people should attempt to shed their emotions—as long as those emotions don't truly interfere with best blackjack.

I have been given an opportunity to buy a concealable, blackjack computer that will keep track of all the cards and signal me the count. The sellers of the computer say it will give me a five percent advantage over the house. Should I buy it? The price is $5,000.

No. First of all, even with a computer, it is unlikely that you'd get a five percent advantage over even the most liberal single-deck games. If such an advantage were so, the guy selling the computer would make much more money using the computers to play blackjack rather than selling them. [This holds true even with a $5,000 price tag and a lot of buyers!] There are computers that can do as your seller claims, however—give an accurate, no, *perfect* count. The only problem is that they are illegal. Get caught with one in Nevada and you face upwards of 10 years in the Nevada State Penitentiary and I've heard that the games there are not known for their good rules. And . . . speaking of computers . . .

A new tool to foil card counters has been developed by Mikhon Gaming called *Safe Jack.* In the guise of speeding up the game and correcting possible errors in payoffs and hand totaling, the system is actually a sophisticated way of checking for card counters. Here's how the *Safe Jack* works. *Safe Jack* is composed of two independent systems: one "reads" the card values and the other "reads" the chip values. For chip reading, the casino must use specially manufactured "safe chips" that have microchips in them. When a player places his chips in the betting circle, they are scanned and the computer accurately records the size of the bet. All possible hands are recognized by the computer and when a player wants to hit, he presses the hit area of the layout. If he wishes to stand, the player hits the stand area. When the players have finished playing their hands, the dealer plays his. When the dealer is finished, the computer alerts him as to who won or lost and how much to pay each. A red light indicates a player has lost; a green light indicates a player has won; and a yellow light indicates that the hand was a push. Unfortunately, the *Safe Jack* system also keeps a running count and will alert the casino as to whether the remaining decks are positive or negative. Thus, every dealer will know when to shuffle up (when the remaining cards are highly positive—thus favoring the players) and when to continue to play (when the remaining cards are highly negative—thus favoring the house) and which of the many players the dealer is facing is counting cards. How will the computer know that a player is counting? It keeps track of your bets and compares them to the count. If the count is low, your bet will be low; if the count is high, your bet will be high. What the casino does with this information is up to the individual casino bosses to determine. My guess is that the paranoid casino executives will bounce the card counters and the enlightened executives will tolerate their action.

There might, however, be a way around this computational monster. If it is programmed to "find" escalations in bets and correlate these with high counts, then a card counter should start with his top bet and go down as the count goes down. Do the opposite of what the computer is programmed to pick up. Stay with your big bet if the count is neutral or positive—thus, you'll have the most money out when the game favors you; and go down to ever smaller bets when the remaining cards are negative—thus, you'll have the least money out when the game favors the casino. In the event that the computer checks and notifies the dealer of all changes in bet size with both high and low counts, then the above strategy won't work. However, so many players move their bets up and down during the course of a shoe that many of them are bound to be betting high when the count is high and betting low when the count is low. The casino that acts precipitously based on this information might find itself banning players or shuffling up on players who don't count and, quite possibly, who don't even play basic strategy.

Indeed, the *Safe Jack* might actually work to the disadvantage of casinos because it might fall under the "equal protection" concept of the law. All players might have to be treated equally when applying *Safe Jack* information. Take a casino that wishes to ban card counters. That casino will have to determine at what point it will ask players to leave when the player is suspected of counting cards. Let us say that when *Safe Jack* correlates 10 high counts to 10 increases in bets for a given player then that player is asked to leave. However, if one player is asked to leave but another isn't—doesn't this violate the principle of equal protection? I think it might.

Are there blackjack systems that can accurately predict what cards will be coming out of the shoe in multiple-deck games? Are little cards expected? Or big cards? Aces? Where can I find these systems?

There are systems for everything in blackjack and you can usually find them in the gaming press. Many systems sellers make glowing claims for their systems but it's "buyer beware" when purchasing these usually overpriced items. The real problem arises as to whether these systems do what they say they do; or, if they indeed do what they say they do, can *you* do them? Can you predict if a whole bunch of little cards or big cards are about to come out? Yes. If you can track clumps of these cards through the shuffle. But if the decks can't be tracked, or if you can't track them, then three or four little cards coming out doesn't mean one, two, three or four little cards are going to come out after these. In fact, logic would tell us that if little cards are coming out, there are more big cards waiting to come out. And that's card counting! I think many system sellers want to take advantage of people's laziness and thus they offer simplistic ways to beat blackjack that actually wind up being self-defeating. Yes, some people can track individual cards and clumps of cards through the shuffle but it isn't an easy thing. The skill required to do this and the practice required to attain and sharpen this skill are much, much greater than learning how to count cards. As for methods that predict what is coming out without using tracking techniques, these can be found by reading the gaming literature. You'll know them by the outrageous claims made by the purveyors of the system in their advertisements. "You can win $1,000 a day or more without counting cards!" "Live like a king on blackjack by using the Special Numbers system!" I'm not the first to say this but it has become a litany of sorts for me—if it sounds too good to be true, it probably is.

As I understand it, the player wins approximately 44 hands, the dealer 48 hands and eight hands are tied for an average of a 100 hands. Does that assume the player is counting cards?

It doesn't matter. The above figures are indeed the averages for a player playing accurate basic strategy. But the number of hands won is not the same as monetary expectation as I describe in chapter seven. Card counting does not change in any *substantial* way how many hands you win or lose over and above the average. It does change how much money you have out in favorable situations. In a multiple-deck game, you will be between +1 and −1 approximately 43 percent of the time. In a single-deck game, you will be in this range approximately 37 percent of the time. In this range, you will lose approximately 43 cents for every $100 bet in multiple-deck games, and 19 cents in single-deck games. The following statistics are what you can expect to win or lose depending on the count (using the Hi-Lo count) for every $100 bet and what percent of the time you will be at these counts. I've rounded the fractions up and down so the percentages might come to more than 100 percent. This chart is based on flat betting in all situations and playing basic strategy. Remember they are approximations and in the real world you might win or lose more or less.

Count	% of Time Single/Multi	Win/Lose Single/Multi
−6 or less	.6% / 2%	−$4.06 / −$4.16
−5	.4% / 2%	−$2.89 / −$3.27
−4	.3% / 3%	−$2.50 / −$2.84
−3	.5% / 4%	−$1.98 / −$2.32
−2	.6% / 7%	−$1.52 / −$1.78
−1	.10% / 12%	−$0.82 / −$1.29
0	.37% / 43%	−$0.19 / −$0.43
+1	.10% / 11%	+$0.84 / +$0.035
+2	.5% / 6%	+$1.43 / +$1.19
+3	.5% / 4%	+$2.18 / +$1.48
+4	.3% / 2%	+$2.68 / +$2.05
+5	.2% / 2%	+$3.49 / +$2.59
+6 or more	.6% / 2%	+$5.09 / +$4.16

It's easy to see that for both single- and multiple-deck games, your money will be made in the plus counts when each $100 bet has a positive return (in neutral and minus counts each $100 bet has a loss). You can win money by only playing in positive situations and flat betting, or playing in all situations but escalating or lowering your bet depending on the count; or you can play some combination of both styles. If, for example, a player only played at counts of +6 or −6 in multiple-deck games, he could make a killing by just tripling the size of his bet in the plus zone. And thus this chart shows the efficacy of counting cards.

Is there a best place to sit at a blackjack table—one that wins more than other places? Is that why card counters like to sit at third base?

Yes and no. Yes, I remember reading someplace (where? I don't remember!) that some research indicates that in a freshly shuffled six- or eight-deck shoe, the first baseman's seat on the very first round, has a slightly better chance of winning than any other position. After the first shoe is finished, all positions at the table have an equal chance of winning or losing. However, the reason some card counters prefer to sit at third base is so they can see more cards before they have to make their hitting and standing decisions. It has nothing to do with whether that position wins more hands.

How often does a dealer have a blackjack when he has an ace showing?
How often will he bust with an ace showing?

The dealer will have a blackjack approximately 32 percent of the time with an ace showing and he will bust approximately 12 percent of the time with an ace up. This is why it is of utmost importance that basic-strategy players ignore the insurance option for as you can see you will lose it much more than you'll win it.

How often does a dealer get a blackjack?

The dealer and the player can expect a blackjack slightly less than five percent of the time. There is a slightly greater chance for a black-jack in a single-deck game than in a multiple-deck game but in a multi-ple-deck game there is a slightly greater chance that both the player and the dealer will have blackjacks at the same time. These are two more reasons why the single-deck game is more favorable for the player.

Which two-card hands win the most for the players in terms of money? Which hands lose the most?

The top five two-card hands for winning money, based on $100 bet, are as follows:

1. Ace-10 (blackjack): +$144
2. Any 20: +$58
3. Any 19: +$27
4. 11: +$18
5. Ace-Ace: +$16

The worst five two-card hands are:

1. Any 16: −$42
2. Any 15: −$40
3. Any 14: −$37
4. Any 13: −$35
5. Any 12: −$32

What's the likelihood of the player busting when he has to hit a bust hand?

When a player has a 16, he has approximately a 61 percent chance of busting. When a player has a 15, he has a 59 percent chance of busting; 14, a 56 percent chance; 13, a 52 percent chance; 12, a 48 percent chance of busting.

Overall, how often will a dealer bust?

The dealer will bust approximately 28 percent of the time.

Overall, how often will the player bust?

A player using basic strategy will bust approximately 17 percent of the time.

What are the real effects on the favorability of a deck with the removal of the various cards?

Dr. Peter Griffin, in his masterpiece *The Theory of Blackjack* (see chapter 23, on recommended books), has compiled an impressive statistical analysis of all aspects of blackjack, including the real effects of card removal on the favorability of the game for any number of decks. This chart is adapted from his work. Plus means favorable to the player; minus means unfavorable to the player.

Number of Decks	Card Removed	Effect on Remaining Deck
1	2	+.38
2	2	+.19
4	2	+.09
6	2	+.06
8	2	+.05

Number of Decks	Card Removed	Effect on Remaining Deck
1	3	+.45
2	3	+.22
4	3	+.11
6	3	+.07
8	3	+.06

Number of Decks	Card Removed	Effect on Remaining Deck
1	4	+.55
2	4	+.27
4	4	+.14
6	4	+.09
8	4	+.07

Number of Decks	Card Removed	Effect on Remaining Deck
1	5	+.69
2	5	+.34
4	5	+.17
6	5	+.11
8	5	+.08

Number of Decks	Card Removed	Effect on Remaining Deck
1	6	+.46
2	6	+.23
4	6	+.11
6	6	+.08
8	6	+.06

Number of Decks	Card Removed	Effect on Remaining Deck
1	7	+.28
2	7	+.14
4	7	+.07
6	7	+.05
8	7	+.03

Number of Decks	Card Removed	Effect on Remaining Deck
1	8	.00
2	8	.00
4	8	.00
6	8	.00
8	8	.00

Number of Decks	Card Removed	Effect on Remaining Deck
1	9	−.18
2	9	−.09
4	9	−.04
6	9	−.03
8	9	−.02

Number of Decks	Card Removed	Effect on Remaining Deck
1	10	−.51
2	10	−.25
4	10	−.13
6	10	−.08
8	10	−.06

Number of Decks	Card Removed	Effect on Remaining Deck
1	ace	−.61
2	ace	−.30
4	ace	−.15
6	ace	−.10
8	ace	−.08

These statistics explain why card-counting systems have been developed to take advantage of card removal. Ideally, you should just memorize the exact percentages of a card's removal and then play and bet accordingly. Of course, in the real world, I'd hazard a guess that only a mathematical savant would be able to do such a thing.

I understand that if you have a one percent advantage over the house you are expected to win one dollar for every $100 wagered in the long run. But what does this mean if I play, say, only 1,000 hands or 5,000 hands with an average bet of $100? Will I definitely win $1,000 or $5,000 dollars?

No. All win estimates are presented as long-term or long-run estimates based on millions of hands where the actual outcomes will be close to their theoretical probabilities. Unfortunately, some players mistakenly think that this is what will happen when they play for the short run. Nothing could be further from the truth. If you are betting

$100 a hand (on average) and playing with a one percent advantage, at the end of 1,000 hands of play you will most likely be somewhere between −$6,480 and +$8,720. At 5,000 hands of play, you will probably be somewhere between −$11,400 and +$22,600. You can see from this that while the game favors you strongly over time, you can still lose in the short run. The best description I have ever read concerning what it means to have an edge over the house was given by the late Ken Uston in his book, *Million Dollar Blackjack* (Gambling Times Books):

> Imagine a game in which there are 100 beans in a jar, white beans and black beans. If you pick a white bean, you win the "hand;" if you pick a black bean, you lose the hand. After each draw the bean is replaced in the jar, the jar is shaken up and you pick another bean for the next hand. The typical player is faced with a game in which he has roughly 48 white beans and 52 black beans (actually this mix gives him a four percent rather than three percent disadvantage, but is used to avoid 'half beans'). The basic-strategy player is faced with 50 white beans and 50 black beans. The advanced card counter has roughly 51 white beans and 49 black beans (again rounding to whole beans, which in this case gives him a two percent advantage over the house).
>
> The typical player, faced with only 48 white beans and 52 black ones, might, in the course of a few hours of 'bean picking,' actually pick more white ones than black ones, thus winning for the session. But if he were to bet on each pick, and pick beans night after night for weeks, eventually the excess of black beans over white ones would be felt and the player would eventually end up a loser.
>
> By the same token, the basic-strategy player, faced with an even game, could easily win (pick more white beans than black) or lose (pick more black beans than white) in the short term. But over a long period of time, he should pick white beans very close to half the time, thus approximately breaking even.
>
> The good card counter can also pick more black beans than white in the short term. Indeed, there are only two more white beans than black beans. Again, in the long term, after many hours of bean picking, he should pick more white

beans, thus winning. I have had a distressingly high number of "black bean sessions."

There are two points to be made here. If the typical or basic-strategy player has been winning heavily, chances are he is picking out a disproportionate number of white beans. He should not expect those results to continue indefinitely.

The second point: if you develop into a good card counter, you will not win all the time. In fact, there are times you will be ready to quit, thinking either that you must be playing wrong or that the gods are against you.

While Uston distorted the actual percentages for the purpose of his analogy (for example, the basic-strategy player rarely has an even game or the card counter a two percent long-run advantage), the black-white bean picking is exactly what a player is doing. Indeed, Uston, in his book *Two Books on Blackjack* (UIB Publishers), uses the bean analogy to describe the real situation of a card counter. The card counter faces three types of bean jars: jar one that has 48 white beans and 52 black beans (a negative deck or shoe); jar two which is one that has 50 white beans and 50 black beans (a neutral deck or shoe); and jar three which is one that has 51 white beans and 49 black beans (a positive deck or shoe). He faces each jar approximately one third of the time. Now, the counter knows which jar is which. Thus, when he faces jar one he'll bet, say $10; when he faces jar two, he can bet $10 or $20; but when he faces jar three, he jumps his bet to $100 or more. Such a betting scheme will give the counter slightly more than a one percent advantage. Card counters know when the bean jar favors them and when it doesn't favor them and they bet accordingly. Unfortunately, the basic-strategy player is stuck playing all three jars the same way since he cannot distinguish among them.

This next question was asked by a dealer at a Tunica, Mississippi casino:

For several weeks now a team of blackjack players has been taking up all the seats at a given table. They bet every square so that no one can come to the table. Their strategy is to never take a card if they can bust. So they will stand on 12, 13, 14, 15 and 16 against all the dealer's up cards—even a 10. They never double down or split. They have been winning a lot of money. Is this a viable strategy or have they just been lucky?

Lady Luck will sometimes favor gamblers playing the worst strategies as the example in the previous question shows. And this, not taking a card if you can bust, is one of the worst strategies. It doesn't matter if they are a team or if the table just had seven bad players playing, the casino will make its money in the long run. The fact that they have been winning is due to luck's fickleness. Sooner or later they will have to pay the piper. Probably sooner. Why? Because this style of play is giving the house an approximately 6.5 percent edge. With an edge such as this, these team players will find themselves going broke.

Say I count cards and I have my maximum bet out—which is one percent of my total stake. Now I get a hand that calls for doubling down—what do I do? If I double I have two percent of my total stake out. If I don't double, I'm missing an opportunity.

I once asked this very same question of the late, great, card counter, Paul Keen. Here's what he told me:

> If you can't afford it or it makes you nervous to have so much money out, don't double. Just take a hit. After all, you already have your maximum bet out and you don't want to over bet your advantage. If you can afford it, then double. You'll experience greater fluctuations but in the long run you'll win more money—and that's the name of the game. A middle-of-the-road approach would be to double when the dealer is weak and you're very strong. The dealer has a five or six up and you have an 11 or 10 with your maximum bet out. Good chance you'll get that 10 or good chance the dealer will bust. You might want to go for it in that case—even if it makes you a little nervous.

What is the single, worst play in blackjack?

If we totally eliminate idiot plays such as doubling on a 19 or 20 (two 10s) against the dealer's six, etc., and stick to plays that a poor player might make thinking he's doing the right thing, then the absolutely worst play in terms of how much you can expect to lose is standing on two eights against the dealer's seven instead of splitting them as basic strategy tells you to. You can expect to lose 70 cents for every dollar you bet in that situation. Why would somebody do this?

Because he figures that the dealer only has two cards that can beat him straight up—an ace or 10 in the hole. All other cards (two through nine) forces the dealer to take a hit on his hand. Thus, the player reasons that he has a good chance if he stands. Here reason is at odds with the facts. The fact is that a player who makes this strategy decision will see his bankroll grow progressively smaller as time goes on.

Since the house wins so much money at blackjack wouldn't playing just like the dealer mean that you would have an even game against the casino?

No! Remember an important thing about blackjack. The player must make all his decisions first. This means that should he bust, the house wins even if the dealer eventually goes bust himself. The mimic-king-the-dealer style of play is a trap that many novice players fall into and it's a trap that comes in with a hefty 5.6 percent edge for the casino.

If the dealer is showing a nine or 10 (perhaps even an eight), why not simply hit your 17 instead of standing? I read somewhere that 18.8 was the average winning hand in blackjack—so 17 seems to be very weak. Why not hit it?

You're right about one thing. Seventeen is a very weak hand. In fact, you have a negative expectation against all dealer up cards when you have a hard 17 with the single exception of a dealer showing a six. That's why you always hit your soft 17s in basic strategy. However, the hard 17 is a different matter. On average you will bust approximately 70 percent of the time when you hit your hard 17. This expectation is worse than if you stand. Here again we see that basic strategy cannot make a losing hand a winning hand but it can diminish how much we lose. We will lose less in the long run by standing on a hard 17 than we will by hitting it.

Why would a casino offer a lot of good rules when they know these rules favor the player? Why allow all the doubling on any first two cards, or splitting and doubling after splits? Why should the casinos give the players an inch?

The good player will indeed take advantage of all the good rules and options. But think of the ploppy—the truly bad player. I'll give you an example. Just the other day I was at the Claridge's high-roller pit and the guy next to me was betting $300 a hand. He received a five (a three and a two). The dealer had a seven up. The guy doubled on his five because in Atlantic City you can double down on any first two cards. He lost. Now, doubling on any first two cards is a favorable rule when you know how to employ it but it can be devastating to the poor player. Give the player all the choices the good rules allow and the good player will take advantage of them and the poor player will lose even more. Since there are more bad players than good players, the more options you give them, the more money the casino will beat them out of. Take the case of surrender, a good option for the player who uses it wisely. But I've seen poor players surrender all their bust hands including 12 and 13 against the dealer's seven, eight, nine or 10. If I owned a casino, I'd have all the best rules. I'd advertise them big time. There's a psychological phenomenon that works in blackjack—poor players are lured by good rules even though they don't know how to take advantage of them. You see this when casinos have single-deck games. Some of the worst players will say: "I always play single-deck because it's the best to play." Yeah, if you know how to play it. If not, it doesn't matter where you play.

What do you think about tipping? I count cards and play a tight game with the casino—to my understanding this eats into my small edge. Should I tip and if I do tip, won't it cut into my edge?

Yes and yes. Yes, by all means tip the dealers who are giving you good service. In the world of blackjack there's the ideal and the real. In the ideal world, dealers make enough money to live the American dream without being tipped (as would waiters and busboys and bell-hops, etc.). Unfortunately, the real world isn't this way. Most dealers make minimum wage or slightly above and must rely on tips to live. I have heard the argument that this is the profession they chose, so let them live with the consequences. I don't buy it. The profession they chose is one where tips are considered a part of the job and customers are expected to give tips. You could call this the tradition of salary expectation. If dealers actually were paid by the casino what they make with tips and tipping were forbidden, you would probably find that the casinos would up the price of their table minimums to compensate—just as a restaurant would have to up the price of its food if it paid waiters and waitresses a full salary. The second part of your question is also "yes." By tipping, you will cut down on your expectation, so you have to do it in a way that doesn't diminish your expectation to zero or less. Here's how I like to tip. When the count is high and the dealer has been friendly (I define "friendly" as just about anything but sullen and nasty), I will put a chip on top of my bet and say to the dealer: "You're riding on top." If I win the bet, I pay the dealer the winning wager but I don't give him the chip on top. I let that ride with my next bet. In this way, a hot streak is a hot streak for me and the dealer. (You obviously have a much better chance of winning several hands in a highly positive deck and thus a better chance for a streak for you and the dealer.) I would not have been betting that extra chip over and over in a hot streak, so one can safely say this is the dealer's money. My tip was really only the initial bet for the dealer. This is not a usual way of tipping and some dealers might tell you to take the chip off the top and bet it in front of your stack. Don't do it. Then the bet only rides once.

If you are a card counter and want to throw the casino pit people off as to your true ability, why not make some bonehead plays that make you look as if you don't know what you're doing?

The reason you don't want to make bonehead plays has to do with the nature of your edge. You have a tiny advantage at best and every intentional (and unintentional) bonehead play eats into that advantage. With that said, in single-deck games the only good camouflage "bonehead" play might be to take insurance when you have a minimum bet out with a stiff hand (and call attention to it) so that when you take insurance with a maximum bet out, it will appear as though you're an insurance taker. In a single-deck game one of the tip-offs that a person is counting cards is the taking of insurance on stiff hands with big bets out.

When should I double on an eight in a shoe game?

Against a dealer's up card of five or six, it would be appropriate to double when the true count is +3 and +2 respectively. Remember, however, that many shoe games allow doubling after splits and thus an eight composed of two fours should be split against a five and six.

When would be the best time to double down on a seven against a dealer's six or five?

You would double in a true count of +8 or more against a six and +9 or more against the dealer's five. These counts would basically hold true for single and multiple-deck games. Card counters should be wary about doubling on such hands as doing so would bring attention to you. Ploppys often make such plays but since a ploppy is essentially brain dead no one seems to care. Which brings us to the next chapter.

Chapter Ten

Ploppys to the Left of Me, Ploppys to the Right of Me

There is one great fallacy in blackjack that I *emotionally* succumb to every now and then—despite the fact that I *intellectually* know better. This fallacy concerns the effect of other people's play on your overall expectation. The fallacy states that other players can affect your monetary expectation. Computer simulations show us quite clearly that this is not so. The play of other players has no real effect on your monetary expectation. You can play with the best players in the world (I have), and you can play with the worst players in the world (I have), and whether you win or lose in the long run will be up to you, period. You can't argue with a computer and you can't argue with the mathematics. In fact, this issue really can't be argued at all. Still, this is an area of blackjack play where theory (proven, concrete, unassailable) and perception (idiosyncratic, subjective, easily disputed) clash head-on.

Many players who know basic strategy get upset when other players make bonehead plays—especially when these bonehead plays seem to cost the basic-strategy player money. It is not unusual to see blackjack players scolding other blackjack players for faulty moves. In fact, it is not unusual when you count cards and change your basic strategy based on the count to have other players yell at you! They do this because they subscribe to the great myth that the play of others can affect their chances of winning and losing.

Take the following example from my own experience and then we'll analyze the whys and wherefores of it to see why it is easy to fall into the trap of thinking that other people's decisions can affect your play.

It was the summer of 1995 and I was playing rather regularly at the Aladdin Hotel and Casino, which had a marvelous two-deck game with great rules, spectacular penetration, and a pit that didn't seem to mind that I was getting a one-to-20 spread (I was following Brian's betting scheme from chapter six). In fact, the game and conditions were reminiscent of the greatest game I ever played, which was at the Maxim Hotel and Casino in the summer of 1991. Of course, the Maxim game stands out as the best game Las Vegas ever offered. Why? Because the penetration was 100 percent. With the exception of the burn card, the dealers dealt out every card. If they used up the cards midway through a round, they just took the discards, reshuffled and continued playing. It was the greatest game ever. To make it even better, the casino tolerated card counters such as myself who were only betting red chips and not spreading more than one to eight. You could split and resplit. You could double down after splits. The dealers stayed on soft 17. It was heaven. I played there every day for more than a month. I made money. I had fun. What more could you ask of blackjack?

I was almost having as much fun and profit for a three-week stretch at the Aladdin until the arrival of the Ploppy from Hell. Now, in my diary in chapter 22 of this book, I will discuss some of the ploppys that I met during a 22-day stretch of playing in Las Vegas. To set the record straight, a ploppy is a moron *with an attitude*. A ploppy is a fool. A ploppy usually looks like what he or she is—something even a cat would think twice about dragging in. Ploppys come in all shapes and sizes (often quite strange actually) and, while most of them have low IQs, some could be bright in a technical way. I have met ploppy doctors, ploppy lawyers, ploppy teachers, ploppy politicians, ploppy book reviewers. But generally speaking, the ploppy population is at the lower end of the bell curve of intelligence, often at the lower end of this same curve in manners, comportment, fashion, and hygiene. Ploppys usually travel alone but when they travel in mated pairs they are a sight to behold and a scent to smell. No one reading this book is a ploppy because by definition, ploppys don't read books about blackjack. They have their own strategies.

The Ploppy from Hell was a giant ploppy. He was six-foot-five if he was an inch and he smelled as if several animals had met their Maker in his clothing. He had a big belly that was exposed because of ill-fitting shirts and his belly button was a lint factory. He looked something like the late, great Zero Mostel on a bad day.

He lumbered into the Aladdin on a Thursday afternoon and stood hovering like some giant hovering thing over the player at third base on the two-deck game. He wasn't drooling, but he should have been. I was at first base, playing my two hands. The previous two weeks had seen me win quite a bit from this casino and I was in a great mood. The beautiful A.P. was next to me and I whispered to her, "Check out the ploppy." She looked at him and shook her head.

"Do you see the belly button?" I asked.

"I'm trying not to notice," she said.

"You think maybe he's an expert card counter and this is some kind of a disguise?" I said.

"Why would anyone want to look like that? Everyone's looking at him."

The guy at third base got up and left several moments later. I met him in the sundries shop the next day and asked him why he had left when he was winning.

"Oh, man, that guy hanging over me," he said. "Man, he smelled. I couldn't take it. I went back to my room and took a shower."

So the Ploppy from Hell sat down and my playing life was irrevocably changed. At first I thought he was a basic-strategy player because he seemed to make the right decisions on the first half dozen hands. But then the dealer showed a six. The Ploppy from Hell scratched for a card and received a 10. I figured he'd put his cards under his chips because, with a 10 showing, he had to have a pat hand against the dealer's six. Instead, he turned his cards over and he had 26. The Ploppy from Hell had taken a hit on 16 against the dealer's six. The dealer turned over her card and she had a seven under her six for 13. She then hit and got another seven—giving her 20. I had 19 and lost.

If I were superstitious I would say that the Ploppy from Hell had taken the dealer's 10. But I was winning and I was in a good frame of mind and I'm not superstitious (because being superstitious can bring bad luck!) and so I remembered that how another person plays has no effect on my expectation in the long run. And I was content to laugh at the stupid mistake the Ploppy from Hell had made.

Three days later, I wasn't laughing anymore.

The Ploppy from Hell always seemed to arrive when I was playing. If I played in the morning, he'd appear, hovering over the third baseman until the third baseman left. If I played in the afternoon, the evening, whenever, the Ploppy from Hell would always make his entrance after I sat down. Once I was at third base and he came. He hovered over me. The smell was indescribably indescribable. But I refused to budge. I put my hand to my nose and doggedly played. When the cocktail waitress came over, I said to her: "Could you get me a small bottle of Vicks vapor rub?"

"What?" she said.

"I need Vicks," I said. I was not about to get up because I was winning quite a bit of money at this particular session. I figured if I got some Vicks, I could put it in my nostrils the way you do when you're watching an autopsy so that the smell doesn't get to you.

"I'm sorry, I can't get that," she said and she rushed off, having gotten a whiff of the Ploppy from Hell. So I turned to him.

"I'm not moving," I said as politely as I could.

"I'll wait," he said.

Great. Just great.

But I played on until I got tired and the Ploppy from Hell just hovered. When I left, he sat down.

For seven days, the Ploppy from Hell was at the table. It wouldn't matter whether I had been winning like crazy before, as soon as he sat down and started to play his ploppy way, I would start to lose. He always played third base and he always hit his bust hands against the dealer's fours, fives and sixes. And every time he did this, it seems, I had a big bet out, he caught a bust card and the dealer made her hands.

Others at the table would say things to him.

"You are a jerk," said one woman from New York.

"He play for house?" asked one Taiwanese guy.

"Jesus Christ almighty, why don't you learn how to play the game?" shouted one Texan.

I never said anything to him because—one, I'm polite; and two, I know that what he was doing wasn't supposed to hurt my chances of winning in any way despite the fact that I seemed to be getting hurt. Sad but true, I couldn't seem to win when he was at the table and, finally, I decided that, despite my edge, despite my intellectual acknowledgement that he had no effect on my expectation, despite the fact that I was substantially ahead at this particular game at the Aladdin, I would not play with the Ploppy from Hell. If he sat down, after rousing the third baseman as he usually did, I'd get up. I'd go to another table.

Was this stupid?

From a strictly professional standpoint, yes, this was stupid. The Aladdin's game was good and it was beatable. Good and beatable and it doesn't get any better than that. But . . .

I'd rather be comfortable. I don't have to play blackjack to make money. I play it for the challenge. It's a game. The money is simply the score.

Was the Ploppy from Hell hurting my monetary expectation?

No. He only seemed to. If we could clean him up and shut him up (he had an irritating voice made more irritating by the fact that I was losing when he was at the table), and I played millions of hands with him at the table, and he was also playing millions of hands, then I would have won just about what I would win if I had been playing with good players at the table. I do recall that many times in my playing career ploppys have sat down, done ploppy things with their hands, and I've won. I recall these things vaguely because when I win, it's only what I expected, but when I lose I remember it because truthfully I never *expect* to lose (see chapter 21). I guess it's human nature to remember all the times some ploppy hit his 16, busted, and the dealer drew to a 21. Emotionally, it feels right to blame the ploppy for screwing up. It feels right to accuse him of making decisions that hurt you. We always like to personify our disappointments and it is just plain easier to blame a person for our bad fortune than to blame some blind force of nature. This is probably why people killed messengers of bad tidings in ancient Greece—if the messenger were dead there would be no more bad tidings from that particular fellow. These things *feel* right even when we intellectually know they're wrong.

Apropos of this, a blackjack-playing acquaintance of mine, Gerard E., was riding me once about something I had written concerning this very thing. K.F., A.P. and I had toyed with the idea [see *The Morons of Blackjack and Other Monsters* (Paone Press)] that maybe the bad play of other players did indeed affect our expectation. I stated quite plainly that intellectually I knew that it did not but then I went off to discuss the issue and give it some credence. Well, Gerard was so superciliously superior in his scorn of this discussion that I thought maybe I should never again write about the emotional aspects of gambling but just confine myself to the numbers and math and all the boring stuff.

Then I played with him at the tables. Lo and behold, a ploppy sat down and did the dirty deeds. Hit all the wrong hands. Split all the wrong pairs. I was winning so I didn't care. But my superior, snide little buddy went ballistic. Gerard started to lose, and every loss *seemed* to be directly related to some dumb move made by the ploppy. He finally screamed at the ploppy. His face got red, his veins popped, I thought my superior friend was going to have a stroke.

When our session was over, I asked him how he could be so scornful of me when I just toyed with an idea and yet he had gone ape over just such a thing. I mean didn't he know that the play of other players had no effect on his monetary expectation? So why had he gone berserk in the presence of the ploppy, when he had criticized me for toying with a feeling in one of my books?

Gerard looked at me and said: "That's different."

Oh.

In the cool calm of the word processor's light as I write this, I can tell you without shame that I do sometimes get irritated by poor play. Especially when I'm losing. I am human. Bad play doesn't bother me when I'm winning. Should I feel this way? No. After all, we are not our blackjack-playing brothers' keepers are we? If they want to kill themselves with poor play, why should it upset us? It shouldn't. But sometimes it does. That is the human predicament after all. We intellectually know something to be thus and so and simultaneously, emotionally, we know its opposite to be true. So it goes.

Chapter Eleven
Face-up
or
Double Exposure
Blackjack

Face-up or Double Exposure blackjack has been available for many years in Las Vegas but it has never really caught on big time across America (or even in Las Vegas for that matter). However, recently Atlantic City casinos have begun to offer this option as have other casinos outside of Nevada. In the past several months, the number of Face-up or Double Exposure tables has increased dramatically in Atlantic City and the game seems to be getting a foothold there. Unlike regular blackjack, all the cards are dealt face up—including the dealer's hole card. The player makes his decisions knowing exactly what hand the dealer is playing. Just like regular blackjack, Face-up or Double Exposure blackjack has basic strategies for every set of rules. Since Atlantic City has taken the lead in this game, I will give you the basic strategy that fits the Atlantic City game. This strategy, with some minor modifications, can be used for the Las Vegas game also. Some of the books I'll recommend in chapter 23 will contain the various strategies for the more obscure Face-up or Double Exposure games.

I have taken this strategy from the charts prepared by John F. Julian in *Julian's No-Nonsense Guide to Winning Blackjack* (Paone Press). It is the optimum *realistic* strategy for the set of rules currently in effect in Atlantic City and elsewhere. The word "realistic" is the key here. The theoretically optimum play, say, of a player's six versus a dealer's 16 is to double down. However, no casino will allow a player to double down on a six because it gives the player too much of an advantage. Indeed, the Atlantic City rules specifically state that you can only double down on nine, 10, and 11. Atlantic City's regular blackjack games allow doubling on *any* first two cards.

In the Face-up or Double Exposure game many hands are automatic losers if you don't hit them. If you have a 20 and the dealer has a 20, you must hit your hand or the dealer will win the push since all ties go to the dealer. Perhaps the reason this game never caught on in Las Vegas is just the fact that for a traditional blackjack player, hitting such hands as 20, 19, 18, and 17 goes so against the grain that it is better not to play the game at all. Can Face-up or Double Exposure blackjack be beaten with card counting? Yes. But you have to make some subtle alterations in your play. For example, if the casino only pays even money for a blackjack (which most do) then you are better off treating that hand as an 11 and doubling against four, five and six in positive counts. Also, the edge for the true count tends to be somewhat stronger in Double Exposure blackjack than for regular blackjack. In regular blackjack every one point of the true count is worth .50 percent for the player. But according to Stanford Wong's *Blackjack Secrets* (Pi Yee Press), in Double Exposure, every one point in the true count is the equivalent of .80 percent for the player. High counts mean more in his game than they do in regular blackjack. Thus, you should wager accordingly.

Player's Hand	**Dealer's Hand**	**Strategy**
4, 5, 6, 7, 8	all dealer hands	hit
9	4, 7, 8, 9, 10, 11, 17, 18, 19, 20	hit
. . . .	5, 6, 12, 13, 14, 15, 16	double
. . . .	A:A, A:2, A:3, A:4, A:5	hit

```
10 . . . . . . . . . . . .9, 10, 11, 17, 18, 19, 20, A:A, A:2 . . . . . . . . . . . .hit
       . . . . . . . . . . . .4, 5, 6, 7, 8, 12, 13, 14, 15, 16 . . . . . . . . . . . . . . . .double
       . . . . . . . . . . . .A:3, A:4, A:5 . . . . . . . . . . . . . . . . . . . . . . . . . . . . .double
11 . . . . . . . . . . . .10, 11, 17, 18, 19, 20, A:A . . . . . . . . . . . . . . . . . . .hit
       . . . . . . . . . . . .4, 5, 6, 7, 8, 9, 12, 13, 14, 15, 16 . . . . . . . . . . . . . .double
       . . . . . . . . . . . .A:2, A:3, A:4, A:5 . . . . . . . . . . . . . . . . . . . . . . . . . .double
12 . . . . . . . . . . . .4, 5, 6, 12, 13, 14, 15, 16, A:5 . . . . . . . . . . . . . . .stand
       . . . . . . . . . . . .7, 8, 9, 10, 11, 17, 18, 19, 20 . . . . . . . . . . . . . . . . .hit
       . . . . . . . . . . . .A:A, A:2, A:3, A:4 . . . . . . . . . . . . . . . . . . . . . . . . . . .hit
13 . . . . . . . . . . . .4, 5, 6, 12, 13, 14, 15, 16 . . . . . . . . . . . . . . . . . . . . .stand
       . . . . . . . . . . . .A:3, A:4, A:5 . . . . . . . . . . . . . . . . . . . . . . . . . . . . . .stand
       . . . . . . . . . . . .7, 8, 9, 10, 11, 17, 18, 19, 20 . . . . . . . . . . . . . . . . .hit
       . . . . . . . . . . . .A:A, A:2 . . . . . . . . . . . . . . . . . . . . . . . . . . . . . . . . . .hit
14 . . . . . . . . . . . .4, 5, 6, 11, 12, 13, 14, 15, 16 . . . . . . . . . . . . . . . . .stand
       . . . . . . . . . . . .A:2, A:3, A;4, A:5 . . . . . . . . . . . . . . . . . . . . . . . . . .stand
       . . . . . . . . . . . .7, 8, 9, 10, 17, 18, 19, 20, A:A . . . . . . . . . . . . . . .hit
15 . . . . . . . . . . . .4, 5, 6, 10, 11, 12, 13, 14, 15, 16 . . . . . . . . . . . . . .stand
       . . . . . . . . . . . .A:A, A:2, A:3, A:4, A:5 . . . . . . . . . . . . . . . . . . . . . .stand
       . . . . . . . . . . . .7, 8, 9, 17, 18, 19, 20 . . . . . . . . . . . . . . . . . . . . . . .hit
16 . . . . . . . . . . . .4, 5, 6, 8, 9, 10, 11, 12, 13, 14, 15, 16 . . . . . . . . . .stand
       . . . . . . . . . . . .7 . . . . . . . . . . . . . . . . . . . . . . . . . . . . . . . . . . . . . . .hit
       . . . . . . . . . . . .A:A, A:2, A:3, A:4, A:5 . . . . . . . . . . . . . . . . . . . . . .stand
17 . . . . . . . . . . . .17, 18, 19, 20 . . . . . . . . . . . . . . . . . . . . . . . . . . . . . .hit
       . . . . . . . . . . . .all else . . . . . . . . . . . . . . . . . . . . . . . . . . . . . . . . . .stand
18 . . . . . . . . . . . .18, 19, 20 . . . . . . . . . . . . . . . . . . . . . . . . . . . . . . . . .hit
       . . . . . . . . . . . .all else . . . . . . . . . . . . . . . . . . . . . . . . . . . . . . . . . .stand
19 . . . . . . . . . . . .19, 20 . . . . . . . . . . . . . . . . . . . . . . . . . . . . . . . . . . . .hit
       . . . . . . . . . . . .all else . . . . . . . . . . . . . . . . . . . . . . . . . . . . . . . . . .stand
20 . . . . . . . . . . . .20 . . . . . . . . . . . . . . . . . . . . . . . . . . . . . . . . . . . . . . .hit
       . . . . . . . . . . . .all else . . . . . . . . . . . . . . . . . . . . . . . . . . . . . . . . . .stand
A:A . . . . . . . . . . . .11, 17, 18, 19, 20 . . . . . . . . . . . . . . . . . . . . . . . . . .hit
       . . . . . . . . . . . .4 to 10; 12 to 16 . . . . . . . . . . . . . . . . . . . . . . . . . . .split
       . . . . . . . . . . . .A:A, A:2, A:3, A:4, A:5 . . . . . . . . . . . . . . . . . . . . . .split
```

2:2, 3:3 . . . . .4, 5, 6, 12 to 17 . . . . .split
. . . . .7 to 11; 18, 19, 20 . . . . .hit
. . . . .A:A, A:2, A:3, A;4, A:5 . . . . .hit

4:4 . . . . .12 to 16 . . . . .split
. . . . .4 to 11, 17 to 20 . . . . .hit
. . . . .A:A, A:2, A:3, A:4, A:5 . . . . .hit

5:5 . . . . .4 to 8, 12 to 16, A:3, A:4, A:5 . . . . .double
. . . . .9, 10, 11, 17 to 20, A:A, A:2 . . . . .hit

6:6 . . . . .4, 5, 6, 12 to 17 . . . . .split
. . . . .7 to 11, 18, 19, 20, A:A, A:2, A:3, A:4 . . . . .hit
. . . . .A,5 . . . . .stand

7:7 . . . . .4, 5, 6, 12 to 17 . . . . .split
. . . . .7 to 10, 18, 19, 20, A:A . . . . .hit
. . . . .11, A:2, A:3, A:4, A:5 . . . . .stand

8:8 . . . . .4 to 8, 12 to 17, A:3, A:4, A:5 . . . . .split
. . . . .9, 10, 11, A:A, A:2 . . . . .stand
. . . . .18, 19, 20 . . . . .hit
9:9 . . . . .4, 5, 6, 8, 12 to 16, 18, A:5 . . . . .split
. . . . .7, 9, 10, 11, 17, A:A, A:2, A:3, A:4 . . . . .stand
. . . . .19, 20 . . . . .hit

10:10 . . . . .13, 14, 15, 16 . . . . .split
. . . . .20 . . . . .hit
. . . . .all else . . . . .stand

A:2, A:3, A:4, ...all dealer's hands . . . . .hit
A:5, A:6

A:7 . . . . .4 to 7, 12 to 17, A:5 . . . . .stand
. . . . .8 to 11, 18, 19, 20, A:A, A:2, A:3, A:4 . . . . .hit

A:8 . . . . .4 to 11, 17, 18, A:A, A:2, A:3, A:4, A:5 . . . . . . .stand
. . . . .12, 13, 14, 15, 16 . . . . .double
. . . . .19, 20 . . . . .hit

A:9 . . . . .4 to 12, 17, 18, 19 . . . . .stand
. . . . .A:A, A:2, A:3, A:4, A:5 . . . . .stand
. . . . .13, 14, 15, 16 . . . . .double

A:10 . . . . .all dealer's hands . . . . .stand

Chapter Twelve
Red and Black Blackjack

Probably the best blackjack option found in the world as I write this is the one where you can place a side bet on whether the dealer's face-up card will be red or black. If it is offered anywhere near you, get to the casino pronto—after first reading this section. It is a simple game to beat, does not require any elaborate new counting system and offers a big bang for your bucks.

The fact that this game is usually dealt from a six- or eight-deck shoe does not lessen its attraction over regular blackjack. The reason for this is simple. The player can get a significant edge over the casino—a much greater edge than is usually available against the regular game because every point in the true count represents almost two percent in favor of the player! (Compare this with the .50 percent for every true-count point in regular blackjack and .80 percent for Double Exposure blackjack.)

You have two approaches to this game. You can sit down from the very first round of play, use basic strategy and count just the red and the black. Or you can back count the red and black and jump in when the count calls for it. You can even employ guerrilla piggybacking by placing a red or black bet on the betting square of someone who is not taking advantage of this option (if the casino and/or the player will allow this). Of course, if you have a partner, as I do (yes, yes, the beautiful A.P.), one of you can count the traditional way and one can do a red-black count, just as I described with the Over-Under 13 option.

The simplest way of red-black counting is to follow traditional *accounting* practices—black is positive and red is negative. Thus, all black cards will be a +1, and all red cards will be −1. Any true count of 2—*whether it be a minus or a plus count*—would indicate that you have an even game. (You figure the true count by dividing the number of decks remaining to be played into the running count just as you do with traditional counting.) The reason you have an even game at +2 or −2 concerns the push on the deuces, which gives the casino an approximately four percent edge off the top in this game.

If you wish to add another side count to your count, you can follow how many deuces of each color have come out. For every deck played, theoretically two deuces of each color should come out. Any time more come out, you have an added advantage over the house of about .50 percent. Keeping track of the deuces is slightly more difficult than just keeping track of the colors but for serious players it might be worth the effort.

Some casinos limit the red-black bet to $25. If your unit of betting is $25 then any count of +3 or −3 or more will call for betting the maximum since it is your lowest unit. If your unit is five dollars, than any +3 or −3 count is a single-unit bet; any +4 or −4 count is a three-unit bet; any +5 or −5 count is a five-unit bet ($25). Should a casino allow a higher maximum bet, any true count of +6 or −6 calls for a 10-unit bet; any true count of +7 or −7 would call for a 15-unit bet. Assuming the casino allows bets higher than $75, you would escalate in units of five with each point in the count.

If this option catches on across the country, and with the growing competition among the casinos it very well could, then a fertile field has opened for the blackjack player—be he a guerrilla player or a traditional player. My guess is that this option will always have certain limitations placed on it because it is so susceptible to card counting—and *simple* card counting at that.

Chapter Thirteen
Over-Under 13

During the past few years in casinos across America, a host of new options, rules and side bets have been offered to blackjack players in the hope of luring them to the tables. Most of these options do not require any change in playing style or strategy. They are passive options and act as incentives for players to play and nothing more. Indeed, most of them are marginally favorable to the players *if the player doesn't stray from basic strategy and/or correct card-counting practices.*

Thus, being rewarded by an extra payoff for a six-seven-eight of the same suit, or three sevens is a pleasant *little* perk in the course of a normal blackjack game. Such a reward is a very, very little perk, of course, since the odds of one of these hands occurring are outlandishly high. Still, all other things being equal, it is better to play at a table that gives you a little here and a little there, than it is to play at a table that doesn't.

One of the new options being offered in casinos, however, is not passive—as they were in my examples above. It is an *active* option because the player must decide whether or not to put up a side bet. And as most astute gamblers know—side bets are usually favorable to the house.

This new option is called the "Over-Under 13" option and it is currently being offered at many casinos in the country. It is a side bet based on the player's initial two-card hand that is paid off before any other action takes place at the table.

Here the player is betting an amount less than or equal to his original wager, that his first two cards will total over 13 or under 13. (Some casinos limit the amount of this bet to a $50 maximum.) The house wins any total of 13. All card values remain the same as for regular blackjack—except the ace only counts as a one! The dealer's hand is irrelevant. You are only betting that your next hand will be over or under that magic total of 13.

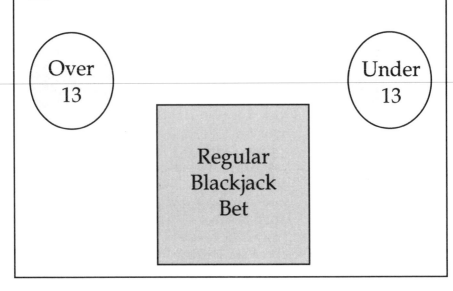

Over-Under Betting Arrangement

This section diagram shows how the Over-Under 13 bet is made. Before the cards are dealt the player places either an Over-13 or an Under-13 bet in the indicated circle. This bet is decided before the play of the hands and has nothing to do with the regular blackjack bet.

Over
13

Under
13

Regular
Blackjack
Bet

For the basic-strategy player, your strategy for the Over-Under 13 option is similar to insurance—never take it. The casino has a strong edge of approximately 6.5 percent on the Over-13 and approximately 10 percent on the Under-13. So for you basic-strategy players this can be a deadly option—worse than some of the proposition bets in craps.

However, for the card counter, the Over-Under 13 option can be a good bet at certain times—if you know what you're doing.

A New Count

The Over-Under 13 option requires a new card-counting system for most expert players since the ace is only valued at one for the Over-Under 13 option and not at one or 11 as it is in normal blackjack. (Please keep in mind—this value for the ace is strictly for the side bet which is decided before the hands are played. Once the side bet is paid off or lost, the ace reverts back to its Janus-faced one or 11!)

Many card counters use the Hi-Lo count which values the cards as follows: two, three, four, five and six = +1; aces and 10-value cards = −1. This is an excellent count to use against both single and multiple-deck games as we have seen. When the true count goes to +1 or more in single-deck games, or +2 or more in multiple-deck games, the player has a slight edge over the house. This edge increases with the increase in positivity.

However, when the count falls into the minus zone, the house begins to see an advantage. The card counter bets accordingly, trying to get more money out during high counts, less money out in low counts. This we have explored.

For the Over-Under 13 option, however, the normal Hi-Lo is not a good counting system for determining when you should bet either end of the option. Indeed, no regular counting system can be considered "optimal" for this option, although the Hi-Opt count (see chapter eight), which values aces as zero, comes closest.

The Over-Under 13 requires new values and a new counting system strictly geared for this side bet:

Aces = +1	5s = 0	10-value cards = −1
2s = +1	6s = 0	
3s = +1	7s = 0	
4s = +1	8s = 0	
	9s = 0	

When the true count is +3 or more, you bet the Over-13 option. When the true count is −4 or less, you bet the Under-13 option. (Remember that you find the true count by dividing the number of decks remaining to be played into the running count.)

If you are a card counter using a traditional counting system, is it better to ignore the Over-Under 13 option or switch to the new counting system? My personal experience and the experience of my fellow card counters in Atlantic City is—switch! You will find many more favorable opportunities for placing an Over-Under 13 bet, than you will find high counts that merit great increases in bet size.

Playing with a Partner

However, the best way to play the Over-Under 13 option is to have a partner. In this regard I've been blessed, as my playing partner is the beautiful A.P.

We have been playing the Over-Under 13 option steadily for many months now. I play two hands starting at the table minimum and moving up as the true count warrants it. A.P. keeps the traditional Hi-Lo running count and converts to the true count, and I do the Over-Under 13 counting system, converting to a true count in that area—exactly as you would do for any counting system.

Of course, the beautiful A.P. signals me what her count is, and I play the hands based on this. However, I put the Over-Under 13 bet up whenever my count calls for it.

What have I discovered?

More often than not, the high positive counts in the Hi-Lo system are reflected by high positive counts in the Over-Under 13 count. And the low Hi-Lo counts, but to a much, much lesser degree, are also reflective of the Over-Under 13 low counts.

Thus, my Over-13 bets tend to be for substantially more money than my Under 13 bets and this part of the option has been more lucrative for me. Remember that when the Hi-Lo count signals an increase in betting and the Over-Under 13 Count also indicates a positive shoe—I can often bet an amount equal to the amount I'm wagering. I always bet an amount equal to my wager. Thus, I tend to have much more money riding on those hands that show a high positive correlation between the two disparate counting systems in the plus counts.

However, the correlation between the two counts is not strong enough to abandon the Over-Under 13 count in favor of the Hi-Lo count if you have to choose one or the other.

Playing Only the Over Option

If you don't have a partner and you don't want to abandon your Hi-Lo count, is there a way to still play the Over-Under 13 option? Yes, but it is dangerous because it involves a small Martingale, and you will only be playing the Over portion of the equation. Any time your true count is +6 or more, go with an Over bet for one-eighth of your regular bet. If you lose this (and the count is still +6 or more), double to one-fourth of your regular bet; lose this, go to one-half of your regular bet; lose this—place a bet equal to your regular bet. In high counts, you have an excellent chance of getting over 13 once in four hands and thus a small four-step Martingale would not be an outrageous strategy. If the count should descend, then you would abandon the Over-13 bet and continue playing regularly. This same strategy is even better for those of you who employ the Hi-Opt count since this count doesn't include aces and thus will be more accurate on the Over end of the equation. How often can you expect true counts in the +6 range? Not very often. Perhaps once every 20 shoes. Still, when the count warrants it, getting a little extra money out with you in the driver's seat is always a good idea if you can afford it.

The above strategy has not been tested against any computer runs but is based on the extensive experience of Hi-Lo counters of my acquaintance who have been using it in Atlantic City. Personally, being the safe type, I would learn the new values and go with the Over-Under 13 counting system. But for those of you with a little more gamble in you, the above Martingale would be an exciting way to get more cash out in high counts. In addition, most Over-Under 13 tables that I've seen are in the $10 to $15 range in Atlantic City—a range that allows players to jump into the game at any time. Thus, this option would make a good game for guerrilla Wonging (see chapter five).

The Over-Under 13 is the type of option that casinos will quickly remove should the players become too astute at playing it. So for those of you who wish to play a beatable game and have the will to learn a new counting system and the bankroll to sustain you during the inevitable roller-coaster blackjack ride, then by all means go over to the Over-Under 13 option.

Chapter Fourteen
Guerrilla Blackjack Strategies

There are essentially two ways to approach the game of blackjack. You can sit at a table and play both good decks and bad decks, letting your card counting and betting variations give you the long-term edge. Most players prefer to play this way. The other way is to use hit and run techniques reminiscent of guerrilla warfare. Blackjack is a game that is made for guerrilla techniques such as Wonging as described in chapter five. There are several strategies that the guerrilla blackjack player can employ—some of which will actually give you a mathematical edge over the casino. Most of these strategies will require some card counting and almost all will necessitate an understanding of basic strategy for any reasonable chance of success.

Card counters will, of course, have the better of it because they have a certainty of playing a favorable game. The basic-strategy player, on the other hand, is hoping for a quick win and then out. All of these strategies require that you have cash (or preferably chips) ready to be laid down at a moment's notice and it is a good idea for all guerrilla gamblers to have a ready supply of chips handy when hitting the casino for a session. To get chips, cash in big at one game, even though you don't intend to stay very long.

Guerrilla Scanning Techniques

The best blackjack game to play is the single-deck and the best way to play it is to hit when the deck favors you and drop out when it doesn't. Most casinos will not allow you to do this over and over, especially if the tables are crowded and especially if the casino thinks you're only playing the positive hands.

Still, the ultimate guerrilla tactics fall into what John F. Julian calls *scanning techniques*. Here the guerrilla blackjack player scans a table for specific situations and plays only one or two hands before leaving and going to another table, and ultimately to another casino and so forth. Scanning works best in single- and double-deck games where the guerrilla player can get a good edge rather quickly.

Scanning techniques can be used by card counters and basic-strategy players alike. Of course, the card counter will be better armed and better able to fully assess the battle than will the non-counter.

Bombing for a Blackjack: Single-Deck Games

The first scanning technique is called Bombing for a Blackjack and can be employed against a single or double deck. First we'll discuss single deck.

You scan the first round and if the count is +1 or more and no aces have been dealt, you come in with a bet of four units on the next round. If you are not a counter, you would scan the first round and if no aces appeared, you would come in with a bet of two units. If the dealer should shuffle up on you, the next time you jump in reduce the size of your bet in half and see what happens. Some casinos are very leery of scanners and are quick to shuffle up if the size of the four-unit bet is substantial—say, four $100 chips. If this happens, just move on. You'll have to judge what size bets you can make when you jump in. A good rule of thumb is to bet the average bet you see the other players making.

In a single-deck game, approximately 16 to 22 cards are dealt to a full table in a round. If no aces appeared, the remaining deck (from 30 to 36 cards) would have four aces. The chances of a blackjack on the next round are comparatively quite high—especially if the count is in the positive zone. If you don't get a blackjack, as most times you won't, you play the hands according to established basic strategy and/or variations based on the count. Regardless, the chances of a winning hand or a desirable winning of a doubling down are quite good.

Bombing for a Blackjack: Double-Deck Games

The strategy is essentially the same for the double-deck game, except that the initial bet after a first round with no aces appearing will be half the amount. Thus, the card counter with a positive true count would only bet two units and the basic-strategy player would only bet one unit. Should the second round yield no aces (or one ace), the counter would increase his bet in a positive deck to four units, the non-counter would increase his bet to two units.

The advantage to card counting here is evident. The card counter will not play after scanning, regardless of whether or not aces have appeared, if the deck is negative. Thus, the counter will always be bombing for a blackjack in decks highly favorable for such an occurrence. The basic-strategy player is somewhat at a disadvantage as he will have to play in both negative and positive decks since he can't distinguish between them.

When you are bombing for a blackjack, you cannot stay at the same table for more than two hands in a single-deck game or more than three hands in a double-deck game. You have to move on to another table and then another game or another casino when you have played your round(s). Remember, if you stay too long at a blackjack venue and only play a scanning game, the casino crew will catch on to you and won't allow you to bet, or the dealer will shuffle up on you every time you jump into the game. You have to scan, hit, and run.

Scan, hit and run. Moving from table to table and then out the door to the next casino.

However, if you decide to employ guerrilla tactics in all the games which give you a decent chance of winning, then mixing up your guerrilla blackjack with guerrilla roulette and guerrilla craps and guerrilla poker, etc., will more than likely prevent the casino crew from suspecting you of counting and scanning. Consequently, you will be able to stay longer in one casino, hitting the various games and, hopefully, running with the money. [See my book, *Guerrilla Gambling: How to Beat the Casinos at Their Own Games!* (Bonus Books) for a complete discussion of guerrilla gambling as it relates to all the casino games currently being offered.]

Guerrilla Wonging

Stanford Wong recommends back counting (counting behind the players and only entering a game if the deck is positive) as the best method for play in multiple-deck games [see *Professional Blackjack* (Pi Yee Press)], but I think it is also an excellent way to play the single- and double-deck games as well.

Stroll through the casino and scan the tables. If, after a first round of a single-deck game, you notice that the count is +1 or above, put up a bet for the next round of two units. (If no aces have appeared, put up a bet of four units.) In a double-deck game, you will put up a bet of one unit if the count is +2 or more after the first round.

Let us say that after the second round the count is still positive, then in a single-deck game you would increase your bet to four units on the third round. In a double-deck game you would increase your bet to two units if the deck remained at a +2 or more. Whether you won or lost your previous bet has no bearing on your next bet.

I am assuming in all these single- and double-deck scan scenarios that there are several players at the table and that you have seen a sufficient number of cards. If there is only one other player at the table, aside from yourself, then sit down and play the traditional game because two players against the dealer is a situation you won't often see in single- and double-deck games.

Chances are that in a single-deck game, three rounds is all the dealer will allow. In the double-deck game, however, this is not so. On the fourth round, if the deck is still positive, you will spread to two hands of two units each. On the fifth round, if the deck is still positive, you will increase each hand to four units. If, at any time, the deck is negative after a round, get up and go to another table or another casino.

Scanning the Multiple-Deck Game

Four-, six- and eight-deck games are much more difficult to beat, whether by scanning or by traditional play. The greater the number of decks, the fewer blackjacks you get and the greater the possibility that the cards that favor the players are all clumped behind the shuffle point. In short, you can't have as much confidence in your true count the earlier you are in a given multiple-deck game. This cuts down on the effectiveness of all scanning techniques.

The best guerrilla attack on the multiple-deck game is a combination of Wonging and progressive betting (but only in *positive* counts!).

Back count in a multiple-deck game until at least two decks have been played and the true count is a +3 or more. (If two decks have been played in an eight-deck game, you need a running count of 18; in six decks you need a running count of 12; in four decks you need a running count of six.) Place a two unit bet. If you win, your next bet is three units. If you win that, your next bet is four units. With each successive win, you increase your betting by a unit. At any point in the progression, should you lose, you will go back to the original two unit bet (again, you are only doing this in *positive* counts). This means that if the initial two-unit bet is unsuccessful, you would simply place another two-unit bet.

The betting ends and you move on if any of the following occurs:

1. You are down after four rounds of play and the true count is neutral or only slightly positive; a +2 or less.

2. The count becomes negative and you are behind, even, or you have lost your last bet.

If the true count is +3 or more, you will continue betting two units.

Now, as long as you are winning you will stay at the table—even if the count becomes negative. However, you will quit the table as soon as you lose your first hand during a negative count. The reason you take a little extra risk and stay for at least one hand in a negative count is to ascertain whether you are in a player-favorable clump of high cards (which, of course, would make the count go down). If you continue to win successive hands in a negative deck, you will continue to stay and play. Otherwise, it's time to seek a new shoe or a new venue.

I've alluded to this before but it bears restating. Casinos have become somewhat paranoid about back counting and will shuffle up if they think you're a Wonger. This holds especially for men and for young men in particular. My experience has been that when I've hit games in this fashion, the pit people watch but when my wife, the beautiful A.P., hits and runs, the pit doesn't seem to care.

Prolonged Guerrilla Blackjack

There is another way to guerrilla hit the game of blackjack. It's more of a money-management scheme. You can play 12 sessions against a single-deck game, six against a double-deck game, three against a four-deck shoe; two against a six-deck shoe, and one against an eight-deck shoe. You will either play basic strategy or count cards. At the end of the allotted sessions, you then take an inventory:

1. If you are ahead 20 or more units, you can quit, or take 10 of your 20+ units and start another round. Should you lose the 10 units, you would quit. However, should you double the 10 units, you would put aside the 10 unit win and continue to play with the original 10 units. As long as you keep doubling those 10 units you will stay in the game, banking your win. Once you lose those 10 units, you leave.

2. After the initial sessions, if you are even or losing, you quit the game and either take a break or play a different game.

3. After the initial sessions, if you are up less than 20 units you quit and go to another game.

Scanning for Blackjacks

If you are going to play any prolonged session in a single- or double-deck game, you have certain advantages off the top, whether or not you are counting cards, that you don't have in multiple-deck games. In single- and double-deck games, perhaps the most important decision you will have to make is whether or not to take insurance should the dealer have an ace showing.

In a single-deck game, insurance is always called for if the deck is +1 or more. On the very first round of play, basic-strategy players and card counters alike can make proper insurance bets by scanning the cards of the other players. What you are looking for is the relation of 10-value cards versus non-10-value cards.

The dealer has an ace showing. That is a non-10-value card. As you scan the other player's hands (or ask them to show their cards), you will take insurance if there is one more non-10-value card than 10-value cards. Thus, there are two more non-10s than 10s on the table because, don't forget, the dealer's ace counts as well. John F. Julian [see *Julian's No-Nonsense Guide to Winning Blackjack* (Paone Press)] has developed great ways of getting players to show their cards without the casino pit personnel catching on to your expertise. It requires you to play the role of happy blackjack gambler—talkative, inquisitive, friendly, and *nosy!* In the double-deck game, you want to have four more non-10-value cards than 10-value cards in order to take insurance.

Unfortunately, you cannot use these techniques on the first round of play against a multiple-deck game because so many cards remain to be played that no scan can give you a good enough confidence rating to risk an insurance bet—which is one more reason casinos prefer the multiple-deck games and one more reason you should avoid them if you can.

Piggybacking or Backlining: Asian Guerrilla Blackjack

Years ago, I was playing at a full table in the Golden Nugget when I felt a tap on my shoulder and a very nice Japanese gentleman asked if he could place a bet on my betting square. I looked at the dealer and she shrugged. I told him it was okay by me but that I couldn't guarantee him a win, even though I had been winning consistently for a while at that table—a fact he knew.

I had a $50 bet up and this man slipped a black chip ($100) under my two greens. He said: "You play the hand."

That was my introduction to a way of playing I had read about but never really experienced, a way of playing that is common in Asian blackjack games, a way of playing that I call piggybacking and is commonly called backlining—where you can make a bet in another player's betting square where that player will play it.

This method of play is quite suited to guerrilla Wongers in multiple-deck games, especially in Atlantic City or other crowded places, where no room exists at a table where the count is positive. Simply ask a player if you can place a bet with him. You have to be willing to abide by that player's decisions, but at a crowded table it would be unusual not to find at least one player who knows basic strategy.

Of course, placing a bet with another player takes a little courage and some charm. If you are the personable type, and somewhat daring, try it. The worst that can happen is that the player so asked will tell you to take a hike. However, as you are back counting, you can size up the players at the table, determine which ones are good players, and which of these (if any) might be agreeable to such a partnership. As play is progressing, talk, discuss the game and if you find that one of the "good" players is starting to win and the count is mounting, you might hint that you'd like to get in this game. When the true count hits +3 with two decks played, make your move. Explain that you've noticed he's winning and you want to get in on the action. Often the player will feel complimented and let you piggyback onto his bets.

Guerrilla Blackjack Bankroll

The size of your bankroll for blackjack has to be determined by the type of play. If you intend to hit and run quickly, you will not need a large number of units. However, if you wish to play longer sessions, then a traditional bankroll is required. For blackjack, a bankroll of 200 to 400 times your minimum bet would be sufficient to sustain you for prolonged periods of guerrilla play.

Chapter Fifteen
Team Play

In 1977, a phenomenal book hit the best-seller lists. It was Ken Uston's *The Big Player* (Holt, Rinehart, Winston), an autobiographical account of the author's adventures playing with teams of blackjack players. What made the book so delightful was the intrigue and the stakes involved. Uston and his teams won millions from the casinos and their cat-and-mouse contests with the casinos' enforcers were spellbinding. His other books, *Million Dollar Blackjack* (Gambling Times Books), *Two Books on Blackjack* (Uston Institute of Blackjack), and *Ken Uston on Blackjack* (Lyle Stuart Inc., Carol Publishing Group) did not have the popular appeal of his first volume. These also recounted his fabulous adventures and his lawsuits against the casino industry. However, with the publication of *The Big Player*, team play became all the rage in blackjack circles.

Unfortunately, Uston opened a Pandora's box with his marvelous book. Now the casinos were alerted to the potential for huge withdrawals from teams of players working together. Paranoia reigned supreme on the pit end of the casino equation and, to some extent, it still does today. Ken Uston died in 1987. But he has left a lasting legacy and he has probably turned more people on to blackjack than any single author writing today. His flamboyant style of life and play are imitated by many young men just cutting their blackjack teeth. These Uston wannabes have many things in common with the late blackjack master. Unfortunately, most of them will never ascend to his Olympian heights or challenge the casino gods to the tune of millions. Indeed, most Uston wannabes just make spectacles of themselves and wind up being barred, since the Uston persona is a well known card-counting camouflage.

Although Uston did not originate the idea of team play (teams had been utilized ever since card counting became a science and not a myth), Uston perfected it and then publicized it.

The conceptual foundation of team play is simple enough to grasp. A team of players pools its monetary resources and plays against a single bank. This allows bigger-than-normal bets for individual players and a lessening of overall fluctuations due to chance. The more players playing the better for a small edge to be realized over a shorter period of time. This is what the casinos do to the players with their slight edge. Team play reverses the normal casino-player relationship for now it is the team that has the big advantage due to the total number of wagers it can make in a specific period of time. It is a winning formula. Based upon Uston's calculations, his blackjack teams played with a five percent element of ruin. That meant they had a 95 percent chance of doubling their bankroll in a given playing period and a five percent chance of going broke. Not bad.

The practical application of team play is a different story altogether. It can be nothing but headaches for the team leader and for his players. Whenever a great deal of money is a stake, personalities tend to clash and problems tend to arise. Ken Uston has much to say on this subject and I recommend his books to you. Some players cheat their teammates. Some honest players are accused of cheating because they have had extended losing sessions. Are all the players of equal skill? Are all the players putting in the same monetary share? The same amount of playing time? Headaches, nothing but headaches.

Team Master

Ray Scott had been playing on blackjack teams for 25 years before his retirement in 1995. You haven't heard of him? Neither have the casinos. That's how good he is. Or was.

Ray: I'm retired. Six months now. I'm 60 years old, I'm ready to enjoy my money.

Frank: How much money have you made, Ray?

Ray: None of your business.

Frank: In the millions?

Ray: Let's just say that my teams made enough money to buy me this home you're interviewing me in, that pool my girlfriend is swimming in, and the ulcer that I'm drinking this elixir for.

Frank: Team play is different from individual play for a number of reasons, not the least of which is the size of the stakes involved.

Ray: Oh, yeah. You're going table max in high counts. We're talking a sizable bank. To be on one of my teams —

Frank: How many players?

Ray: Ten to 30. You want to put in a lot of play in a short period of time. But getting back to the stakes. In the beginning, each member of a 10-man team would put up anywhere from $10,000 to $20,000. We expected to double that investment or even triple it if the conditions were right. When you're playing against a $500,000 bank, in high counts you can go to $5,000 on a single bet. You can have many players playing against that bank and your ups and downs . . .

Frank: Fluctuations.

Ray: I'm from the old school, I call them ups and downs or good days or bad days. I don't say stuff like negative fluctuations or any of that because that doesn't tell you what you're going through on a bad day.

Frank: So when you go to the dentist, you experience pain and not discomfort?

Ray: Pain with a capital "P." And when I lose in blackjack I'm not having a negative swing, I'm having a rotten day. Those early teams were group efforts. Later on, I bankrolled the teams and paid the card counters to play.

Frank: I want to talk about your recruitment philosophy, the types of players you recruited. Then the various team strategies, the signals you used, that type of thing. And then I want your assessment of the future of team play since this seems to be the one area where millions of dollars are won—

Ray: And lost. You don't always win.

Frank: That's something that always has to be remembered. You started with quite a bit of money.

Ray: That was a basic philosophy of mine, that you don't get players who are struggling in life and put them on a team. You don't get players who have a hard time coming up with $10,000 to $20,000 to contribute. There's too much chance that they'll cheat you. And when I was paying people, I still wanted people who had money or were successful in other fields. Success breeds success. There are a lot of screwballs hanging around the fringes of the blackjack scene. A lot of losers. A lot of crossroaders [cheats] and the casinos know most of these guys because as cool as they think they are, they've been spotted on previous occasions or they have records or, as is often the case, they are idiots who just think they're talented gyps. I don't want to be involved with that kind of person. And I never was. I always recruited solid players with solid bankrolls. Often I would recruit non-counting basic-strategy players who were already known to the casinos as big players, legitimate players, and these would become my big players if my team was using the big player approach.

Frank: Explain the "big player" concept.

Ray: On certain teams you have two distinct types of players. Men and women who count but play for relatively low stakes and "big players" who hop into the middle of a shoe when the count is sufficiently high to warrant a big bet. The counters at the table will signal the big player who is usually walking around that specific pit, pretending to drink or socialize or whatever. The big player jumps in, makes a few big bets and leaves.

Frank: Can you still get away with this?

Ray: Not really. The casinos are very much aware of the big player and the hit-and-run tactics of some counters so they are likely to shuffle up or not allow mid-shoe entry. This technique was big in the early 70s before Uston's book. You could do the big player routine for days without a peep from a casino. Now, moderate players who can't count jump into a shoe and the dealer shuffles up.

Frank: But you would recruit big players who were known players?

Ray: Guys who had lost thousands to the actual casinos we wanted to hit. I'd approach these fellows and explain that I could set them up to make a decent score, all legal, and all they would have to do is bet when they are told to. Many went along with it. You'd be surprised how many people in their heart of hearts really want to beat the damn casinos. You see these guys who love blackjack and pretend not to be bothered by their losses? Well a lot of that is bull. They are just pretending that losing doesn't bother them. You should see these same guys jump at the chance to nail the casino. So I'd train them and they usually performed well. I mean they actually were big players to begin with. So our big players would come into their favorite casino, win big, and the casino executives just figured they were having lucky nights that were bound to happen sooner or later and also bound to end. What's funny is that a lot of these guys that I recruited became so interested in counting cards that they learned the skill and went on to become winning players in their own right.

Frank: What other types did you recruit?

Ray: I tried to stay away from young people, young men in particular; even great players, if they were young, I'd avoid. For obvious reasons, the casinos used to get very suspicious of young players betting big money or even being around when big money was being bet. Where did a young person get this kind of money? How come this kid is always around when these big players appear? Young players also found it hard not to show off. They also drop little hints about how good they are. Young guys are always trying to impress the girls. I stayed away from them. So, I preferred to recruit middle-aged men and women. Teachers made good team players and they had the time off to actually put in the training and then put in the hours. I had lawyers, dentists, mailmen, construction guys who were off in the winter. I liked to have as many women on my teams as I could, especially in the role of signalers. We never used women as big players because very few women would play that way in real life. Maybe today you might get some women who play that way—roaming around the casino, placing big bets as the mood hits her—but for most of my career, women were not associated with that style of play. I always tried to have my teams blend into the natural landscape of the casino. It was just another night as far as the casinos were concerned. And I'd even make sure that the betting levels on the high end were in keeping with the casino we were hitting. At Caesars Palace, you could bet $5,000 a hand but at other casinos the pit crew would drop dead if you did this. So you'd go to $500 a hand in high counts and have two or three hands going if it didn't bring too much attention. You had to be adaptable. There were times when the pits would get suspicious and I would pull the team immediately. If I had the least doubt, I'd pull my teams out of a place. There may have been times when I was just overreacting, but I wanted to keep playing and making money and I was willing to sacrifice a given night in the interests of longevity. In the last 10 years, I've used a lot of Asian players. The Asian players have a reputation for wild bet swings, table-hopping, and this kind of behavior is not associated with card counting. It's their style of play. So I recruited quite a few Asians for my teams in the past decade. As a group they are great players with nerves of steel. They love to play and they are very loyal to the team concept. I had very few personality problems with them. I never had to worry about being cheated.

Frank: I've heard a lot about stereotyping of blackjack players. You've already given me two—young people and Asians. Any others?

Ray: Oh, yeah. I said about women. That women are not usually the big player types. Women tend to sit in one spot and socialize, even women who play for big money. So it would look peculiar if a woman was bipping and bopping and table-hopping. I liked to recruit black players too. The casinos don't associate them with card counting either. One of my best big players was black and he'd bet thousands and thousands and never get any heat. The casinos don't think of black players as tough. They think of them as suckers. Or drug dealers laundering money. You know, all the negative stereotypes. So I had this guy, he was a professor of history or something, and he'd dress up in these pimp suits—pink, purple, orange—and strut through the casinos placing giant bets. No one paid him any mind. The pits would laugh at him. Meanwhile, our counters would signal him and he'd table-hop like crazy. He was one of my best big players in the 70s and early 80s. He died a couple of years ago. Outside the casino, he was the ultimate conservative, voted Republican no less.

There are other stereotypes too. Not just ethnic. How people dress, what part of the country they come from. All of these things signal to the pit whether they should watch someone or not. So I would often dress my signalers in ways that made the casinos think of them as nothing players. A lot of this stuff is head games really.

Frank: You talk about signalers. Other than a big player, who did they have to signal?

Ray: Well, not all the techniques we used were card-counting techniques. I'd have several players at a table who would keep track of the location of the aces. This was called keying in on the aces.

Frank: Explain that a little more.

Ray: Whenever you have an excess of aces in a given clump of cards, the tendency of that clump will be to favor the player. On the first round of a shoe—this technique works best with four decks and six decks—you see five aces come out. Some guy splits aces, gets an ace on one, some other guy has a blackjack, you know. Now, what other cards are on the table? Say you have six players and the dealer. Now you have five aces in a clump of 20 cards or so. That's a great thing. So one of my team would check out all the key cards in those 20 and remember them. He would remember the other 15 cards. Now, a few hands later another batch of aces comes out. The second team player would remember all the cards associated with these aces. After the shuffle, the cards surrounding those clumps of aces, and those clumps of aces themselves, will be relatively close to each other. The sloppier the shuffle, the greater the tendency for the clumps to stay intact. The team players themselves play basic strategy and just wait for the clumps to come out. When they see the key cards appearing, they alert our big player or our two big players and they put up big bets. The size of the bets will be determined by two factors—the aces coming out and the actual count.

Frank: So the big players are counting down the deck in the traditional way and the signalers are just keeping track of the location of the aces?

Ray: Yes. If the count is positive, they'll put up a bet according to Kelly—bet their advantage. But if the aces are about to come out and the count is positive, we might go two or three Kelly. If the aces are about to come out and the count is negative, we'll up the bet one Kelly. [One Kelly is one percent of the total bankroll, two Kelly is two percent and three Kelly is three percent accordingly.]

Frank: I've always been fascinated by these card-tracking techniques but they seem awfully hard to do.

Ray: One player playing alone would find it difficult to keep track of the count and also try to remember clumps of cards. It might be possible but I personally think it would be beyond most people to do. But two people could do this. One plays according to the count, the other keeps track of the clumps and key cards.

Frank: How often do you find shuffles and dealers that you can track? How often are dealers sloppy enough to keep the key cards close to the ace clumps?

Ray: Not that often, maybe five to 10 percent of the time. But if you want to win money, you look for these things. Even if one in 10 shoes has a traceable ace component, it's worth its weight in gold—or chips!

Frank: Are these techniques still viable in the casinos? I mean, the casinos must know everything the players know.

Ray: With the exception of the roaming big player, which will work with Asian players today but not most others, all these techniques can still work if the people executing them are skilled and professional and wary but relaxed. Remember, the pit crews have a million things to do, especially in casinos that cater to big money. So only a part of their attention is on any given game at any given time. Anyone playing big money as my teams do will bring attention to themselves but my players act as if this is what they want. They ask for comps, they're friendly to the crews. They act just the way any big player would act. Remember that some of these players really are regular big players. When my team is hitting a casino, I'm usually there watching for the telltale signs of real heat as opposed to normal interest in big bettors.

Frank: Explain real heat as opposed to normal interest.

Ray: Normal interest. Some guy is making $100 bets, sometimes up to $1,000 on a given hand. The floorman comes over and asks for his name. Strikes up a conversation. Then says, "Let me know if there's anything I can do for you, sir." A regular gambler will be flattered and talk to the floorman and maybe even ask for a comped meal to the best restaurant. The floorman will watch the way the guy plays in the off chance that he is counting. But when the floorman is there, my big player will play a moderate game with no huge spreads but he still will move his bets around. Only if I have a key-card signaler will I let him move the money around big time because often this won't conform to the count. The floorman will watch the game but all this is normal interest. Another thing here is if I'm using a regular customer of the casino, there will be no heat because they already know the guy. Then you can really spread the money.

Real heat will involve an intense scrutiny from the floor and phone calls to the eye in the sky. Phone calls not necessarily from the phone nearest your players. New suits [executives] will arrive and check out the game. Then everyone disappears. Suddenly there is all this activity. Then you don't see anyone near your players. That means they are being filmed and the play is being analyzed. I don't ever get to that stage. When I see the new suits arriving, I have the players ask for a comp and then they leave. You short-circuit the order of events by making a quick exit.

Frank: Is team play still a viable option for people wanting to really attack the game of blackjack for big money?

Ray: Hard to say. It's harder to do everything today. The casinos know that we're out there and they are on the alert. It used to be that multiple-deck games were easy to follow [clump card following] because the shuffles were so sloppy. The casinos used to think that just because they had multiple decks, that was enough to thwart experts. Now they know better. So now you have very rigorous shuffles in most casinos. That hurts our efforts. Of course, the casinos aren't helped by rigorous shuffles when they are facing your average player because these shuffles take a lot of time to perform. While the dealers are shuffling, the casinos aren't making any money. I think smaller teams can still make out if they are selective in their strikes and use a host of techniques. The picture for team play is not as bright now as it used to be but it still can be done.

Frank: Are you aware of other teams working the casinos?

Ray: Yes. But I stay away from them. I stay away from everyone associated with blackjack. I read all the books and I play but if I notice some counters at my table, I leave. I actually hope the public stays ignorant of how to really play this game because that allows me to win. I know two other team masters who have had my kind of success. One has kept a relatively low profile as I have. I know him by reputation only. The other one has been in several publicized brushes with the law and the casinos. Smaller teams undoubtedly exist and I'm sure some of them are highly successful but I'm not interested in knowing them. Anonymity is the key to victory in team play as far as I'm concerned.

Mixed Doubles

For most of us, playing on a team like Ray Scott's is out of the question. Time restraints, bankroll, and personal taste will all conspire to keep us in a one-on-one battle with the casino. However, the next best thing to being on a big team is being on a small one. In fact, one of the best ways to attack the casino coffers is by playing with a partner—preferably one of the opposite sex. Your wife or girlfriend; husband or boyfriend. I talked to two husband-wife teams: the first, Bill and Billie (no kidding) play a traditional game of blackjack. They both use the Hi-Lo count and their betting mirrors one another. They play for relatively low stakes ($10 to $50) and while they have been hassled a few times by paranoid pit crews, they enjoy the game and play it all over America. Bill, 34, is an electrical contractor; Billie, 31, is an elementary school teacher. They live in Tennessee.

Frank: How often do you get to play?

Bill: Basically we follow Billie's school schedule. So on the longer vacations like Christmas and Easter and, of course, the summer, we go to Las Vegas or Reno. Weekend trips to Tunica or Biloxi.

Frank: How many days a year would all that add up to?

Bill: Oh, maybe, 80 days of play. We love it.

Frank: What system of play do you use?

Billie: We both use the Hi-Lo count with some variations in basic strategy. Our spread is one to five.

Bill: But we bet 20 off the top, then double it at +2 and go to 50 at +3 or more. In any negative count we go to 10.

Billie: With one bathroom break each hour in an extremely low count.

Frank: Do you play at the same table or at different tables?

Bill: Doesn't matter. I like to play with her at the same table but half the time we play together, the other half we play separately.

Billie: I prefer playing at the same table with Bill because, after all, this is why we do what we do. Our marriage is based on our togetherness. I couldn't be one of these wives whose husband goes off with his friends and I go with mine. Blackjack is our mutual hobby.

Frank: I like that idea. You look upon blackjack as a hobby.

Bill: It's nice to have a hobby that makes you money.

Frank: Can you give me an idea of what you make?

Bill: An hourly rate?

Frank: I think that would be more helpful than what you've made in your career. How many years have you two been playing?

Billie: Five years.

Bill: I'd say we're each averaging about $15 or $16 an hour. So maybe 30 between the two of us.

Billie: There are wild streaks though. I once went 20 sessions without a loss. During that same time, Bill only won seven of the 20 sessions.

Frank: Do you tend to win more sessions than you lose?

Billie: Overall, we win many more sessions than we lose.

Bill: Except that some of those losing sessions are big. It seems that you have a lot of little winning sessions and then a big losing session. At the end of that, you're up a little. I don't know what causes that.

Frank: Other counters have commented on this, too. Your biggest losing session always seems to be bigger than your biggest winning session.

Billie: Maybe you didn't leave the game soon enough.

Bill: Or you didn't stay long enough to see it turn around.

Frank: So between the two of you, you're averaging about $30 an hour in profit with a betting spread of $10 to $50?

Billie: That's about right. Blackjack isn't a gold mine at our level of betting but it's fun.

The next couple, Gene and Jennifer, could legitimately be called "casino killers," as they employ a host of advanced techniques in their assault on the casinos. They also play for rather large stakes—sometimes as high as $500 a hand. Both are college teachers in New Jersey. She teaches math; he teaches literature. They have been playing together for 10 years. Despite the fact that they have other careers, I tend to consider them professional blackjack players, as they average some 150 days in the casinos each year.

Gene: Our life is teaching and blackjack, not necessarily in that order. We play almost every weekend in Atlantic City. We spread our action around. There are 12 casinos in Atlantic City and we hit each one, one weekend at a time.

Jennifer: We hit one casino each weekend. Thus, every 13th weekend we're back at a given casino. We're known but, thus far, no one has realized the extent of our playing.

Gene: Or how much we've actually won.

Frank: Atlantic City isn't known for its great blackjack games. Yet, you play there.

Jennifer: Every casino has six-deck games in their high-roller pits and many of these games are decent, some are even good. We play carefully and take advantage of every opportunity. Gene is able to track aces when the deal is lax and sometimes he can shuffle track.

Gene: When we first started playing, we had some difficulty because we were playing the regular way—big bet swings in high counts.

Jennifer: Our minimum bet would be $25 or $50 and we'd go to $500 in a high count. That was way too much because it's noticeable. So early on we realized that if we were to last in Atlantic City without having terrible cuts or shuffle-ups on every hand, we'd have to get the betting spread done in more subtle ways. So now we flat bet $100 on two hands then double it in a high count to $200 and double that to $400 if we're winning and at the opposite end, we'll go down to $50 in a low count. We take the bathroom breaks in low counts. [Note the similarity between their style and that of Bill and Billie.]

Gene: In neutral counts, however, when the casino has little or no advantage over us, we spread the money around. Sometimes we'll bet $200, sometimes $50, sometimes $100. We're always moving the bets around in the neutral zone so when we do pump them up to $400 per hand in high counts, it isn't out of keeping with our style of play.

Jennifer: If we've followed aces, we'll up the bets in low counts. If a clump is coming out right off the bat, we'll have a large bet up on the·first round. We don't seem to be expert players in our bet sizing because we aren't all that predictable. I think predictability is what does a lot of card counters in. Big money brings down scrutiny but if you seem to have no real rhyme or reason to your bet swings or if you seem to be parleying bets, then the casinos welcome you with open arms. Every casino comps us. We get the full treatment—the limos, the gourmet meals, the shows, the special parties. But we're cautious.

Gene: We do keep our distance, however. We aren't all that close to any of the hosts or hostesses that we deal with. We select our parties judiciously.

Frank: Following clumps, tracking aces, all these things are advanced skills. You do everything at once? Each of you?

Gene: No, we have a division of labor. She counts and signals me the count. She doesn't play. She acts like the typical girlfriend. She hangs over me. We laugh, we talk. All the time she is counting and signaling me. Now, if we have a sloppy dealer, I'll try to track the shuffle. If a lot of aces come out on one round, I'll remember the key cards. I place the bets. It's all very innocent-looking because most times I don't really have to follow the game too closely, so I'm free to talk to the dealer, the floorman, the other players.

Frank: How does she signal you?

Jennifer: Everything I do is a signal. We have verbal signals and physical signals. I mix them up. At any given moment, I can give him the count per deck [true count] and he plays according to the count.

Gene: Based on the count, or whether or not aces are coming out, or whether we're hitting a favorable clump, I move the bet up or down.

Frank: Give me an example of what you mean by verbal signals.

Jennifer: Well, I'm talkative at the table and I sprinkle in my conversation certain cues that tell Gene what the count is. Let's say that the dealer has just finished a round and the count per deck is +3. I'll make any kind of reference to temperature. For example, I might just say out of the blue: "God, it's getting hot (or cold) in here." Or, "I wonder what the temperature is outside." I can say: "I hope the deck gets hot, or stays hot," or that "the dealer cools off." Any reference whatsoever, even to saying that so and so is a hot actor or such and such leaves me cold. Or any synonyms to the effect that this is frigid or that is torrid. Say we're talking about actors and actresses, or politicians, you ask about their love affairs. "I think Princess Di's popularity has cooled," I'll say. Those are verbal cues.

Frank: And physical?

Jennifer: I touch his hair.

Gene: What's left of it.

Jennifer: That's three.

Frank: What's four?

Jennifer: His shoulder. I touch his shoulder or rub his shoulder. Or I'll start the sentence with an "f" as in "From what I can see, we're having a good night," or, "forget it, we're losing our shirts." Any sentence that begins in 'f' when the dealer puts the last cards in the discard rack. We also let words beginning in "p-h" stand for "f."

Gene: You'd be surprised at how easy it is to remember the signals and how effortlessly we can incorporate them into a running conversation with other people. It took us maybe six months to get really proficient but now it's like second nature. We talk to the pit crews and dealers, real conversations but when I have to place a bet, Jen just drops the cue and I know what the count per deck is.

Frank: Are you exclusively Atlantic City players?

Gene: During the school year, yes. In the summer and winter vacations we'll go to Vegas and Reno.

Jennifer: I love Tahoe.

Gene: We've basically tried every area in the country, including Mississippi and the riverboats.

Frank: Do you always play the big stakes?

Gene: Well, in some locales we reduce the bets. Stay with greens and no more than $200 on a hand. We've found that when you go to $400, you get too much attention in most other places.

Frank: Do you use your real names when you play? Obviously, the casinos must look to comp you.

Jennifer: I have three different names that I use. I have my maiden name, my married name and a third name. I have credit cards in all three names and also picture ID. But you have to be careful. These casino people move around a lot and one time you may be Ms. Jones to a certain casino and the next time you're Ms. Smith to a different casino but someone is working the pit there who used to know you as Ms. Jones. With each name I have a certain demeanor and a certain look that is distinct.

Gene: I wear my toupees. Some places they know me as a bald guy, in others I have this big head of curly hair.

Frank: Do you really think it's important to have various personae?

Gene: Yes. In Atlantic City, we use the same names for the Bally's properties—we sign in as Mr. and Mrs. Gene Jones. For the Trump properties we use a different name—Mr. and Mrs. Smith—Jennifer's maiden name. For the other casinos, we use a third name. Even if we should run into someone who knows us by one name or another, it's easy to explain. In some hotels we are comped on my wife's name, on some mine. That's the explanation, if we ever have to give one. So far, it hasn't happened. Each casino property has us as regular players who come in once every three months—which is not a lot. Even if related properties should see that we came last month to one of their properties and the next month to another—that's still no big deal.

Frank: Give me an idea of what you're earning per hour.

Jennifer: Seventy-seven dollars and 36 cents per hour in Atlantic City.

Gene: On a given weekend we'll play seven or eight hours, so we walk away on average with between $500 and $600.

Jennifer: Our yearly winnings fall between $35,000 and $45,000. That's not enough for us to live on, but as a supplement to our teaching salaries that's not bad.

Frank: But to make that money, you must have a large bankroll to sustain such high betting levels.

Jennifer: Yes, we play against a $40,000 bank.

Frank: That's a big bank. You didn't accumulate that bank playing blackjack did you?

Gene: No, we had the money already. It was part of an inheritance that I received when my parents passed away. I took that amount and put it aside to play blackjack.

Frank: Do you use some variation of the Kelly system to decide on betting spread?

Jennifer: Actually, we use what we are able to get away with. Our maximum bet, if everything is going well and the count is high, will be two hands of $400. That's a total of $800 or two percent of our total bankroll. However, if we're losing we don't go to that top bet but we stay at half that amount. At the end of the weekend if we've lost—and we've had many losing weekends—we take money from a reserve blackjack fund of $20,000.

Frank: So your reserve of $20,000 gives you $60,000 to play blackjack with?

Gene: But we only play against that $40,000.

Jennifer: We created the reserve fund from our winnings—so that we could keep our level of betting at its present rate without sweating it out.

Gene: We actually use our winnings to buy things. Despite the fact that we both have careers, being college teachers is not the most lucrative of professions. So that extra money is a part of our working income. But we never touch the blackjack money, never.

There you have it. Two couples who enjoy the game of blackjack for the fun and profit. And there's a simple lesson to be learned in their cases: to wit, two minds are better than one—especially if you're trying to incorporate advanced techniques into your play.

Chapter Sixteen
Counterattacks

There was a heart-warming story recently reported in the media about a card counter—one Anthony Campione—who was awarded over a million dollars in damages as a result of his being arrested at Tropworld in Atlantic City in November of 1987. His crime? Simple. He was a skilled player.

Of course, that was not the technical charge. Tropworld couched the charges as trespass and disorderly conduct when Campione became annoyed with being constantly harassed by the pit personnel and dealer. He was arrested because he had made a ruckus over the fact that every time he increased his bet in positive counts, Tropworld pit bosses changed the limits on the game and wouldn't pay him what he had won. Their claim was that he was betting over the maximum—a maximum that they kept changing depending on the count. This is the economic equivalent of preferential shuffling where the dealer, who is counting along with the player, shuffles the deck any-time it becomes positive. If a card counter can't make his big bets in high counts, the casino has effectively eliminated the card counter's advantage.

There are three ways to take away a card counter's natural advantage over the house (there is a fourth—beating the card counter to a pulp, as has been done in some Vegas casinos in the past but I'll let that one go): the first is to shuffle the decks every time a counter makes a big bet. But this procedure can be costly to the casino since a shoe game requires a lot of time to shuffle and, while the dealer is shuffling, poor players are not losing money.

The second way is to simply ban the player. Tell him that his action isn't wanted and he'd better get his butt out of your casino. This is used in Nevada and Mississippi casinos (and in the New York Indian casino from recent reports). But the casinos can't throw people out in New Jersey, ever since the late Ken Uston took them to court in 1982 and the New Jersey Supreme Court ruled that it was illegal to ban someone from a game because that someone had skill.

So Tropworld took the third option. Change the limits every time the counts favored the counters and make Mr. Campione as uncomfortable as possible as he played. In short, harass him until, hopefully, he left of his own accord. It didn't work and Campione stayed, thus setting up the subsequent court appearances and Tropworld's plea that its huge profits were seriously in danger because a lone counter wanted to bet a few hundred dollars when the decks favored him by a couple of percentage points.

But Judge Barry Weinberg was not buying what Tropworld was selling in this case and ruled that, indeed, Tropworld was in violation of the law every time it told Campione that he couldn't increase his bet to a certain amount when others at the table were allowed to do so. He also wrote: "It is discriminatory to allow others at the same table to play two hands while limiting Campione to one."

Weinberg also hammered the casino because at times the dealer was told to skip over Campione during a round and at other times the dealer was told to short pay him.

Once Campione had a $350 bet up but the pit boss claimed that the new maximum was now $100 for Campione. Although others at the table were betting well over the $100 limit, when Campione won the hand, the dealer would not pay him his $350. Instead he slid him a single black chip. Campione demurred. Then the pit boss called over security and Campione found himself arrested. This after enduring hours of nasty treatment.

Now, you would think that there would be a general uproar when this report hit the media. Not so. The Atlantic City casinos' public relations departments went to work to put the "proper" spin on the event. Newspapers and television were given reports that blackjack was in danger of being removed from the casino floors if this judgment remained. Stories were released stating that card counters were making millions and hurting the casinos' profits in Atlantic City.

Instead of the casinos hanging their collective heads in shame for the despicable way Tropworld handled a patron, suddenly it was the victim who was the villain. Those damn card counters were going to cause the end of blackjack. This tactic is reminiscent of what defense lawyers subject women to in rape cases. They try to show that the victim of the crime forced the perpetrator to commit the crime. That the perpetrator is the real victim! "Hey, pal, if your nose wasn't there in the first place my fist wouldn't have hit it now would it?"

Sad to say, this propaganda worked. I actually had blackjack players ask me if I thought Atlantic City would remove blackjack from the casinos. I told them not to worry—that the Atlantic City casinos' collective blackjack profits are staggeringly high and that the casinos would be insane to kill the golden goose just because a handful of skillful players have obtained a small share of a single egg shell. I mean, Atlantic City's BEST games are six-deckers for crying out loud! Most of their games are lousy eight-deckers. It's not as if they're offering single deck dealt to the bottom while paying two to one for a blackjack!

If you really want to get a perspective on the real blackjack situation in Atlantic City and not just the self-serving viewpoint of greedy casino flacks, just look at the casinos' own win-rate figures for the past few years. Take a look at their individual win rates at blackjack. A win rate is easy to understand. It's a simple percentage. For every $100 bet or cashed in for (in slots it's "bet," in table games it's "cashed in for"), the casinos will keep "X" amount. In the latest win rates for Atlantic City, there is very little difference from one month to another and the averages for a few years are all within a couple of percentage points of these figures. These figures are an average of six months of play. Peruse them and tell me if Atlantic City blackjack games are in any danger from those evil card counters. Keep in mind that the dollar figure is for every $100 that players buy in with. So if a casino has a win rate of $15, that means for every $100 the casino exchanges for chips, it keeps $15. As I write this the following are the latest win rates for Atlantic City:

> Bally's Park Place: $15.40
> Caesars: $12.90
> Claridge: $14.20
> The Grand: $19.40
> Harrah's: $17.60
> Resorts: $14.80
> Sands: $13.50
> Showboat: $15.70
> Taj Mahal: $18
> Tropworld: $13.50
> Trumps Castle: $12
> Trump Plaza: $15.90.

The average win for all Atlantic City casinos combined during this six month period was $15.50 for every $100.

Now, the casinos in Nevada, a state that has competition and therefore offers much better games, are also in no danger of folding their blackjack hands and calling it a day. Here's some recent figures concerning blackjack wins in the state of Nevada. Note that Nevada does not break down the win rate by individual casino but by area. That doesn't matter, you'll get the idea. Again these are six-month averages:

> Boulder Strip: $14.40
> Carson Valley: $16.26
> Churchill: $20.10
> Clark: $12.85
> Elko: $16.83
> Humbolt: $23.77
> N. Lake Tahoe: $14.78
> S. Lake Tahoe: $15.72
> Las Vegas Downtown: $10.92
> Las Vegas North: $13.62
> Las Vegas Strip: $12.87
> Laughlin: $14.28
> Nye: $15.20
> Reno: $16.18
> Sparks: $15.75

Washoe: $16.10
Wendover: $15.22

The total win rate for all the tables in Nevada was $13.50. This rate is as low as it is because the venues with the best blackjack games, the Strip and Las Vegas Downtown, have the greatest number of tables. The win rates are not dramatically different anywhere in the United States. Blackjack makes a fortune for the casinos and not all the combined power of all the card counters on the planet has had much effect on the casino treasury.

Now, this next statistic might shock you inveterate blackjack players but here it is—THE AVERAGE WIN RATE FOR ALL THE ATLANTIC CITY CASINOS' SLOT MACHINES WAS (hold your breath) $8.60. That's right, for every $100 put in slot machines, Atlantic City kept $8.60. In Nevada, where again competition forces the casinos to offer better games, the combined slot machine win rate for all denominations was—five dollars for every $100. For Atlantic City blackjack the average was almost double the slot figure and for Nevada the average was more than double the slot figure (Do these statistics mean that it's better to play the slots than to play blackjack? No. The win rate for slots is the actual rate per $100 put in the machine. The win rate for blackjack reflects the casino hold. So for every $100 a player buys in for, the casino wins $15 of it. But that $100 goes back and forth across the table so that the player is actually betting much, much more.) So who is kidding whom when the casinos cry poverty? Whose petard is being hoisted when the Atlantic City casinos claim they might have to remove the blackjack games? Blackjack pays the casinos handsomely. So you casino PR people, please, don't insult our intelligence by saying you might have to remove blackjack because a few skillful players have managed to eek out a few lousy bucks.

The only reason casinos want to get rid of skilled blackjack players is greed. Instead of making $15.50 or $13.50 for every $100, they want to make $15.51 or $13.51! That extra penny means a lot to them. They want it badly. So badly that they'll mistreat their patrons and even go so far as to have them arrested. Are the massive numbers of card counters really only worth a penny on the bottom line? Is that what we're talking about? No. We're talking much less than that!

I will say one good thing in defense of Tropworld. As Atlantic City casinos go, Tropworld has offered decent games over the years and maybe someday it will again. But when you are skilled, the pit crews can be boorish. Mr. Campione is not a singular incident. He just had the guts to file a suit. There have been dozens of Mr. Campiones. Decent citizens who play a game with exceptional skill. For this they have been pilloried. Unfortunately, the news media—especially the television and radio media—have ever been the lackeys of the casino publicists, and thus have ever been too lazy to really explore a story, so they were spreading the word that Atlantic City blackjack was in danger. Bosh. When you're making $15.50 on $100, you don't stop. Mr. Campione, I hope you enjoy your million dollars.

But the Campione case is only the latest in the casinos' counterattacks. I don't want to scare off any would-be counters but, in the past, counters have been physically as well as verbally abused.

War Stories

"In the early 1970s, I was 26 years old and I had just learned to count and I was good, damn good," one old pro, let's call him Jack Harkness, told me. "I was taken into the back room of one of the downtown casinos [Las Vegas]. You see this scar?" Jack pointed to a scar just above his eyebrow. "I needed 20 stitches to close it. The security guard *accidentally* hit me in the head with a big, metal ash tray. We settled out of court."

Harkness continued:

Now, all I was doing was playing good blackjack. I wasn't cheating. I wasn't a member of a team. Today I cheat. Today I am what the casino thought I was back then. Because I hate the casinos. This wasn't the only time casino guys roughed me up or made me feel like a chump when I was being honest and just using my brains to beat them at their own game, but it was the first. You always remember the first time for everything. And at this time, I wasn't even betting all that much—just going from $50 to $300 and sometimes going from one to two hands.

There was this one casino boss there, he's dead now and may he rot in hell, who was a mean son of a bitch. He liked being a mean son of a bitch. He didn't want anyone to win on his shift because he thought he'd look bad. He should have looked in the mirror. I was winning a lot. So finally this big security guard comes up to the table and nudges me. "Come with me, sir," he says. I started to object and then he said, "Come with me if you know what's good for you, kid." So like a dope I went with him. I was young then and stupid and I obeyed authority. He took me to the manager's office and in walks this pit boss. The pit boss calls me a couple of dirty names and says that I was a known cheater. I tell him I never cheated. That I was a good player and if he didn't have any more to say I was leaving. He started to tell me that if I ever came back in the casino while he was there I would be considered a trespasser and I'd be arrested. This pissed me off. So I told him to eat something unpleasant. That's when the ash tray accidentally hit me in the head! I was dragged out back and thrown out. The next week I initiated a lawsuit but the casino gave me a couple of thousand bucks to forget the incident and my lawyer said to take it. I think they gave my damn lawyer more money to tell me to take the thousand.

If you learn how to count cards, will you be brought into the back room and accidentally clobbered with an ash tray? I asked one blackjack pro to tell me what he thought. He said:

There's always a danger that if you're a big player, you'll be eighty-sixed from the casinos and have your picture taken and maybe even have the picture sent to other casinos. I don't think you have to worry too much about being beaten up because today's casinos wouldn't want the bad publicity. I don't think they would anyway. At least I haven't heard of any beatings of legitimate card counters lately. I'm talking about an individual counter, playing alone, who is not on any list of cheats or anything like that. For team play, it's another story. If you are a member of a known team and especially if that team has some unsavory characters, anything can happen. The casinos have seen legitimate card counters who have become cheats in order to win more money. So team play can invite some scrutiny. I think now they would just tell you to leave and read you the trespass law.

But another counter countered this assertion:

Despite the casinos' attempts to freshen up their image and become good guys, there are still unsavory types—not necessarily criminals or mob guys, just guys who don't like to have their casinos lose money—who will take it upon themselves to make sure you don't win too much money from them. When I was playing steadily for a couple of weeks in Vegas my room was broken into—entered is a better word—because the door wasn't smashed or jimmied—and my notes were stolen. The next morning, after I had called security I get a call back saying they didn't want me at the hotel. I'm not a criminal, I just play for big money and I'm good.

A recreational counter told me: "I was playing in a Strip casino, spreading from $25 to $150. I don't think that's much of a threat to the casino's profits. I was asked to leave."

Another recreational counter tells this story of the notorious Barbary Coast casino on the Strip: "I was only betting $15 and going to $35 on a two-deck game. The guy next to be was betting $100 a hand. I was up maybe $25 when the pit boss comes over and pushes my chips back to me and says: 'That's all for you.' I felt like a jerk."

In Atlantic City, at an eight-deck game at Bally's Grand, one counter encountered trouble:

I was playing $50 on one hand off the top. As the count went up I'd go to two hands of $50 and then two hands of $100, then two hands of $200, with my maximum bet being two hands of $350. If the count went down I'd go down to one hand of $25. The shuffle point was about 75 percent, which for Atlantic City isn't so bad. I was up maybe $400 at the time. Well, after the shuffle this one floorman comes over and takes the plastic card out of the decks and places it at the 50 percent mark. I got up and went to another table. This guy followed me. A new shoe was beginning. I sat down. The floorman stopped the game and had the dealer shuffle. Then the floorman put the shuffle point at that 50 percent mark again.

I knew I had a choice. I was quite angry. I could just keep going from shoe to shoe and force the floorman to follow me. I had a flash fantasy of doing just that. I fantasized that every time I sat down he would stop the game and make the dealer shuffle. I could just move again and the dealer would be shuffling all those decks and I'd now be at another table where the same thing would happen. Shuffling up all those decks every time I sat down would cost the casino a fortune. I really thought of doing that. My mind was saying: "Screw you, Bally's Grand, how much can I hurt you with my play? Okay. Now, I'll really hurt you." Like a little kid, I was throwing a temper tantrum in my mind.

I thought of getting together a team of 100 card counters and placing them at every table in the casino. I don't even know 100 card counters. I know one other guy who counts and he isn't too good at it. But I had these visions of making the casino shuffle after every hand. Killing the casino's bottom line. But I quickly calmed down and realized that the best thing to do was to go to another casino that wouldn't harass me. So that's what I did. Of course, I told six of my craps-playing buddies, guys who bet big at the craps tables, to stop playing at Bally's Grand. They did. So what little they saved by backing me off, they lost 10 times as much because my friends don't play there anymore.

I let the old pro, Jack Harkness, read the above account of the Atlantic City counter. He said:

You see here, that's what did it to me, that's what turned me around and created the casino cheat I am today. I would have been content to play alone and mind my own business. I would have been content to bet enough to win a few hundred a week, maybe a thousand a week if I got lucky. I never thought of cheating the casinos when I first started playing blackjack. But after a few years of constantly being harassed and after a few more back-room incidents, I became a blackjack outlaw. As far as I'm concerned now I don't think it's wrong to steal from a casino. I know it's illegal but they embarrassed me, harassed me, and hurt me. That guy at Bally's Grand had that fantasy of screwing up the bottom line. Well, I went the whole nine yards. I joined a team of criminals, that's what they were, and we stole from the casinos. After getting hit with an ash tray, after being abused, I feel no guilt. I'm the Jesse James of the casinos. Who knows, 10 years from now that guy from Bally's Grand might just be a member of my team of cheats if he keeps experiencing bad things at the hands of the casino bosses.

Of course, I don't subscribe to the "I was victimized, I can now do whatever I want" school of thought. But I understand the pain and embarrassment that players suffer at the hands of casino personnel because these players are skilled at a game. The casinos are stupid for doing this. It is just as stupid becoming a casino cheat. You'll only wind up in jail and the blackjack games there aren't all that good—and the players aren't too friendly, either.

Still, the casinos shouldn't be let off the hook in their mistreatment of card counters simply because some card counters have crossed over into criminality. The overwhelming majority of card counters are just like you and me—honest people. Still, the casinos are paranoid about card-counting players who can theoretically beat the game, so much so that common, ordinary citizens—taxpayers, people who have fought for America in wars, lawyers, police officers, teachers, doctors—in fact, a whole cross section of the American populace—are often asked to leave gambling establishments because they are "too good." It's happened to me and to friends of mine. It's embarrassing and demeaning and demands redress. Yet, most of us will continue to play blackjack in casinos under a cloud; feeling as if we are thieves because we can play a strong game against an overwhelming opponent. And the bannings will continue. We've seen some individual stories to that effect in this chapter.

To me this situation is nothing less than a disgrace; a despicable, un-American disgrace, whether it occurs in sawdust joints or in the plush pleasure palaces. Players who can play the game well are often asked to leave, sometimes they are threatened with arrest under the trespassing law should they return, and quite often they are embarrassed in public—treated as common criminals.

In fact, they are treated worse than common criminals. The common criminal has a host of rights, and court-appointed attorneys to defend those rights. The lowly card counter has no one to defend him or her. Indeed, the expert blackjack player is a man or woman without a country since his or her rights stop at the casino's doors. Illegal aliens have more rights in America than do taxpaying, American-citizen card counters!

Two people who do not agree with this sorry state of affairs are blackjack expert Dr. James Wallace and his wife, Michelle Finbar-Wallace [these are pseudonyms]. Michelle is not only a gaming enthusiast but a highly successful civil rights lawyer.

"I believe that as an American citizen the actions of the casinos violate my rights under the Constitution," states Michelle, a card counter in blackjack. "Although I have not personally been banned from any casinos, I know people who have. The first casino that bans me will have a high-profile lawsuit on its hands."

"My attitude is very simple when it comes to the question of banning skilled players from play," says James. "Since a casino can determine what kind of games it wants to offer, it should not have a right to also determine who can play those games—except of course in the case of actual cheaters and the like who are violating the law or acting in a disorderly manner."

James continued: "Once the game is offered, the casino should have only two options when it comes to skilled players—either cease to offer the game in that manner or change the rules. But, first, it would be wise to determine whether the few people who can beat them are actually hurting the profits. I don't think the casinos should have a third option—getting rid of the good players."

But Michelle, ever the fighter, goes even further. "I think if a serious case were brought against a casino in Vegas, the United States Supreme Court would back the player—in fact, I'd say it's five to one in the player's favor. Naturally, you'd have to go through all the Nevada appeals courts and get it out of the state because there's no way you would win in Nevada. From my experience, you have the United States and its laws and then you have Nevada and its 'practices.' So to redress this crime against American citizens you would definitely have to get the case heard outside of Nevada."

In fact, James doesn't think it has to go that far. He cites the casinos' bottom line as indicative of their misdirection in banning skilled players. "I think in blackjack the answer is obvious. The casinos make a hell of a lot of money on that game and there aren't enough skilled players out there to really hurt the bottom line. And if they do, simple, don't offer the game anymore."

This solution was tried once already. When Dr. Thorp developed the first card-counting system in the 1960s, the casinos literally flipped out. They immediately changed the rules to make it impossible to beat the games. What happened? Indeed, the good player stopped playing but, surprise!, the bad players stopped playing, too. The casinos immediately reinstituted their old rules and it's been a gravy train ever since—for the casinos. Just reread the casino win rates in the beginning of this chapter. Still, the casinos want it both ways. They want to haul in boatloads of money from the suckers but they don't want a few skilled players to take out even a thimble's worth of profit.

If the casinos should continue their banning policies, how would Michelle structure a lawsuit?

"Card counters should not be banned," she says. She added:

The people who ban them should be held personally accountable for their actions. The key to any lawsuit against the casinos is to bring it against the organization *and* against the individual employee who actually does the banning.

The Nuremberg Trials can be used as a precedent in a way—if the orders are illegal or immoral it is the obligation of the subordinate to refuse to carry them out. It is immoral and I believe illegal to deny an American citizen the right to play a game that is openly available to the public. So every floorman, pit boss, eye-in-the-sky spy, every shift manager should be made to answer for his or her crimes.

Remember that these people have choices to make. Do they put heat on the players? Do they take the step to ban that person? If they do, then they are personally responsible for their actions. I say, drag them into court. Their actions have caused shame and humiliation to a law-abiding citizen and they should be forced to make restitution. It's also a case of the equal protection concept. Why should someone be discriminated against because of a skill? [Michelle smiled] Or something to that effect.

But aren't the casinos in Nevada, for example, considered private clubs?

"I've heard this argument for years," says Michelle. She continues:

How can you have a private club that is open to the public 24 hours a day? It's nonsense. There's no criteria for membership in this club is there? No. Although it's obviously nonsense, it is the kind of nonsense that some Nevadan judiciary and legislative individuals will cotton to because it maintains the status quo.

I think you can handle the private club issue as a clear cut case of discrimination based not on race or sex but on intellectual capacity. A private club cannot discriminate against individuals on the basis of race, for example, if it is receiving any federal or state funding. Well, what about liquor licenses? The state dispenses these and indirectly gives the establishments money by so doing.

So a subset to the main suit would be to challenge the private club idea by stating that it is discriminating based on an arbitrary criteria, an intellectual skill, and that it is therefore exploiting individuals who do not have skill. In short, it is a scam.

If indeed the casinos wish to continue to create their own criteria for membership in violation of civil rights laws, then fine, but forget your liquor licenses, forget your restaurants. After all, when a card counter is banned, especially if it's a full-fledged reading of the trespassing statute, he or she is usually banned from the entire establishment. Since when is eating in a restaurant illegal because you can count cards? Why can't you use a restroom? Listen to a band? Go to a show? And remember we are not talking about criminal behavior here. We're not talking about some rowdy drunk, some pickpocket, some thief stealing other players' chips. We're simply talking about someone who can play a card game using the intelligence the good Lord gave him or her. We are talking about someone being penalized for something going on in his or her head.

I realize that some of these arguments might sound silly, I mean I am getting excited and rattling off constitutional issues all because of a card game. That's because the whole situation is silly. Casinos are public places, often publicly traded places on the stock market. Imagine owning stock in companies that won't let you play their games? That would be like owning Pepsi stock but not being allowed to drink the product. Indeed, that would be another way to approach the issue—as a stockholder. Get enough well-heeled card counters to invest in a given property or properties and have them put pressure on the management to stop the practice of banning. This practice is unconstitutional.

James has a slightly different slant:

With the explosion of gambling around the country, you have many new players. Most will never learn how to play skillfully. I think the casinos should just forget the whole issue of card counting and instead keep polishing their slot machines because most new players will be slot players and they won't hunt for loose machines. [See my book *Break the One-Armed Bandits!* (Bonus Books) for how to find loose machines.] Rather, they'll put their hard-earned money in the first machine that catches their fancy and probably lose all of it. The profits in the future from the mechanical monsters will dwarf the minor withdrawals some skilled players will make.

And if the casinos continue to ban skilled players?
States Michelle:

Sooner or later this will wind up in a court outside Nevada. Picture the case on Court TV. Picture the American public watching casino executives trying to explain that they are banning American taxpayers, war heroes, housewives, lawyers, teachers, clergy, from playing blackjack because these American citizens are too good or too smart.

Would you want to gamble in a casino if you knew the casinos allowed you to do so because they felt you were too stupid to win? The casinos will not only lose the case but they will lose whatever support our legislatures are currently giving them nationwide.

Indeed, every state that is considering legalizing casino gambling should stipulate that no one can be asked to leave an establishment because he or she is too good. If the casinos can't agree to this stipulation then they can't operate in that state. There is a time coming when casinos will be at the saturation point. They'll have to back off the bannings because of competition. There's only one thing worse than a card counter to a casino—and that's an *empty* casino. To be an exciting place, casinos need people in them. When the saturation point comes, the casinos will be scrambling for people and card counters might then get treated properly.

Of course, Michelle Finbar-Wallace is a maverick in this area, as most skilled blackjack players have no interest in bringing expensive and time-consuming suits against the massive casino industry. Most just want to play and win.

Dr. James Wallace himself prefers to let Michelle do the legal pioneering. "I'm interested in seeing justice done but I'll leave that to Michelle. I enjoy playing, and winning and I even enjoy the cat-and-mouse game I have to sometimes play with the casinos."

Strangely enough, not all blackjack experts think the casinos should be stopped from barring players. In the June 1995 issue of Arnold Snyder's *Blackjack Forum*, a panel of regular contributors to the magazine had a diversity of views. I recommend you get this issue for a full exploration of the subject. However, the arguments in favor of the casinos' "right" to ban or otherwise harass players fell into the following categories:

1. If the casinos know they can ban players if they have to, they will offer good games. Note that New Jersey, which has outlawed the banning of card counters [but not the harassing of card counters!] has the worst games, and Nevada, which can ban them, has the best games.

2. Barring players prevents casinos from cheating players that could be a threat to win.

3. The best players enjoy the cat-and-mouse game almost as much as they do playing blackjack.

4. The casino industry offers a gamble, as does an insurance company. You insure your car because you're betting that you'll win if you get into an accident. If you do get into an accident or enough accidents, the insurance company bans you from playing with them. Insurance companies can also change the nature of the game based on demographics or other statistics. This is what casinos do. If it's not illegal for insurance companies to decide who they'll gamble with, why should it be illegal for casinos?

5. If you owned a casino, would you want to be forced to deal to a team of players betting in the millions? Or would you want the right to ask them to leave?

The *Blackjack Forum* discussion was interesting, lively and intelligent, as *Blackjack Forum* discussions usually are. The experts made some telling points for and against banning, preferential shuffling, cut-card placement, etc. My own personal feeling is that casinos should have the right to do the following:

1. Set the game limits—minimum to maximum bets.

2. Change these limits if they give the player a half hour notice—but all players must be subject to the same new limits.

3. Decide the number of decks to be used.

4. Decide the shuffle point.

5. Decide the rules for doubling, splitting, etc.

I don't buy the idea that it's necessary to ban or harass people to have good games. Many of the most paranoid casinos in Las Vegas have the worst games, not the best! Atlantic City could offer single-, double- and four-deck games and by manipulating the shuffle point, minimum to maximum bets, and the rules, assure itself that it would win from the suckers and basic-strategy players alike. Actually, my bet is that Atlantic City could offer wonderful two-, four-, six- and eight-deck games with terrific rules, deep penetration, and wide bet spreads and still maintain the win rates discussed earlier in this chapter. The Aladdin Casino in Las Vegas has been offering just such games with terrific rules and outstanding penetration for several years now and the Aladdin's bottom line is the best on the strip. What the casinos should not be allowed to do is have one set of rules for the suckers and another set of rules for the expert player. If the maximum bet at the table is $100, then it's $100 for the ploppy and it is $100 for me. If the ploppy can jump his bet from five dollars to $500, then I can too.

In truth, I think the casino fears are only marginally justified when it comes to mega-players and teams. Yes, a team of blackjack pros can take the casinos for millions. But they can't do that in a half hour! If a casino thinks it's being hit by pros, it should have the right to lower the maximum bets—after that half hour notice. I keep going back to the figures for blackjack win rates, not a one of them was under $10 for every $100; most were in the $14 to $17 range. Come on! Who's crying wolf?

Are there millions of hungry card counters out there waiting to jump on the casinos should they stop their vigilance? Nope.

In an informal survey I took in the summers of 1994 and 1995 in Las Vegas, out of the 603 people I observed playing blackjack (or questioned as to their strategies), only 97 were actually playing basic strategy. In a winter survey of Atlantic City in 1994, of 758 people I observed playing, 205 seemed to be playing basic strategy. In the combined group, I found a mere 17 card counters. If these informal surveys are actually accurate (and I have no idea if they reflect the real statistics) then one in 80 blackjack players can count cards, getting between a .50 percent and 1.5 percent edge; while approximately one in four can reduce the casinos' edge against them to between zero and .61 percent. The rest are playing against casino edges that allow for the staggering win rates recorded above. Do the casinos really have to worry that after you read this book, they are in danger of going out of business? Nope.

Chapter Seventeen
The Million-Dollar Bum

Here is every gambler's dream. You come into the casino, down on your luck, with your last few dollars in your pockets and suddenly the lightning strikes and you win hand after hand in blackjack. You can do no wrong. Double downs. Splits. Insurance. Every move you make works to perfection.

You had started out betting several dollars a hand and you worked it up until you were betting several hands of several thousand dollars each. The hotel suddenly realized your powers and comped you to the finest room. You want dinner? The finest gourmet restaurants were at your beck and call. Room service? A butler? Right away, sir. And shall I bring the limo around for your afternoon of shopping?

There is a nightmare version of this story which is the flip side of the dream. You've won all this money only to give it all back. You play hand after hand and nothing goes right. So you increase your bet in the hopes that you can recoup everything you lost with a few big wins. You lose those too. Now you have to reduce your betting level from a few hands of a few thousand to one hand of under $100. Then you're down to one hand of $25. The casino executives who laughed at your jokes and were super-serviceable now frown when you ask for a comp to the coffee shop. Sorry, sir, you'll have to pay for your room. Limo? There's a bus that comes by the casino every half hour. It'll take you where you want to go.

Finally, you move over to the lower-limit tables where you bet your last dollar and lose it all. As you leave the casino, a thoroughly beaten and depressed human being, you can hear the dealers snickering; you can feel the scorn of the cocktail waitresses and change people. Look at that big dope! He won a million and gave it all back.

Now, unfortunately, most of us will never experience scenario one. We will have our good nights and, perhaps, some great ones, but we will never walk into a casino with a few bucks and work it up to a million or more. Fortunately, many of us will never experience giving a big win back either. True, many gamblers have had good streaks in a given night only to keep playing and lose it all back eventually. Still, most of us just have to settle for the mundane ebbs and flows of luck with a small "L".

But that doesn't mean on rare occasions some lucky fellow (or woman) isn't gifted with the golden touch. Nor are the gods of chance all that particular when they choose the recipient of their largess. Murderers are treated with the same amount of *élan* as saints. To paraphrase Shakespeare: "Dame Fortune is a whore."

Such was the case of the bum who won over a million dollars at Treasure Island in Las Vegas in the spring of 1995. Although the story is shrouded in secrecy, and that is because Steve Wynn, the owner of the casino, has bought the "rights" to it and has informed his employees to keep the lid on it, I was able to talk to the people involved—the dealers, waiters and waitresses (whose real names do not appear here)—who were more than happy to give me their versions of these extraordinary events.

It was a Sunday in April 1995. A tattered old man walked into the casino at Treasure Island, which is upscale and family-oriented. This man was anything but. He was dirty and disheveled. His aroma on this spring day was reminiscent of anything but a spring day. This is the kind of guy you expect to find in the seedier casinos downtown, not in an elegant place such as Treasure Island. He cashed his social security check of $400 and sat down to play at a five-dollar table.

Peggy, the dealer: It was my understanding that he had been thrown out by his wife and told never to come back. He came in with a chip on his shoulder. He was cursing and scowling. He was nasty. No wonder his wife threw him out. He just had that $400 with him. My guess is that if he lost it he would have just gone outside and slept in the street, which is probably where he is now.

Mike, the dealer: He ordered some strong drinks and some cigars— foul-smelling things. Then he started to play. He was winning right away, not a lot, but enough to be noticeable. He'd go to the bathroom frequently. If you want a description of him, he looked like the shriveled manager in *Rocky*.

Unlike Rocky, who just wanted to go the distance with Apollo Creed, our hero went for the KO. He began to win hand after hand and as his winnings increased so did the size of his bets. This man had a gambler's blood and a gambler's conscience.

Sal, the dealer: Oh, yeah, I remember how he played. He was crazy. He would win maybe nine out of every 10 hands. But he didn't know how to play. He stood on two deuces and would double down on a six or seven. He'd split fours against a 10. He'd split 10s. I mean the guy was just lucky. He played at my table, six or seven hands of $2,000 to $5,000 each. I think he took me for $60,000 or $70,000 in a few hours. He bet wildly and went with his luck, which was great at the beginning and bad at the end.

Ellie, the dealer: He was vile, just vile. But he couldn't lose a hand. He would call the female dealers names. He used the "C" word a lot in referring to us. We—the female dealers—were about to request that we not have to deal to him when the management, who were watching him closely, realized that we shouldn't be subjected to his viciousness, and they proceeded to have only male dealers deal to him. If I had told my husband some of the things this guy said to me, he would have come here and killed the bum.

Steve, the dealer: I'm proud to say that I took $80,000 from him. I hated him. He was the most disgusting human being I ever met. Once he came to my table and there was a really nice man playing at the table. This man was playing green chips. He was doing okay but win or lose he was a gentleman. He was quiet and refined. Then this creep comes to the table and announces that he's taking over and he tells the nice man to move over to first base or to get off "my table." The nice guy moved over to first base but after awhile he left. I got the bum as he was starting to lose. I'm usually rooting for the players because it isn't my money and the casino wins in the end anyway. So I like to see players have good nights. But this guy, I was happy every time he lost a hand. As far as I'm concerned, I'm glad he lost it all back. God should never have given him the good luck in the first place. So many other people would have been so much more deserving.

Deserving or not, at the height of his winning streak, the "bum"—as he was referred to by just about everyone—won between 1.3 and 1.6 million, no one knows for sure—except for the casino executives who weren't speaking. This streak lasted between one week and 10 days. Regardless, this is a man who had over a million dollars in his hands and blew it all. But no one sympathized with him because of his behavior. It was a tragedy without a tragic hero.

Denise, the waitress: He came in and had a comped meal one night. He ate like a disgusting pig. Then he calls over the waitress, my friend Gail, and he puts a $500 chip on the table. Now Gail's face beams. I mean a $500 tip! But then he says: "Naw, that's too much." Then he picks it up and puts a $100 chip down. Gail is about to pick it up when he grabs it and puts a $25 chip down. Then he pulls that back and puts a five-dollar chip down. Then he takes this back. He didn't leave a penny. He was a cruel bastard. He was cackling when he left the restaurant.

Brian, the waiter: He always had a couple of security guards with him because he liked to carry his money around. I don't know how he treated these guys but he treated the rest of us like garbage. He did drive the security guys crazy though, because at any hour of the day or night, he'd want to leave the casino and go somewhere. I heard that one night he had the limo driver take him to a local park, where he slept on a bench. The security guys had to stay up all night and watch to make sure that no other bum stole his money. I waited on him a few times. I ignored his insults and served the food. He never tipped and he always complained and called you names. I was secretly hoping he would choke. He didn't.

Paul, the dealer: He was a fool. He gambled like a fool and that's why he lost it all back. I understand that when he got down to his last $50,000, Steve Wynn pulled the plug and told him to leave with his winnings and to never come back. If Steve Wynn did that then Steve Wynn's a nice man because this bum didn't deserve to win even a penny. Really, if you had won that much money wouldn't you take at least half and say, I'm never touching this, I'll gamble with the other half? Come on. Wouldn't you at least be a little pleasant when you were winning so much?

Martina, the change person: Once he took the bus downtown to go see his friends. He took all his money with him on the bus. The security guards got on the bus with him. They wanted him to take the limo but he was hardheaded and insisted on taking the bus. So here he is on a public bus with a million dollars. Once when he was walking through some of the machines, he spit right on the floor.

One might wonder why card counters, who are usually polite, quiet and unobtrusive, are banned and a smelly bum is given the royal treatment.

Mike, the dealer: The bosses aren't fools. This guy's luck would change and when it did, they wanted it changed at Treasure Island, not someone else's casino. So give him a presidential suite, give him comped meals and a limo. Give him anything he needs to keep him playing in your casino until he loses. Then boot his ass out. Which is what they did. Of course, a guy like that, if I owned the casino, I wouldn't deal to him in the first place. When he came in here, and I was here that first day, he smelled like death. He was just disgusting. That was the time to get rid of him.

When his luck ran out and he was asked to leave Treasure Island with his $50,000, he vanished from the scene.

Steve, the dealer: I heard he went over to the Gold Coast [casino] and was arrested for abusive behavior. I heard he dropped a few thousand there.

Peggy, the dealer: I think when he left, he had about $10,000 in cash with him. I heard he went downtown and blew it all. Got drunk and had a heart attack.

Brian, the waiter: I think he was arrested for urinating in the street. Someone told me he got hit by a car.

Paul, the dealer: I believe that he made a deal with Steve Wynn. That Wynn has the movie and book rights to his story. Really, no one talks about him because it was a weird week here. Actually that bum played here for a little over a week. It was an embarrassment. I was embarrassed for the other customers.

Although the fate of this formerly "lucky bum" is unknown, at least by the people I spoke to, the fact remains that one of the most incredible gambling streaks in the history of casinoland came to a halt somewhere around April 19, 1995. This piece of lore will probably take on a life of its own, as other such stories have. When and if they make the movie, he'll probably be portrayed as some cantankerous but lovable curmudgeon with a heart of gold.

Denise, the waitress: I really wish it could have happened to a nicer guy and that he could have walked with most of the money. Then the story would have had a great ending because it happened to a great person.

Steve, the dealer: As far as I'm concerned, the story did have a happy ending because the guy is probably broke and sleeping in a sewer somewhere, which is where he belonged in the first place.

If you like the stuff of dreams, then this true story is the stuff that can fuel your fantasy. Since you're a nice person, you can picture yourself being gracious to all the help, tipping the dealers, having the smiling casino executives slapping you on the back and laughing at your witticisms and then, when your luck started to change just a little, you can picture yourself leaving with your million dollars intact.

Could this happen to me? Probably not.

Here's why.

I would never escalate my bets the way the "lucky bum" did. I don't have that gambler's blood. My lucky streak would have to last a hell of a lot longer than his because I would never get to a point where I was betting several hands of several thousand dollars each in such a short time. Remember, this guy wasn't counting; had no strategy; just went with the flow. In his case, doing everything wrong turned out right, in the beginning—until everything wrong turned out wrong in the inevitable end. That monumental good luck won't happen to me but that rotten ending won't either. Truthfully, I'm better off. But I can always dream.

Chapter Eighteen
What is the Long Run, Anyway?

About a year ago I was playing blackjack regularly at a Las Vegas casino that had a wonderful single-deck game. My wife, the beautiful A.P., and I would play two sessions there a day, one early in the morning after our walk, one in the late afternoon just before our nap. Each session lasted an hour, maybe less, maybe more—especially less, if we were able to get the money and run.

One particular morning I noticed an Asian woman who seemed to really know her stuff. She was losing but I could tell from her bet sizing and her play that this was a woman who not only counted cards but varied her strategy based upon the count. She was good.

That afternoon the delightful A.P. and I went back for our afternoon session of play and there she was again.

"You don't think she's been playing all day, do you?" I asked A.P.

"She's wearing the same clothes," said the observant A.P. "She looks tired too."

"That she does," I responded.

The next morning, the lady was there again. And again the following afternoon. As it so happens, A.P. and I had sat down at her table and fairly soon A.P. had struck up a conversation.

"I'm so tired," said the Asian woman as the dealer shuffled.

"How long have you been playing?" asked A.P.

"Today," she looked at her watch, "10 hours so far. Yesterday, I played 16 hours."

"Sixteen hours!" I said. "Sixteen straight hours?"

"Yes, except for a lunch break and to go to the bathroom."

"You're a good player," said A.P., "hasn't the casino put some heat on you?"

"I would think they would throw you out, as un-American as that is," I said.

"They know us. If we keep our bets under $100, they don't bother us," she said.

"Us?" I asked.

"My husband," she said, then pointed. "He's over there."

He was a middle-aged guy, balding, a little paunch, a little mustache. Could have been any one of a million visitors to Las Vegas. Any one of a million tired, burnt-out, bleary-eyed visitors.

"Does he put in those long hours, too?" asked A.P.

"Yes, we are trying to get into the long run," she said. "In the long run, we are supposed to have the edge and win."

"How long have you been playing—how many years?" I asked.

"Eight months," she said.

"Every day?" asked A.P.

"No, we live in California and we come every other weekend. We are on vacation this week so we came for the week."

"And you put in 16 hours almost every day on those weekends and during this vacation?" I asked.

"Yes," she said. I could see her eyes were bloodshot.

"That's a lot of playing time," said A.P.

"We have to get into the long run," said the woman.

Maybe it was her fatigue but the woman was fixated on the idea of the long run. Then she told us her story.

A year ago her husband had discovered blackjack. He had read many books on the subject. He had taken a course with one of blackjack's gurus, a reputable and quite expert player and analyst. Then the husband had taught his wife how to play. For two months he drilled her every day in basic-strategy and card-counting techniques.

Finally it was time to hit the casinos—which this couple did with a vengeance. The husband booked rooms in Vegas for every other weekend for a year. And they flew to Vegas.

For the past eight months they had put in enormous amounts of time and Herculean efforts into playing blackjack.

They were down many thousands of dollars. Many, many thousands of dollars (which would explain why the casino tolerated their action up to that point).

They were both exhausted and frustrated.

They had not yet made it into the long run, where they believed they were guaranteed a victory that would last a lifetime.

"What if there is no long run?" asked A.P.

The woman looked at A.P. as if she had been struck with an axe.

Asking a novice card counter and blackjack guru follower to consider whether there is such a thing as the long run for a flesh-and-blood player in the real world, would be like asking a religious fundamentalist to play with the idea that there is no God. It's heresy. It's unthinkable.

It's also the fundamental question that must be asked by those individuals who are killing their health and, often, the health of their bankrolls, by playing countless draining hours in smoke-filled casinos. Better, perhaps, to hunt the unicorn than to hunt the long run.

What is "the long run" anyway?

The idea of the long run is easy to assimilate. As the number of trials of a given event—say hands in blackjack—begins to approach infinity, the *actual* outcomes of various events will begin to reflect their *theoretical* probabilities. Of course, for practical purposes, a run of a million hands in blackjack would be enough to figure out the theoretical advantage in a given situation.

Say you want to discover what the best possible move would be if you had a 12 and the dealer was showing a two. With no other information other than your hand and the dealer's upcard, a million runs says hitting your 12 would be the best move. In a million runs of 12 versus a dealer's two, you will lose less if you hit your 12. This now becomes the basic strategy for a 12 against a dealer's two. For card counters, you do the runs based upon the composition of the remaining cards. Thus, when the composition favors the player to a certain degree, a million runs would say the best move would be to stand. These options are considered the best theoretical moves.

Now, the likelihood of one player playing a million hands of 12 against the dealer's two is remote. Just playing a million hands is tough.

I did some quick calculations. If the couple I had witnessed played two days every other weekend (26 weekends = 52 playing days), plus spent two vacation weeks (say, 14 playing days) in Vegas, all this time playing 16 hours a day apiece, how long before they hit the long run—if we defined the long run as a million hands? They were playing 66 days × 16 hours, which equaled 1056 hours of play. However, they were playing two hands (one apiece), which gave them 2112 hours of play. For argument's sake, lets say they played a hand a minute, or 60 hands an hour. So in 2112 hours of play, they would play 126,720 hands of blackjack in a single year. To reach a million hands, they would have to play eight years!

But they would reach the long run, correct?

Not necessarily. The long run is just a theoretical construct. It's necessary for establishing the parameters of play. But no amount of time is a guarantee that every hand will work out exactly as theory supposes. Remember, that each hand must be analyzed based upon the theoretical long run, but in reality, to expect each hand played to conform to the long-run projections is silly. Probably no hand will reflect the exact probabilities.

So why play basic strategy?

There is no other choice. You have only a (reasonably) optimal way of playing or a bad way of playing. There is nothing else. You play optimally or you play foolishly, period. The totality of your hands, all the hands you will ever play in your whole lifetime, if played optimally, will give you the best chance for success. Not a guarantee, mind you, just the best chance. That is why you use basic strategy and count cards.

So what about our couple, plugging away, endless hour after endless hour, in a desperate attempt to get to the "long run?"

My advice is to relax, play half as much, and go to a show. Playing blackjack is the equivalent of being in the forest, among the trees. The long run is the entire forest. As an individual wandering in the woods, you will never see the entire forest through the trees, yet you are in it. Thus, I think of every moment as a point in the long run. In fact, everything is the long run and nothing is the long run. The long run is a useful myth to establish the priorities of your playing strategies. But it is not something to lose sleep over.

Chapter Nineteen

Some Tricks and Some Treats

Blackjack is a well-researched game. The mathematics, charts, graphs, tables, and esoteric debates that have been published in books and newsletters would make one think that somewhere along the way the secrets of the universe will be discovered when the question of whether to double down on a five versus the dealer's two in a true count of +48 is answered. Unfortunately, mathematics is not the be-all and end-all of best blackjack play. There is, after all, the real world, where certain things can happen that can add or subtract from the probabilities inherent in the math end of the game.

In short, there are tricks that can make you a better player, tricks that can secure for you an even bigger edge on the casino. All of the tricks I will recommend are legal but you will have to decide if they are moral. Often situations will occur at the table that an astute blackjack player can take advantage of, if he knows what he's doing.

Let me give you an example. I was playing at the Claridge Hotel and Casino in Atlantic City. The dealer had a nine up. I had 13. The player next to me signaled for a hit—or at least the dealer thought she wanted a hit and the dealer gave her another card—an eight. When the lady explained that she was surrendering and that her hand-signal meant "I surrender," the pit person came over and said: "Next time, lady, you have to call out surrender loud enough so we can hear it. Got that? Now, the next player gets the card." That was me. I had 13. I was getting an eight. That made 21. I held up my hand and said: "Wait, I want to double." I took my chips and doubled down. The dealer said: "Very smart, sir." The pit person frowned. I won the double down.

Was I cheating? Or was I merely taking advantage of a situation that presented itself? I say it was the latter. And that's what these upcoming tricks are—simply things to look for that you can take advantage of. Some will happen rarely, if ever, some will happen quite often. All of them can be exploited by the astute player. And when you are exploiting these things, you are playing the best blackjack.

Some of the following topics can all be lumped under the heading of "Hole-Card Play," as you are using techniques to discover what the dealer has in the hole. They are all perfectly legal and eminently practical.

Front Loading

Most hand-held games will have the dealer give himself his first card face up and then give himself his second card face down. To do this, the dealer has to slip the face-down card under his face-up card. Remember that the dealer's hands are above the table. In the shoe game the dealer merely has to slide the card along the table. But in a hand-held game he has to go from up to down. Most dealers can do this seamlessly, and fast, most of the time, so that it is impossible to get a peek at what the card is that is going in the hole. But a few dealers often, and some dealers occasionally, will get sloppy and place the down card in such a way that the quick-eyed player can get a peek at it. Of course, knowing the dealer's hole card is a huge advantage. For example, if the dealer has a 10 showing and you have a bust hand, knowing that the dealer has a six in the hole allows you to stay on your bust hand instead of hitting. Knowing the dealer has a bust hand will allow you to split pairs and double down. These moves will not make you look like an expert but rather a fool—which is great cover if you're a good card counter.

In the rare event that a dealer is readable throughout a session, you might not want to hit certain hands that would be dead giveaways that you're reading his hole card. No one, not even the biggest ploppy in the world, will hit a 19 against a dealer's 10. So even if you know another 10 is under it, you should take the loss. But on splitting and doubling, I've seen it all and so has the pit. Bad players double on many occasions against all sorts of up cards. They also split like mad. Go for it. When you know the dealer's hole card you can look as though you are joining the ranks of ploppydom. In reality, you are taking advantage of extra information.

There are optimum seating conditions for front loaders. Let us assume a seven-seat table, the middle seat being number four, the third-base seat being number seven, and the first-base seat being number one. For right-handed dealers, you want to sit in seats five or six, preferably six. For left-handed dealers, you want to sit in seats two or three, preferably two. When a dealer is placing the hole card, he usually has it covered by his fingers in front and by his palms on the side. This leaves a tiny margin of visibility for you to exploit—usually near the pinky knuckle.

Often with a front loader, you won't be able to see all the hole cards all the time. Often certain cards will be difficult to read. Sometimes you can only see the markings and not the actual denomination. You can practice with a set of cards so that little clues will yield big results.

An acquaintance of mine, let us call him Mr. Yueh, can tell with very few clues what the denomination of the cards are. Mr. Yueh states: "I practiced for years. A quick flash of the side and I can tell if I'm dealing with a five or a six, an ace or a deuce. If I hit a front loader, I don't need the guy to show me what's there entirely, just give me a hint of it and I'll know what card the dealer has going in the hole."

Some dealers, a rare few, front load from the front! That is, you can read the hole card perfectly if you sit in seat number four—center field. These are the best dealers to face because it is difficult for the pit people to see what's going on. When you are playing a front loader from either the first-base side of the table or from the third-base side of the table (say, spots two or six respectively), you have a tendency to hunch down to get a better look at the cards. A tall player suddenly sliding down the chair is a dead giveaway that something is up. But a *front* front loader is almost impossible for the pit people to see. More importantly, this type of front loader usually reveals the exact card more often. You won't have to make educated guesses from the markings, as Mr. Yueh does.

Dealer Tells

A "tell" is any conscious or unconscious signal from dealer to player (or player to player in games such as poker) that *tells* the player what the dealer has in the hole. Cheating dealers at casinos where dealers check under their 10s and aces can set up signals between themselves and players to give the player the knowledge of the hole card. Something as simple as the following:

Dealer peeks under 10.
Dealer blinks once.
Dealer deals.
Dealer has a bust card (2, 3, 4, 5, 6) in the hole.
Or:
Dealer peeks under 10.
Dealer doesn't blink.
Dealer deals.
Dealer has a pat hand.

It can get much more elaborate than that. Signals between cheating dealers and cheating players can give the actual card that is under the 10 or ace. Obviously, this kind of conscious "telling" is illegal and immoral. There's no fine line here, no moral quibbles; any dealer or player who sets up this kind of situation deserves to be arrested because he or she is a crook.

But what of unconscious tells? Where the dealer doesn't know he's giving away information and where you haven't asked to be given any information about the hole card? Where you are able to tell what he has in the hole because you've picked up something subtle in the dealer's behavior? Is that cheating? Nope.

Unconscious Dealer Tells

In many blackjack games the dealer will check under both his aces and 10s to see if he has blackjack. Any time he does this, the astute player has an opportunity to find out what the dealer knows—which is what the card underneath is. Naturally, if he looks under an ace and sees a 10 then you and everyone else at the table will know what he knows in a split second. He'll turn over the hole card and show his blackjack to the accompanying groans of the players. But what if he's looking under his 10 and there isn't an ace under it? Is there any way to figure out what the dealer knows?

In front loading, you know the dealer's hole card but the dealer doesn't. When a dealer peeks under his aces and 10s, he knows what he has but you don't. Is there any way to read the dealer?

Yes.

This happens to be one area of arcane blackjack play that I'm particularly good at. Maybe it's because I was an actor for a dozen years and I can see chicanery in the faces of those who know one thing but are projecting another. Whatever the reason, I've been quite successful reading the tells of blackjack dealers. Some of this may be instinct, perhaps, and that part of it I won't be able to share with you. But the reading of other types of tells can be learned. One good thing about learning how to read tells is that you will know if you're right or wrong fairly quickly—when he turns over the hole card. Practice, therefore, can make perfect because you can play your basic way (basic strategy and/or card counting) and keep a mental note of how often you were right when you guessed the hole card. If you discover that, with certain dealers, you're right 90 percent of the time, then by all means play accordingly.

Here are some tells to look for:

The Chinese Blackjack Double Take

A dealer taking a quick peek under his 10 will often confuse certain low cards for aces. This is called a Chinese Blackjack in honor of the Chinese players who squeeze their cards. When the top card is a 10 these players often think they have blackjack when they have bust hands because, as they squeeze the bottom card out, certain small cards give an ace-like appearance. These players will often slam their cards down and shout: "Blackjack!" only to have the dealer say as he spreads the cards: "Sorry, sir, that's a 14."

But dealers can make the same exact mistake when they are peeking at the hole card. There will be a lightning-quick double take as the dealer tries to ascertain if that was, say, a four or an ace under there. Sometimes dealers have been known to actually turn over their hole card thinking they have a blackjack only to be embarrassed by players saying: "What are you doing? That's a 14!" Usually a two or four will be the culprit, but any low card looked at quickly enough can look as if it is an ace. When you see that double take, you know that the dealer has a bust card underneath.

The Hesitation and the Blush

Sometimes the double take is extremely subtle. No more than a brief hesitation as the brain sorts out what it thought it saw with what it actually saw. The dealer *freezes* for a half a heart beat. It's almost as if his soul goes away and comes back—just like that! At other times, a small blush will appear because the dealer is embarrassed that he mistook a low card for an ace. He didn't do a double take; nor did he freeze, but he did realize internally that he was mistaken for a split moment and that is why the blush appears. This is a strictly unconscious reaction and when you find a blusher, don't be bashful about taking advantage of him.

Blinking, Winking and Nods

Then there's the blink and non-blink tells. Dealers are just like players. When they get a 10 as their up card they expect to have a pat hand underneath. When they don't, they either blink or don't blink. When they do have a pat hand, they either blink or don't blink. The tell is that some dealers do one or the other consistently. Like this:

Dealer "A" peeks under 10.
Dealer "A" sees another 10.
Dealer "A" blinks as he puts cards back down.

The reverse:

> Dealer "B" peeks under 10.
> Dealer "B" sees a bust card.
> Dealer "B" doesn't blink as he puts cards back down.

Dealer "A" gives a tell because he consistently does a blink on a pat hand, and doesn't do a blink on a bust hand. But dealer "B" does the reverse. He blinks when he has a bust hand, and doesn't blink when he has a pat hand. Consistency in this case is the hobgoblin of small tells.

Some dealers give a slight nod when they have a given kind of hand. Usually, it's a pat hand. The nod—just a slight little one, mind you—is to say: "There, I have a pat hand." On rarer occasions the nod says: "Oh, all right, I have to hit." Again, dealers who nod their tells are consistent one way or the other.

I once played with a dealer who had an unconscious wink. Actually, it was a reverse wink. When he looked under his 10, his left eyelid was slightly lower than his right eyelid. When he had a pat hand, that eyelid jumped up and was equal to his right eyelid. When he had a bust card, his left eyelid remained the same. Thus, a reverse wink.

There are other physical tells. I've had dealers who grind their teeth whenever they get a bust hand. Or dealers who are always moving their jaw muscles but suddenly stop for a brief second as they see that they have a pat and/or bust hand. I've had dealers whose nostrils flare if they have to hit. All these tells are unconscious and generally last for the life of the dealer—unless someone alerts him to the fact that he's doing it. And keep in mind that one dealer's jaw muscle twitching can be a pat hand, another's jaw muscle twitching can be a bust hand. You have to read that dealer correctly, know that your reading is accurate, and then play accordingly.

The Prim and the Proper

Sometimes the way the dealer leaves his cards after peeking is a tell. Some dealers, when they know that they have a pat hand, actually pat their hands! It goes like this. They peek under the 10. See that they have a seven, eight, nine or 10. They realize they will not need a hit but will merely turn over the card when the players are done with their decisions. So they put the cards back down on the table and make sure that the edges are flush with one another. There is almost a subtle patting motion that is made as if to say: "Well, I won't be needing a card and when I turn over the hole card it will be perfectly aligned to the top card."

The opposite is also true. If they know they are going to have to hit, they don't square the edges because they know they might have to move the cards somewhat on the table before the final decision is rendered. Why waste that minute amount of energy lining up the cards perfectly when you're just going to have to mess around with them anyway? So they don't. The edges don't exactly meet. There's a hint of sloppiness. That could be the signal that there's a bust card in the hole. And, you might run into a dealer who does the exact reverse. Pats his bust hands, and keeps his pat hands sloppy. But dealers are creatures of habit and they will tend to do the same thing over and over. If you've read them correctly, those dealers' tells will be consistent.

The Hole Card in Mouth Syndrome

You've heard of people putting a foot in their mouths, well there are some dealers who actually give verbal tells. Just recently, I was playing with one woman who did just this type of thing. Every time she had a pat hand under her 10 she would look at the player on first base and say: "Okay." It was her signal that she was ready to deal. If she didn't have a pat hand, she didn't say anything or she'd say: "You want a card?" But whenever she had a pat hand, it was that "okay" that gave her away.

It's Good to Have a Friend

If you are the friendly type, as the beautiful A.P. and I are, then sometimes dealers will actually root for you to win. Often as you study them, you can see subtle signs on their faces, in their body language, in their eyes, that can alert you to their hole cards. In my experience, women dealers (sorry, don't mean to be sexist here) tend to give the best tells when they are rooting for you. When a rooting dealer is peeking under the 10, her body and/or face tenses a bit. If it stays tense, she has a pat hand. If you see that slight relaxing at the moment of peek, she has a bust hand.

Often her eyes give her away.

I once read a scientific study that showed that men are highly attuned to the eyes of a woman. A woman whose eyes are dilated tends to be alluring to us, a woman whose eyes are not dilated tends to seem cold. Advertising agencies have evidently read the same studies because in products aimed at men but sold by a female image (automobiles, beer, etc.), the females in question will often have their eyes noticeably dilated. Now, in the normal course of shooting a commercial or a photo, a woman's eyes will be anything but dilated because of the enormous wattage needed for professional photography. So in the lab, the eyes are fixed to make them look dilated. Men respond to that and drink more beer and drive fast cars and ultimately, like giant cicadas, kill ourselves trying to impress the females of the species. (Sorry, I get carried away sometimes.)

Now, emotions can dilate eyes also. A strongly positive emotion creates a glow. A negative emotion creates the opposite. So if you are a male who is attuned to the female signals, you might find yourself reading a dealer based upon these subtle sex signals. This dilate/non-dilate phenomenon has a strong sexual component.

I Look and You Look

The best of all possible worlds are the dealers who look under their 10s and aces in such a way that they show you the card too. Usually the person sitting at third base or in the number six position gets the benefit of this hole-card information. The dealers who do this kind of thing are just plain sloppy, or tired from a long shift, or have arthritis. When they peek, they don't cover the hole card sufficiently to block your view. I'm not joking when I say that dealers who have arthritis (or carpal tunnel syndrome) will often be good candidates for tells. Because of the handicap to the hands or wrist, their procedures will be slightly off. These people can be exploited. Yes, in this situation it's okay to take advantage the *hand*-icapped!

Best Burns

As a counter, knowing what the burn card is—especially in single-deck games—can determine the size of your first bet. If it's a low card, you would increase your bet. If it's a high card, you would bet your lowest bet. Some dealers flash the burn card unknowingly. If you find yourself at first base, which is the best position to get a view, look for the burn card. This happens a lot so always be on the lookout. Even some dealers who are otherwise perfect will, on occasion, flash the burn card.

Coin Play

Notice the dealer's tray. Quite often he'll have dollar slot-machine coins in front of each stack of chips. Sometimes these coins are relatively shiny; shiny enough to pick up the reflection of the dealer's hole card when he lifts his 10 or ace. An otherwise perfect dealer is rarely aware of the fact that you are picking his hole card out by this method. And I've yet to meet a casino pit person who has ever suspected such a thing. That's because the player can see it clearly reflected in the coins fronting the dealer's stacks, but both the dealer and the pit crew are oblivious to these coins because they only see the tops of them. The best coin view is usually from seats five, six and seven.

Forced Tells

The following technique will often work against new dealers and will sometimes work with old pros. The dealer does a perfect peek of his hole card. You look him right in the eye and say: "I know you have a bust card under there." Gauge his reaction. Does he blink? Blush? Grind his jaw? Now, match the reaction with the hole card. If he has a bust card, it's possible that this reaction will occur every time he has a bust hand. Next time he peeks under his 10, look him in the eyes again and say the same thing. Gauge his reaction again. Now he has a different reaction—he purses his lips, say. Does he have a pat hand? If he does, you might just be getting a good read on this particular dealer. On his next 10, don't say anything. Just stare at him. What's his reaction? Does he give one of the two reactions you saw before? If he does, did it match the hole card as it did before? There are times when you can force a dealer into tells by creating situations where the dealer must unconsciously react to you and these reactions (blinking, winking, blushing and so forth) will be readable if they are consistently exhibited with certain types of hole cards. These could be tells of the day for some dealers who would otherwise never give a thing away. Many of these forced tells will wear out once the dealer gets used to your act. Fine. But while it lasted, if it was accurate, you were reading the hole card and getting a good edge.

No Telling for You

As Lady Macbeth said to Macbeth: "Your face is a mask where men may read strange matters." Once you find a dealer who is *telling* you his hole card, don't "tell" him you know this. Don't be like Macbeth and wear your face on your sleeve or sleeve on your face or whatever the right expression is. I have seen players do just that. Oh, they don't say: "Excuse me, Mr. Dealer, but every time you peek under your 10s, you cough when you have a bust hand, and take a deep breath when you have a pat hand. Stop it! I don't want to know what your hole card is."

Although it may not be as grossly ridiculous as the above, some players kill the goose that laid the golden eggs because of their own telling stupidity. I had one dealer at the Aladdin a while back who was always showing me her hole card when she lifted up those 10s and aces. I made it a point to sit at third base, where I'd get a good look. However, this dealer was so sloppy that she alerted the players at seats six and five to her hole card, also. (She lifted her hand high instead of bending her head low. Her hands barely covered the cards at all.) I played with her for about a week, until some ploppy ruined the "hole" thing. The ploppy was at seat six and, like me at third base, he was in heaven, getting a peek of the card she had under her 10s almost every time. He was guffawing like a baboon every time she got a 10 up. He wanted everyone to know that he knew the hole card. He'd roll his eyes, giggle, make weird noises. He'd raise his eyebrows à la Groucho Marx. He'd say stupid things like: "I'll bet you got a low card under that 10, yuck! yuck!" Of course, she had a low card under that 10 because we had seen a six under the 10. (This is *not* the same technique as forcing a tell!) He once turned to me and in a stage whisper (to make the people on the other side of the table jealous?) said: "Boy this is GREAT! Keep checking for that hole card, honey!" I told him to calm down. He didn't. Finally I begged him: "Please, be quiet." But it was too late. The dealer realized that she was giving away her hole card and took measures to stop it. I played at the Aladdin for weeks after that and she never revealed her hole card again.

If you run into a dealer who gives tells, front loads, peeks poorly under 10s and aces, keep it to yourself. Play at the person's table and enjoy the advantage but don't be a Ploppy Macbeth and reveal it for the world to see. That kills it. As Lady Macbeth said: "Look like the innocent flower but be the serpent under it!"

Strategy for Hole Card Play

The dealer looks under his 10. You know the dealer's hole card is a six or less because he "tells" you. What do you do? Well, if you have a bust hand, you stay. If you can double down on nine, 10 or 11—you double down. Feel free to split nines, sevens, sixes, threes and twos because those poor ploppy players who you are imitating do just this sort of thing. However, if the casino personnel know you and know that you play basic strategy, suddenly becoming a ploppy in your playing style will be a little too obvious. So you might have to forgo certain moves in the interest of not giving away what you're doing. You won't want to hit your 17 against the dealer's 18, 19, or 20, even though you should. If you are known as a good player, you'll have to be careful. In tell play sometimes you have to give up a little of your advantage to keep the rest of your advantage.

Knowing the dealer's hole card when a 10 is showing can give you an enormous advantage in the long run—upwards of 10 percent. But it's not a guarantee that you'll win. I once had a dealer who I read like a book. One day I played for four hours at his table and lost. In a given session of play, bad luck can even overcome tells, as good luck can overcome bad play.

A Caution on Tells

Playing tells can be fun. It can also be a highly rewarding experience. However, some caveats must be put in place before you consider risking money on your ability to accurately read another human being or on your ability to accurately read a quickly-flashed card. Tell play is not a substitute for proper basic strategy and card counting. Don't go into a casino figuring your plan is to find a dealer whose tells you can read. There's a good chance you won't find any. There's also a good chance that you'll merely *think* you've found one when, in actuality, you haven't found one. In such a case, you will probably lose a bundle before you realize that you were mistaken.

Take a slow approach. If you think you can read a dealer's tells, don't bet money right away. See if you're right. If you think the dealer has a low card under his 10 when he peeks, see if he actually does before you assume you've read him. Do this several times in similar situations with the same dealer. Has he had small cards when he looked under his 10s as you thought he had all those times? If the answer is yes, then you have a real tell worth risking money on. If you were right some times and wrong at other times, forget it. Just play the correct basic strategies against this dealer. Mere guessing will allow you to be right some times and wrong at other times. For extended and serious tell play you have to have around a 90 percent accuracy on your ability to read a given dealer or a given situation. Otherwise, you are taking too great a risk.

True, some tells are singular moments (for example, the Chinese Blackjack) and might not be duplicated at the same session or by the same dealer. The first time you see a dealer hesitate and double peek, figure he has a small card in the hole. Make a notation as to whether you were right or wrong. After you've seen what you believe to be 20 Chinese Blackjacks with 20 different dealers, see how many you were correct about. If the answer is 16 or more, there's a good chance that you are able to pick this quirk up accurately. Otherwise, play against the dealer's 10 card as basic-strategy and/or card-counting variations suggest.

Cutting the Cards and Clump Play

As a card counter, you look to take advantage of every situation at the tables. One of the best abilities to have as a player is the ability to follow clumps of cards in four-, six-, and eight-deck games through the shuffle and then cut them into play early on. This allows you to bet big off the top (thereby not looking like a card counter) into a clump of high cards.

I know a few people who have mastered this technique, which is formally called shuffle tracking. Unfortunately, unless the dealer is extremely lax in his shuffle technique, I have not be able to do it. Nor do I really desire to put in the incredible hours learning all the different kinds of shuffles and how to track clumps in them. As I said, if the dealer is sloppy or lax, I can follow a small clump in a four-, six- and, sometimes, even eight-deck shoe; but if a dealer does a decent job of shuffling, I'm lost. (If you want to learn this technique, Arnold Snyder did a series on it in his excellent newsletter, *Blackjack Forum*, which he is now selling as a complete set. See chapter 23 for further information.)

However, what I can do is cut the cards in such a way as to give me two pieces of information. The first is what the bottom card will be. This card will, of course, be out of play since it's on the bottom. You do this by slightly elevating or angling your cut card as you stick it in. This is usually enough to give you a peek at the card above it, which is the card that will wind up on the bottom. You then count this card. Sometimes, you can even get a peek at the card that will be the card just before the "shuffle card" as the dealer rearranges the decks. The shuffle card is the plastic card that is put into the decks to alert the dealer that it's time to shuffle. This card comes in a variety of colors—most usually green, yellow, or red. As the dealer gets down to this card, you can accurately gauge who will get it and who will get the card just before it—a card whose value you know in advance. If that card is an ace and if you know on the next round that you're going to get it, you up your bet. If it doesn't appear on this round, you know that the dealer has it as his hole card. (Remember that the appearance of the shuffle card just means that this is the last *round* of play for that particular shoe. A round-in-progress doesn't stop simply because the shuffle card has come out.)

Some shoe games are completely covered and you have no idea where the shuffle card is. The above technique obviously can't be used for those. Sometimes the dealer hands the pack to you with the cards facing him and the backs of the cards facing you. Again, if this is the procedure, you won't be able to cut and peek. You have to have the sides of the cards facing you for the above technique to be effective.

If it is possible for you to shuffle cut in such a way as to see the bottom card, or if you can get a glimpse of the bottom card as the dealer puts it into the shoe (this is quite easy to do from first base) and you can also get a glimpse of the burn card (in some shoe games, such as Atlantic City, the dealer will show you the burn card if you ask to see it) then you have two cards for your count that you would not have had otherwise.

Unfortunately, more and more casinos are aware of shuffle trackers and shuffle cutters and they are making it difficult to beat them this way. You will note the elaborate shuffles that many casinos use in their shoe games. In some casinos, the dealer has to call over the floorman to observe the cards in an alternating stack in order to ascertain that the cards are thoroughly shuffled with no big gaps between cards. This is to discourage clump-card play. And some casinos have even stopped offering the players the opportunity to cut the cards. Still, there are opportunities for mastering these shuffle techniques and effectively putting them into play, since many casinos do an ineffective job of mixing the cards.

Tracking Aces

There's no secret that when aces are due to come out, the advantage rests with the players. That's because the player is paid three to two for a blackjack. Also, soft hands can often be doubled in certain situations—again improving the player's monetary expectations. One of the premier advanced techniques is to follow aces through the shuffle. This isn't quite as difficult as it sounds (certainly it is a much easier thing to do than to follow clumps) because you are only keying in on a small portion of the decks. Here's how it's done. Anytime four, five or more aces come out in a given round—quickly memorize all the cards that have come out with them; or, if that is too daunting a task, memorize the several cards nearest the aces. Usually at a full table of seven players plus the dealer, you'll have to memorize eight to 15 cards. These are called "key" cards, as they will key you into the locale of the aces if they start to appear after the shuffle. Fewer players, fewer key cards. Now, in a shoe game there are many denominations of these "key" cards and that's why you have to get a handle on all or as many of the cards that are associated with your clump of aces as possible. When a bunch of them come out on the next shoe, say six to eight of the 15 you memorized, then you will increase your bet for the next round in the expectation that some of those four, five or more aces are about to come out also. Properly applied, this is a great tool for increasing one's edge.

No-Mid-Shoe Entry?
Try These Entry Techniques

In the attempt to stop guerrilla gamblers from jumping into shoes that have turned positive and Wonging their way to victory, and to forestall the possibility of blackjack teams using the Big Player techniques, many casinos have instituted a "no-mid-shoe-entry" policy. Once the dealer starts to deal, the game is effectively closed to new players. If a player who has been playing sits out a round, he is not allowed back into the game until the next shuffle. This rule was also put into effect because many gamblers are superstitious and they feel that the "order of the cards" will be changed by someone jumping in and out of their games. Counters who prefer to sit at a single table and play negative and positive counts also get annoyed when guerrilla players jump in during the positive counts. You will note that almost all the tables that have this no-mid-shoe-entry policy have minimum betting requirements of $25, $50, and $100 on up. The casino is not as concerned with the small bettors getting annoyed when the "order of the cards" is disturbed.

There is a way around this particular rule. When the count goes sufficiently positive to warrant jumping in, jump in as a partner to someone who is already playing. Piggyback on his bet. In fact, you can even ask the guy or lady to now play two hands and you'll put up the cash. After all, you aren't taking up a new spot, a regular player is playing your money. Some casinos that have the no-mid-shoe-entry rule will allow this. Often they haven't seen someone attempt to piggyback a bet and they'll permit it until they find out from the pit boss or shift manager whether it's allowed or not. No matter, you've gotten some money out in a good situation.

If they are not allowing piggybacking and you have the intestinal fortitude for it, give your chips to someone at the table and tell them to bet yours with theirs. If you can do this quietly while the floorman is looking elsewhere, you can get into the game without much fanfare and get out again without undue notice. The only problem with piggybacking is the fact that the player upon whose back you're riding gets to make all the playing decisions. So don't ride on a ploppy.

Jail Bait: What *NOT* to do at a Blackjack Table

Sometimes there's a fine line between cheating the casinos and merely taking advantage of situations that arise at the tables. This next section crosses the line. All the following techniques I'll discuss are illegal and immoral. For some reason, some gambling writers, and many gamblers, feel that the casinos are operating under a different moral law or, rather, that they are operating under a different moral law when it comes to the casinos. They believe that since the casino gives itself the edge wherever possible, this is immoral and therefore, they have the concomitant right to cheat them out of their money any way they can. With the exception of banning skilled players (an immoral activity) and using card mechanics to fix the game (generally a thing of the past), the casinos are not doing anything wrong by offering games you can't beat in the long run. Although the casinos don't publicize the fact that their games are player-deadly, only a fool would think he's getting an even break from them. The information on how much the casino takes on each game is readily available and we do, after all, live in a country where you can go to your local bookstore and buy a book that will explain exactly how much of an edge the casinos have over you. Then you can choose to play or not to play. Or, you can choose what's the best way to play for you. The casinos have to make money to exist and to make money they have to offer games where they have the long-term edge. That's the unwritten contract that you sign when you cash in your money for chips. You're playing their game.

This makes some people very angry.

But they don't have a right to cheat. Period.

Still there's a fine line between cheating and advantage play. The best description of that fine line was given me by a blackjack pro who wishes to remain nameless and pseudonymless. Here are his fine-line distinctions:

> When I go to the bank, if the bank teller gives me too much, I will tell him he made a mistake. I once found a wallet with over $1,000 in it. I returned it without even expecting a reward. But if a dealer in the casino pays me more for a bet than I deserve, I don't say a word. If a dealer pays me twice for the same bet, I don't say a word. I rationalize this easily.

No casino person ever tells the player playing foolishly not to do something suicidal. "Sir, you really want to split those fives against the dealer's 10?" "Ma'am, doubling on a 14 is dumb." Nope. You'll rarely catch a dealer doing that. [Author's note: Some good dealers will hesitate when a person is about to make a truly poor play and ask that person if he really wants to make the move indicated. I have seen this happen on occasion.] The fools are allowed to be plucked. So I rationalize my not saying anything when I get something I don't deserve as a case of what's good for the casinos is good for the player. If the casino takes advantage of stupidity or mistakes, then the player can take advantage of the same thing. I rationalize this a second way. Unlike a bank teller, who is eternally grateful when you inform him of an error, dealers are usually unhappy when you point out their mistakes. If the bank teller gave you $100 too much when you made a withdrawal, all you have to do is give it back to him. He takes it, says thank you, and that's the end of it. But this isn't what dealers have to do when they are found to be in error. Usually they have to call over the floorperson and make a big deal out of it. Dealers can be fired for making too many errors. So if a dealer makes an error in my favor, I would never embarrass him or in any way make him look bad in front of his superiors. After all, we all make mistakes.

Of course, if the dealer makes an error in favor of the casino, well, that's a different story altogether. I'll call over the president of the casino if I have to but, damn, that error better be fixed and I better get my money and so what if the dealer is embarrassed. Hell, he shouldn't be making those kinds of mistakes.

Still, I have never gone into a casino with the thought of cheating them out of their money. I've never tried to force a dealer to make a monetary mistake. I don't consider reading tells, forced or otherwise, to be cheating. I've never actively done anything that constitutes cheating. I have a clear vision of what I consider to be my fine line between cheating and advantage play.

The following techniques are techniques that you'll never find me using. They constitute *real* cheating and I doubt if even the most liberal ethics philosopher would consider any of them to be on any fine moral line. I write about them merely to inform you of what is out there. If you use them, you open yourself to having your blackjack-playing career shut down, perhaps forever.

I also give you a friendly warning. Some blackjack experts think nothing of cheating the casinos or of cheating their fellow players. I'm not talking about the famous, rich authors, mind you, but some members of the loosely-knit community of blackjack professionals can often be turned to "the dark side of the Force," to use *Star Wars* terminology. Many of these professionals don't make great livings (despite what they claim) and are always on the lookout for scamming opportunities—be they against casinos or against other players. Systems sellers fall into this lot, by the way, because the systems that they are selling are usually worthless or, at least, not worth the price they're selling them for. I once had a very good blackjack pro tell me he could hook me up with an incredible card-counting system for "just $500." It would make what I was doing look like "child's feed" (he mixed his metaphors) and I would increase my hourly win rate by a "fraction of 20!" (he meant "factor"). Of course, I turned him down. Through some fluke of fortune, I met someone who had bought this fellow's system. It was merely the Canfield system (a good blackjack counting system but certainly not better than the Hi-Lo you've learned in this book) which can be learned by buying Richard Canfield's excellent book, *Blackjack Your Way to Riches!* (Lyle Stuart Inc., Carol Publishing Group), for a fraction of the cost. [A word of warning. Canfield's book is terrific but he overstates how much of an edge you can get. The book is some 20 years old and quite a few of the blackjack-playing conditions have changed in that time.] Blackjack hustlers are a part of the professional blackjack world and while I know some of them, interviewed others, I don't really move in those circles. I prefer the straight and narrow.

Past Posting

The oldest, simplest, and easiest cheating method in hand-held games is past posting, the placing of bets after a decision has been rendered, or, in the case of blackjack, once you have seen your hand and the dealer's up card. Since you are holding your cards, you can easily bring your hand over your chips and deposit a few more chips should your hand warrant it. Usually the dealer will warn a player to take his hands away from the chips but by then it's too late. The deed is done and the extra chips are out there.

Many cheats also put more money on a double down. Let us say you have three five-dollar chips (reds) in your betting square. Now, you get an 11 against a dealer's six. Obviously, you want to double down. The cheat takes a green chip and two reds and places them to the *left* of his stack and nudges his original three-chip stake as far as he can towards the edge of the betting circle or off it if he can. Then he waits. When the dealer comes to him, the dealer will either say: "Sir, your original bet was for $15." The player then admits to making a mistake (see the "oops" plays). Or the dealer will say: "Doubling for less," as he will think the player's original bet is the $35 bet (one green, two reds). If the dealer does that, the player says, "Wait, I want the same amount," and he retracts his original $15 wager and substitutes another $35. He's in an excellent position, as an 11 against a six is a strong player hand. This technique is done in hand-held and shoe games.

The Quadruple Down

Bryce Carlson, in his wonderful book *Blackjack for Blood* (Compu-Star Press), relates an interesting way to get more money on the table in high counts or in favorable situations. Interesting but wrong. It's called quadrupling down.

The player sits at third base. Usually if you have a double-down hand, you'll wait until the dealer gets to you before placing your cards on the table and putting up the extra money next to your original bet. However, in this method of cheating, you place your double-down hand on the table immediately and your extra bet as well. But, instead of placing your double-down bet next to your original bet, you place it *on top* of your original bet. Now, the dealer might see you out of the corner of his eye and tell you that your bet has to go next to the original bet. In that case, you look sheepish and do as you're told. However, sometimes he won't notice. When he gets around to you, there's your double-down hand but no extra bet next to the original bet. The dealer will inform you to put up another bet. You do so. Thus, you have quadrupled your original bet in an advantageous situation.

The "Oops" Plays

I was once playing at a casino in Las Vegas known for its mistreatment of card counters. I received two aces and, as I was about to lay them out on the table to split them, I accidentally rubbed one card against the other. The dealer thought I was signaling for a hit and he hit me—with a 10. I said: "Wait a minute, I was splitting." I then separated my aces. The floorman who had been watching the whole thing came over.

"Let him split," said the floorman to the dealer. Then he turned to me and said: "And after that, buddy, *you* better split."

I realized then that he thought I was cheating. I didn't bother to argue. When a casino thinks you're cheating, you won't be able to convince them otherwise, so you might as well leave.

I didn't realize at the time but there's a time-honored tradition among blackjack cheats of giving false signals and taking extra hits and then claiming they didn't mean to do that or they really meant to do something else. These are called "oops" plays because you usually say something to the effect: "Oops, I didn't mean to do that. I meant to do this." The idea behind them is that if they work, you get extra value, and if they don't work, you are forgiven and no harm done.

Here are some examples of "oops" plays.

The player has a 17 and the dealer has a 10, nine, eight or seven up. The player takes a hit and, if he busts, he then says: "Oops, I didn't mean to take that hit, I didn't know what I was doing. I thought I had 16." Often, the dealer and/or floorperson will realize that this was an honest (!) mistake and let the player stay with his 17. I mean what player in his right basic-strategy mind would hit on a 17? Of course, if the player catches a four or less, he just stays. If the dealer should notice that he had hit a 17, the player just looks at the dealer sheepishly and says: "I wasn't paying attention but I lucked out."

Some players go so far as to hit 18s and 19s and then go "oops". One player I saw at the Aladdin in Las Vegas did a "semi" hit on a 20 against the dealer's six, got a 10 and then before I could blink, he had turned over his cards as if he intended to split his 10s all along. The casino allowed it. When another dealer was on, he pulled the same thing against the dealer's eight, but this time received a six. He promptly said: "Oops [actually, he said 'Damn'], I didn't mean to do that!" Obviously, no one would hit a 20, so he got away with it again.

Here's a second "oops" play. The dealer is showing a 10. The player puts up an insurance bet. If the dealer is on automatic pilot, he might not notice it. He checks for a blackjack. If he has one, he'll pay off the player's insurance bet at two to one and take the player's original bet. The dealer might not realize that he didn't have an ace showing. If he realizes that the player can't insure against a 10, the player just says: "Oops, I was so afraid you had blackjack that I didn't know what I was doing. Sorry." If the dealer doesn't have a blackjack and he takes the player's insurance bet, the player stops him and says: "Oops, wait a minute, what a dope I am! I just insured against a 10! Ha! Ha! Sorry about that!"

And finally a third. The player has a 12 made up of anything but a 10-value card and a two. The dealer is showing a four, five or six. The player puts his 12 on the table and says: "Double on 11!" If the dealer is on automatic pilot, he'll accept the player's double down because he'll think it's 11. If he hits the player with a nine or less, the player just stays. After the player has received the card, the dealer might say: "Wait a minute, you doubled on 12!" The player just smiles and says: "Oops, well thank God I didn't bust." If, however, the dealer should hit the player with a 10, thereby busting the double down, the player will suddenly realize what a ploppy he is and cry for mercy: "Oops! Oh, my god, I thought I had 11. Oh, I wouldn't ever double on a 12!" He would then beg for his double down not to count. Most of the time, a player will be told before the double down that he's actually doubling on 12 and not 11. Most dealers are specifically trained to call out the double down to avoid such mistakes. In that case, the player just withdraws the double down and thanks the dealer profusely for saving him.

Low Count Card Crunching

As every card counter knows, sometimes you have to play negative counts where the dealer will tend to hit and make his hands owing to the excess of small cards remaining in the deck. You want to get this deck over with as fast as you can. So card-counting cheats who have busted their hands just keep hitting in the hopes that the round will end sooner this way.

Goes like this: The player has 16 against the dealer's 10. He hits and gets a six. He hits again. Then he realizes that he went over and sheepishly turns over his cards: "Oops, I took an extra card." The dealer discards this batch and there's one fewer card remaining. If the player really has chutzpah, he'll take a couple of extra cards.

Here's a wrinkle on the above. If Player "A," the player who's hitting after he busts, has an accomplice, Player "B," sitting next to him, they can play this scam. Player "A" acknowledges that he took an extra card. Let us say that the extra card was a 10. Now, let's say that player "B" has an 11. Player "B" gets all upset and says: "Wait a minute! I was going to double down on my 11 [he would not have doubled down on an 11 against a 10 in a negative count] but now *he* took my card! That's *my* card!"

Sometimes, after a little charade like this, the floorman will let Player "B" have his double down. Another wrinkle on this is for Player "B" to accept the card and double down on any hand that comes to 21—as I did at the opening of the chapter. The difference between the two situations is obvious. Mine happened by accident, while Player "A" and Player "B" are in collusion to cheat the casino.

Naturally, if Player "B" doesn't like the card that Player "A" caught, he rejects it if the floorman offers it to him.

BIG Cheats

Some players won't settle for the little wins an honest card counter grinds out day after day. Some crooked players won't settle for cheating in small ways to increase their edge. Some players want to make killings against the casinos. Unfortunately, the only way to do that, short of winning a jackpot or having phenomenal luck, is to cheat and I mean cheat BIG. In blackjack BIG cheating is a complicated affair because the cheater usually has to have someone on the inside, usually a dealer or floorperson, in on the deal.

The most common form of BIG cheating is simply replacing the shoe in use with a shoe that has been perfectly stacked in advance. A diversion is arranged to take place at the critical moment when the cheaters want to introduce their own shoe into the game; a diversion that will (hopefully) take everyone's attention off the game at hand. Then the cheating blackjack players remove the old shoe and replace it with one they have carried into the casino. The cards in this shoe have been arranged so that the players will win every hand (or almost every hand). Usually the players will take up all the spaces at the table so that they can hit the casino fast and get out of there before anyone is the wiser.

Little Cheats

The beautiful A.P. and I saw this scam at the Golden Gate in downtown Las Vegas. A dealer and two players (who were themselves dealers at another casino) were in cahoots. When one or the other player had a pair of face cards, he would put them face up on the table as if the hand were a blackjack. The dealer would scoop up the cards and then pay off the player as if it were a blackjack. In this way, every 20 composed of two face cards that these players received was paid at three to two. At first we thought the dealer was just a new dealer and that she was making a mistake. But how many 20s can one dealer mistake for blackjacks? We were so uncomfortable watching this that we finally left the table.

No, I didn't tell the casino management, and perhaps I was wrong there (I'll leave you to decide the moral issue here), but I just couldn't watch such blatant cheating. I also realized that if a dealer was willing to cheat the casino to help her friends, she would certainly be willing to cheat another player to help herself.

Card Mechanics: They'll Fix You Up Good!

A "card mechanic" is a dealer who can manipulate the order of the cards during a shuffle, and/or deal from the bottom of the deck, and/or deal the second card of the deck—until such time as a specific card is needed either to help a confederate or to nail a big player for the casino; that specific card being the card at the bottom or at the top. The techniques the card mechanic uses take years to master and dealers with these skills were in great demand during the heyday of the mob in Vegas during the 1960s and 1970s. Today, you won't find all that many of them around. Here's what to look for just in case. If you are a big player and you've been winning big, suddenly you discover that your dealer has been taken off your table before the normal rotation and a guy (sometimes with no name tag) has taken his place. This guy deals fast and snappy. Indeed, he "snaps" those cards when he deals. He also watches his shuffles closely. Suddenly, you find yourself busting. Suddenly, you find the dealer is making all his bust hands. Suddenly, you realize that the money is crossing the table in the opposite direction than it was before. You are now beginning to lose. My friend, you are facing a card mechanic. The tell-tale "snap" means he's dealing seconds. Watching the shuffle shows him the order of the cards. He'll shuffle until he sees an order he likes or an order he's arranging. It's rare to find these mechanics today but in the past 10 years, I played against two of them. I didn't play for long. That "snap" was enough for me to pop out of the game and move to another casino!

Chapter Twenty

Coupons and Comps Are Cash in Your Pocket

If I told you that you and a partner could make $732 in a little less than three hours of gambling, what would you say? What if I told you that the money was almost as good as guaranteed? What if I said that the method I was about to show you would give you a staggering edge over the casinos—a bigger edge than the casinos have over their worst players? I know what you would say. You would say that I'm scamming you like those scammers I've written about in my newsletter, *Chance and Circumstance* (Paone Press). And—you would be wrong! Because I've done just that in Las Vegas.

In the summer of 1995, the Imperial Palace in Las Vegas was offering the most incredible coupon deal. In their "Fun Book" was a five dollar match-play blackjack coupon. You bet five dollars with this coupon and if you won, they paid you $10. If you got a blackjack, most dealers would pay you $15.

You also could split and double down with most dealers for the full amount of the coupon.

So the beautiful A.P. and I played four coupons each—one at each day shift and two during the night when the casino was packed. That gave us eight opportunities to win.

The value of this coupon is close to 50 cents on the dollar. That's right. The coupon player will win 50 cents for every dollar bet (remember you get your dollar back plus 50 cents!). That's some edge. Put another way, let us say that blackjack is almost a 50/50 game (with the three to one payout on a blackjack, it's close). That means we win one of every two bets. We lose five dollars but win $10 for a net gain of five dollars.

Mathematically, that worked out to an average of $20 per day on this coupon. That translated into a $420 theoretical win for three weeks of play.

The Imperial Palace was also offering a three to two payoff on the even-money bets at roulette. This translated into 37 cents on the dollar, or $14 for every 38 spins of the wheel. In roulette even-money bets, you will win 18 times, lose 20 times. Thus, on two dollars bet, you will lose $40 but win $54 because of the three to two payout! Net gain: $14!

So in roulette, we did eight spins a day at the Imperial Palace. For three weeks that translated into 176 spins. That translates into a $65 win.

So for three weeks at the Imperial Palace, we were theoretically given $485. (We actually won a little more.)

We combined this with three to two coupons at craps, big six and roulette at several other casinos in Vegas during this time for a grand total of $732.

This was all done without going out of our way to take advantage of the coupons available in Vegas. If a casino offered a good coupon deal while we were there, we took advantage of it. We didn't travel high and low looking for coupons. We didn't have to. Many of the casinos where we played hawked their coupon books. They were practically begging us to take their money. And we obliged.

I know some people who do nothing but couponing when they are in Vegas because it's guaranteed money. At any given time, there will be 10 or more casinos offering coupons with incredible paybacks as an incentive for you to gamble in their establishments. One retired fellow I know makes about $35 a day doing his "coupon run."

For those of you who enjoy beating casinos, the "fun books" are a fun way to put extra cash in your pocket with little or no risk. Play enough of these "fun books" in a given vacation and you are practically guaranteed a win.

The art of using coupons has been dubbed "couponomy" by blackjack expert and publisher Anthony Curtis. His excellent book, *Bargain City* (Huntington Press), goes into detail on how to become a coupon expert—a "couponomist." If this appeals to you (and it should—after all it's free money!), then I recommend you get his book.

Comp Runs

In Atlantic City, where "fun books" are somewhat rarer, you can make a comp run. If you go to Atlantic City on a rather regular basis, spread your play among several casinos. You'll be delighted to discover that most of them will send you coupons for cash in the mail as an incentive to come back to them. When you go, you can make a comp run—collect your cash and whatever other goodies the casino has set aside for you. (And by all means take everything they offer.)

Unless you have a specific reason for limiting your action to just one casino (great penetration in blackjack, 10 times odds in craps, etc.), there's no reason not to spread it around a town like Atlantic City. You'll get a better return in comp coupons for your investment.

In point of fact, most casinos in most casino towns offer monetary incentives in the local papers where they advertise. Often these are discounts for food and beverage. But sometimes they are match-play coupons every bit as good as the coupons offered in the fun books. Take advantage of them. Even if you aren't going to stay or play at a particular casino, walk over (if it's close enough) and use the coupon. Your edge is worth the exercise.

Some high rollers think it's beneath them to take $10 here, $20 there. Nonsense. If that same $10 or $20 were sitting on the sidewalk, wouldn't you pick it up? Of course.

Match Play and
Special Pay-Back Promotions

There is another type of promotion that merits a close look by the sharp player seeking a sizable edge. Some establishments will give you a special cash bonus for playing a given number of hours (usually four hours in a 24 hour time period) in their casino. Often these promotions are done in conjunction with a travel agency as a part of larger public relations scheme. For example, one such promotion was recently featured at the Sands in Las Vegas. If you played a minimum of four hours at five dollars (or more) a hand you would receive a $40 cash bonus at the end of the four hours. Now, you could choose your game (double-deck, six-deck) and you could flat bet that five dollars or vary your bet with the count (the Sands was a little paranoid about players who spread too much, however). This double-deck game had approximately a .30 percent advantage for the house (you are expected to lose 30 cents for every $100 risked). Figuring that you would play 60 hands an hour or 240 hands in a four-hour period (risking $1200), that meant the basic-strategy player could expect to lose $3.60. Since the casino was giving you $40 as a bonus, you could expect to come away with $36.40 profit. If you were counting cards and spreading, increasing your bets when the game favored you, you could expect to win even more.

One friend of mine, K.F., played this game every other day. For four hours of play at five dollars a hand (he spread from five dollars to $15 in high counts), he averaged $67 a day for two months. That might not seem like much but . . . the Sands also offered certain other comps along with the cash bonus. You received two free tickets to the show, two-for-one breakfasts and lunches and an occasional fully-comped meal.

The Sands was just one such promotion at the time. Let K.F. tell it:

> I played one casino where you bought $200 worth of match-play chips for $150. The only stipulation was that you had to lose those $200 worth of match-play chips, you couldn't cash them in. You could do this promotion once every 24 hours. Another casino was offering a whopper. You bought $1,500 worth of match play for $1,100. Again, you had to lose that $1,500, you couldn't cash them in. With both of these promotions, you had to bet an equal number of your chips and match-play chips, the minimum bet being $10—five dollars match play, five dollars regular. Both promotions were leery of card counters since they were looking to capitalize on tourists and poor players. A card counter has a nice edge in a

promotion like this. So I limited myself to a one-to-three spread in a double-deck game. I did quite nicely.

How to Play and Win at the Comp Game

[Much of the material in this section first appeared in *Guerrilla Gambling: How to Beat the Casinos at Their Own Games!* (Bonus Books). It's been adapted for *Best Blackjack*. To be the best blackjack player you can be, the advice and attitudes of the guerrilla gambler are just as important to you. The comp game is worth playing when it works to your advantage. It isn't worth playing when it hurts your style of play.]

American gamblers have gone comp crazy. Players will lose thousands to win a comp worth $100. The casinos know that many players want to get "free" food and lodging, or, for lower rollers, substantial discounts on same. The casinos have set their comp policies with one thing in mind—making you play at a certain level for a certain period of time to lose a certain average amount of money to get a comp worth maybe one percent or less of your total action. (Total action is the total amount of money you bet during your session or stay at a casino.)

I recently heard the story of a great, high-rolling Australian billionaire with a love for blackjack. It is typical of Las Vegas high-roller stories and you can substitute Japanese, Chinese, Texan, movie star, baseball-team owner or whoever for the Australian lead character. This man likes to bet $50,000 a hand—and play all seven hands at a table. That's $350,000 in action per round! He prefers shoe games. The casino of his choice flies him and his party in first class, puts him and his party up in the most luxurious of suites, lavishes him and his party with gifts and gourmet meals. Nothing is too good for Mr. High Roller. A casino host told me in private that the hotel spends $30,000 a visit on this individual.

Sound like a lot? The last visit Mr. High Roller lost—nine million dollars! That's nine million. NINE MILLION DOLLARS!

The casino made nine million dollars for an investment of a lousy $30,000! Mr. High Roller could buy a lion's share of the hotel for nine million dollars. Sadly, in their desire to be treated like kings, many high rollers will bet their kingdoms.

To a lesser extent this is what the casinos try to do to everyone. Even the lowliest of low rollers wants a comp. To get it, the casinos demand action. They demand you bet high enough and for long enough to justify "giving" you a freebie. For low rollers this comp often comes at the expense of their dignity for, unlike the high roller who gets everything "up front," the low roller must literally beg for every comp. While the high roller is fawned over in a sickening manner, the low roller must grovel to get a few crumbs. I can't tell you how often I have heard the following conversation:

Low Roller: You think I could have a comp for lunch?

Pit Person: [pretending to look a little surprised but quickly pretending to cover his astonishment that such a plebeian would dare to ask for a comp] I'll have to see about that. [pause for effect] One?

Low Roller: [embarrassed by his lowly stature in the eyes of the casino world, stammers] Two. Me and the wife. [seeing the pit person's eyes narrow in horror] For sandwiches, you know. [Low roller feels that if he specifies sandwiches, the pit person might take pity on him.]

Pit Person: [frowning ever so slightly] I'll have to check your action. [Subtle hint that the man might not have played sufficiently long enough to merit a sandwich.] I'll be right back.

Low Roller: Thank you. [Low roller continues to play.]

Now, the pit person writes something on a piece of paper. If the casino where this little charade is taking place is computerized, the slip of paper goes to a rather bored man or woman who types some information into the computer. While this is happening, the pit person goes to the farthest end of the pit and busies him or herself with something or other. (If the casino is not computerized, the pit person takes the slip of paper to the farthest end of the pit and busies him or herself with something or other.) Ten, 15 or 20 minutes later, the low roller asks the dealer what happened to the pit person. The dealer will shrug or say something to the effect that he'll be right back. A little while later, another pit person walks by and the low roller calls out to him or her to come over.

Low Roller: I asked for a comp about 20 minutes ago and the guy disappeared.

Pit Person: [looking suspicious] Who did you ask it of?

Low Roller: The guy at the end of the pit, all the way down there. [Pit person eyes the low roller. Low roller, feeling awkward, blurts out . . .] It was just for sandwiches.

Pit Person: I'll see what I can do.

Now the new pit person walks down the pit, stopping to chat with the dealers, talk to high rollers, breathe in the smoke-filled air. In five minutes he gets to the other pit person and a long conversation ensues. The low roller looks anxiously down the pit. He thinks they are making a big decision about his comp. In fact, they are talking about the barbecue held by one of the dealers the previous week. At the end of a discussion of how drunk so and so got, the new pit person says to the previous pit person, "Oh, player A at table B seat two wants a comp." Of course, the decision had been made earlier by the original pit person. Sure the guy was going to get a comp—if they could keep him playing another 20 minutes to half hour! The little charade of giving it to the computer person and walking down to the end of the pit was to get the low roller to play more.

Now, the original pit person comes back and either hands the comp to the low roller or takes a comp from the computer person and hands it to the low roller.

Pit Person: Sorry this took a little while. I had to get this authorized [which means that the low roller's action was so low that only one of the casino gods could authorize a comp for a sandwich] and the boss wasn't here. I can't authorize comps at your level of play. [By saying "your level of play" the pit person shoots home the message that next time there won't be a comp and maybe Mr. Low Roller should consider betting more heavily.]

Low Roller: [feeling grateful as he takes the comp from the pit person] Oh, thanks.

Pit Person: [magnanimously] You're welcome. [pause] Enjoy your meal.

Low Roller: [grateful] Thanks, really, thank you so much.

The low roller takes off for the cafeteria with his $15 comp. The pit person whispers to the dealer, "How much did he rebuy for?" The dealer whispers back. "Another hundred." The pit person marks the following on the slip of paper: *Mr. Low Roller cashed in originally for $100. Played a half hour, asked for comp. Cashed in for another $100. Half hour later. Cashed out for $50. Loss $150. Comp $15.*

Scenes like this occur quite frequently in casinos. The pit crew's job is to get you to play as much as possible. When you ask for a comp, if you are a low roller, they will delay, hem and haw, to get you to play overtime. Don't do it.

In fact, the guerrilla gambler attempts to play less and get more. The guerrilla gambler wants to extend his body time at the table but not his at-risk time. The casinos generally rate players on two criteria—*how long* you play and for *how much*. They multiply *how long* by *how much* and come up with a bettor's profile. Once they have a profile, they can determine how much in comps this particular individual's play deserves. Thus, your goal as a guerrilla gambler is to distort the profile, so that you appear to be a much bigger player than you actually are.

This can be accomplished in any number of ways—depending upon the game you are playing. In craps, the *5-Count* automatically extends your body time but not your "at-risk" time [for those of you who enjoy craps or want to master it, see my book, *Beat the Craps Out of the Casinos: How to Play Craps and Win!* (Bonus Books)]. Let us say that as a low roller, you place the six and eight for six dollars apiece after the *5-Count*. If you can stay at a table for two hours but only risk your money for one hour *and* have the casino rate you as a two hour player, you will get more comps. More reward for less risk!

The following are techniques that extend your body time but not your at-risk time. Included will be some methods designed to deceive the casinos into thinking you bet more heavily than you actually do. I have used many of these methods with varying degrees of success. I have not used some of the methods, but acquaintances have. I can't state unequivocally that all these methods will reap in the comps for you but you have nothing to lose by trying them.

If you feel that the more devious methods of getting comped are "cheating" and "immoral," then don't utilize them. I used to think that all of these techniques bordered on the shady until one time at the Taj Mahal in Atlantic City showed me the error of my thinking. There was some poor, pathetic blackjack player, obviously drunk and stupid (a lethal ploppy combination) who had just signaled for a hit on an 18 against the dealer's six. He had a $100 bet up. The dealer hesitated and said: "Are you sure you want to hit that?" The drunk nodded. The dealer still hesitated.

The pit person came over and nudged the dealer. The dealer gave the drunk a card. Obviously, the drunk busted. The pit person whispered to the dealer. "You're not here to help the players." For the next half hour that poor, pathetic drunk hit all manner of absurd hands and lost thousands of dollars. The pit person hovered near the table at all times and the dealer kept his peace. Finally, the drunk staggered off and the pit person very matter-of-factly wrote down the drunk's losses.

I turned to A.P., my beautiful and quite moral partner, and said: "I guess all is fair in love, war *and* gambling." She agreed. And I thought to myself, *How many times have you seen players do suicidal things and the casino honchos just snicker into their rating pads? Answer: too many. How many times have you seen low-rolling players who have taken substantial losses—for them—of $50, $100, $150 and when they asked for a comp the pit crew let them stew and wait and wait and wait? Answer: too many.* Well, I say, to hell with playing by the casinos' rules. As long as you don't steal chips, mark cards, substitute dice, hit slot machines with sledge hammers, or do anything *illegal*, leave morality to the saints.

I think of these tricks the same way a poker player thinks of a bluff. If I can make the casino think they have a better edge over me than they really do and their misconception leads them into giving me more than what they would otherwise think I deserve—so what? Casinos do the same things to the players with their psychological warfare departments—better known as public relations and advertising departments. Casinos attempt to get you to bet over your head and bust out. That's why more gamblers have gone belly-up than have casinos. So bring on the comps!

Getting Your "Fair" Share

1.   Always join as many players' clubs as the casinos offer. If you are a slot or video-poker player, join the slot clubs of as many casinos as you enjoy playing in. Casinos compete for players and you will find that, with little or no action, you will be offered discounts on many things during promotional periods. A great disguise for a card counter is to give the casino a little machine action on the side. If you look for loose machines or play a strong game of video poker [see my books *Break the One-Armed Bandits!* and *Victory at Video Poker!* (Bonus Books)], you have a natural camouflage at work.

2.   As a basic-strategy blackjack player, you should never begin playing until you have either asked to be rated *and* given your name in, or handed in your player's comp card. Some casinos, especially in Atlantic City, have pit crews that watch a player cash in and play for several minutes *before* ambling over and picking up the player's card. The player then has missed part of his rating. So when you sit at a table, cash in but don't place a bet until your rating begins! You want every second you've earned!

If you are a card counter, sometimes you don't want to draw attention to yourself. One of the best ways *not* to draw attention to yourself is—*to draw attention to yourself!* A regular gambler wants a comp and wants to be rated. The pits know this. They also know that many card counters are somewhat timid and withdrawn in the face of pit scrutiny. The pit people are going to notice how you bet—whether you give your name in or not. So give them your name first. "Hey, Molly, can I get a rating?" "Hey, Joe, don't forget to take my card!" "My name is Jimmy Jackson, can I get rated?" Of course, if you are playing for serious money and you are a brilliant card counter, you might not want to give in your real name. But don't hesitate to give in a name. Let the pit crews think you are just one of the sheep wanting a comp for your shearing.

3.   Try to have three or four player's comp cards in your name. An acquaintance of mine puts her cards in machines of players who are not getting rated. This gives her their time. She thinks of this little maneuver as the equivalent of donating blood. The player is donating his or her time. She sees nothing wrong in doing this—after all, she rea-

sons, the machines are being played, time is building up, comp units are being earned. Why not have someone get them?

4.   In blackjack, during low counts, or when you have to go, make sure you head for the bathroom in *mid-shoe*. Don't wait for a shoe to finish to go to the bathroom (especially if you are counting cards and the count is in the basement). Your rating points will still be accumulating but your risk will be nil. A visit once an hour in a low count can really reduce the casino's edge and increase your comp value. If you aren't in the midst of a torrid streak and winning bundles of money, make your pit stop mid-shoe. In some places, such as Atlantic City, when you leave the table to go to the bathroom, the dealer will put a clear plastic disc in the spot or spots you are playing. In other places, such as Las Vegas, the dealer will say he'll save the spot(s) as long as you leave some money on the table. Spots will usually be saved for 15 to 20 minutes.

5.   Put up a larger than usual bet when the pit person comes over at the beginning of a shoe. If your normal bet is $20, then make the first bet $40 and the next two $10 each. Your risk will still be $60 (albeit skewed on that first hand) but your rating will be double. (In a single-deck game, you are even with the casino off the top so in the long run that first bet is an even proposition.) In a shoe game, the pit person does not observe every hand. He moves around. If you want, whenever he comes to you, up your bet. If you are counting and the count is low, don't up your bet—up your body and go to the bathroom. First, however, start pushing out a $100 bet (or whatever you consider a big bet) and at the last minute indicate that your bladder is about to burst and head for the restroom. You might even get that $100 bet down in the ratings.

6.   Once you have asked for a comp, *stop playing*. Either that or ask for the comp 10 minutes before you intend to finish. Never play one second longer than you want just to be comped. If they make you wait, *sit* and wait. You might even want to loudly call out every few minutes: "Hey! How's my comp coming?" The reason you want to sit is to speed up the process. If they know you aren't going to play any more hands, they will get the comp to you sooner to free up a chair for the next player.

7.   Don't be afraid to grovel. Oh, yes, the beggar who grovels the most is sometimes the beggar who gets the most. Think of asking for a comp as an act, that's all. It doesn't reflect on your dignity. You're an actor and this is Academy Award time. Also, when you get the comp, try to be effusive in your praise of the pit person who gives you the comp. And always use that first name as if the two of you are best buddies. "Oh, *Billy*, thanks for the comp. Really, *Billy*, thanks so much. Billy . . . Billy, Billy, *Billy*."

8.   If groveling is not your style, then ask for the comp in such a way that the pit person knows that not only do you *expect* a comp but you have *gotten* a comp before, perhaps even from him, for this level of play: "Comp for two for lunch, Willie." Remember, always talk to the casino pit people as if they are your buddies. They will do that to you, so you do that to them. Sometimes it's hard to turn down a buddy.

9.   Put up a large bet at the time a casino pit person is observing, but take it down *before* actual play. I once put up a $300 inside bet in roulette in an Atlantic City casino that I rarely frequent. It was an accident. I had reached for the wrong pile of chips. The only reason I had a pile of black chips at the roulette table was due to the fact that I had played a Big Number which had hit several times in slightly more than several spins. The dealer yelled out: "Blacks in action." I looked over at the layout and thought to myself, *what idiot would put a $300 inside bet at roulette?* and low and behold those were *my* black chips sitting on number four! The ball was not as yet being spun, so I just left the bet there. The pit person asked the dealer who had placed it and the dealer nodded towards me. He wrote something on the pad and turned away. I took the bet down the moment the dealer began to spin the ball and replaced it with three blue chips (roulette chips worth $15 total)—a far cry from the three black chips! Several weeks later I received an invitation to *fly to the casino at the casino's expense!* Okay, it wasn't an invitation to fly to Vegas, but still, the casino was willing to put me on a plane at their expense and fly me from New York to Atlantic City. And I believe this was all the result of one inadvertent bet.

10.   As stated previously in this chapter, always look for coupon books and play the coupons that give you a better game. If you are guaranteed $20 to $30 a day with almost no risk—go for it! Think of your coupon trips as breakfast money.

11.   Don't be afraid to sell a comp to someone else. The Frontier in Las Vegas was offering an incredible deal during its rancorous strike with the culinary workers union. If you played blackjack for a minimum of five dollars or more, every time you received a blackjack, you got a special silver coin. Collect a certain number of silver coins (originally 10, then 11, and by the time you are reading this—who knows?), you got a free room! You had to collect a few more for a free room on a weekend. Well, several of my Las Vegas buddies who play the Frontier game found a way to add to their advantage. They sold the silver coins! For two dollars or more, they gave you their coins for a free room! This deal appealed to low rollers who could truly benefit by a "free" room. Some Las Vegans had quite a business going selling "free" rooms. They hoped the strike would never end.

Say you are playing at one casino and your friend is playing at another. Both of you get a comp for two for lunch. One of you sell the comp for half price! There's no end to the ingenuity with which you can approach resale in America! If two of you are playing at different tables but at the same casino—then both of you ask for comps for *two*. Then sell one comp. You can usually sell the comp as you wait on the line to the restaurant. If the casino has a rule about selling comps, and they stick it to you as you are peddling your comp—give it away! Make a donation to the poorest slob you can find. He deserves a gourmet meal, too, no?

12.   Some casinos offer free shirts, jackets, vases, picture frames, bookends, mugs, wine glasses or what have you to regular players. Even if you have more of the aforementioned items than you could ever want—collect it. The casinos record the fact that you are interested in receiving their merchandise and thus they will tend to keep offering it. I have a wardrobe full of jackets and shirts with casino logos. Wearing them in a casino makes the casino pits look at you as just another dopey gambler.

13.   If you are *not* a card counter, always cash in for *much, much* more than you intend playing with. At craps I always cash in for four times what I'm actually willing to lose in a session. This makes it appear as if I'm a higher roller than I actually am because the pit person always writes down your initial buy-in. The figuring goes that what a person cashes in for is what that person is willing to lose. What you are willing to lose sometimes helps the casinos decide what they are will-

ing to give you. Especially after you have a winning session, the pit will want to get a handle on what you would have been willing to lose had you been clobbered. That would be your buy-in.

Card counters should be wary of doing this, as astute pit crews know that card counters like to have enough backing them so they can withstand the inevitable swings of luck—those "fluctuations in probability" the mathematicians are always writing about. So if you count cards, cash in for much, much *less* than you expect to play with!

14.   Always collect whatever coin vouchers are offered by the casinos. In Atlantic City, for example, the players comp clubs are always mailing players coupons for coins. I know some members of the Captain's Crew who used to ignore these generous coin offers. After all, what do mega-rollers need with some coins? Then one day, the Captain himself added up what he collects *weekly* from Atlantic City casinos in coin vouchers—a staggering $120! That is truly free money. So always collect your coin vouchers and redeem them. I always set aside a part of any trip to tour the casinos where I have coin vouchers waiting.

15.   Never be afraid to ask for a comp. When I first started my war against the casinos, I was embarrassed to ask for something for free. It was my upbringing, I guess. Now, I ask for comps even if I play for 15 minutes in a casino. I don't consider a comp a freebie, I consider it a part of my game. The worst the pit people can do is say no. Big deal. One caution, however, for high rollers. Don't make a pig of yourselves when you are fully comped. If you can't eat it, don't order it. Some high rollers are such oinkers that many casinos have tightened their comp requirements for their gourmet restaurants. This hurts medium rollers who like a gourmet meal now and then.

I'm sure there are other ingenious ways of getting more for less that you will come up with in your own personal attack on the casinos. The key to remember is that you don't want to alter your game, except as I've indicated, just to get comps. For card counters, comps are the icing on the cake of their advantage over the casinos. For basic-strategy players, a comp can be the thing that makes you a winner for a given session. As K.F. once sang: "I play tight, I play strong, then I sing my old comp song!"

Chapter Twenty-One
Emotional Blackjack

You have been playing blackjack for many years and you use a strong point count and you know the important variations of strategy based on the true count. You are a winning player in that time and you've vacationed free of charge in Las Vegas and Atlantic City, not because you're comped and lose bundles, but because you win enough at the tables to pay for your meals, travel, entertainment and hotel accommodations—and you bring something home in the bargain.

You are a truly skilled blackjack player.

Now, tonight the dealer shows a six as his up card, the count is highly positive, and you have your largest bet up. You split your threes and get a seven and an eight. You double down on both and receive a 10 and a nine, respectively. You now have two hands of 20 against the dealer's (supposed) 16. You now have four times as much money on the table and you are in an enviably advantageous position.

You feel your heart pounding and the muscles in your stomach tighten.

The dealer slowly turns over his hole card and indeed it is a 10! Thanks to your threes and seven, the count is in the stratosphere. The deck is loaded with bust cards for the dealer.

Your heart pounds even more. Then you remember that not many fives have come out of the deck. In fact, you don't remember seeing a five. You dismiss the dread. The deck is loaded against the dealer and he'll bust. (*Please, God, he has to.*) A bead of sweat forms on your forehead.

In seeming slow motion, the dealer takes his hit. A *five!* He now has 21 and he's beaten your two hands—your two *double-down* hands with your maximum bet out! You feel your heart slowly merging with your trachea and your large intestine. If you had enough strength, you'd like to reach out and strangle the dealer but two things prevent you from doing so—you're too weak and the dealer is much bigger than you.

Also, your intellect tells you that the dealer didn't *purposely* give himself a five. He didn't *purposely* give you hands that called for splitting and doubling. He didn't *force* you to put a maximum bet on everything. And you certainly imagined that snicker cross his lips for just a brief moment as he saw that look of defeat in your eyes. He didn't really snicker. He wouldn't dare. (Would he?)

No, the dealer was merely the messenger of fate. He was the herald who revealed the blackjack gods' will on this particular hand. Now you realize, naturally, how emotionally satisfying it must have been to live in ancient Greece and be able to kill the messengers who brought bad news!

Instead, you go back to your hotel room, curl up into the fetal position, and wonder why you subject yourself to this torment. Gone is the realization that you fly free, eat free, room free. Free? You've paid a big price this afternoon—and you're not thinking about money. Why do you do this? Play this stupid game? So you fall asleep in the fetal position and, if you weren't over 40 years old, you would suck your thumb for peace. But you can't.

For you expert players out there, you know what I'm talking about. For you novices—welcome to the world of *emotional blackjack*.

Every skilled blackjack player knows that the game, despite the favorable long-run percentages, is an emotional roller coaster. My contention is that the emotional lows are greater than the emotional highs in direct but inverse proportion to one's skill and financial expectation. Put another way: the *emotional expectation* of blackjack for the skilled player is negative, while the *financial expectation* is positive.

Now, let's take a look at the scenario I painted just before. Suppose the player in the preceding example had won his two double-down hands of 20 because the dealer, as expected, busted. The player would have felt great but he would not be ecstatic—the dealer is *expected* to bust more often in a situation like that. Emotionally, you got what you expected. Thus, your high is tempered by your expectation. The high is not *as high* when the dealer busts as the *low is low* when the dealer does the unexpected and draws to a 21 in a high-count situation from a bust hand of 16.

This is the emotional difference between hope and expectation.

Intellectually, you know that in the long run you will win. That is your *mathematical expectation* based on millions of computer runs. But *emotionally* the "long run" is every session, every hand you play. You also know intellectually that on any given hand, any given session, any given extended period of play, the normal fluctuations of the game can produce losses. You intellectually accept this. But emotionally you expect to win! Thus, an interior battle rages inside the skilled blackjack player. What you intellectually accept, you emotionally reject. You don't *hope* you are going to win—you *expect* it. And when you lose it can be devastating.

Most gambling is the reverse.

Craps, for example, has different emotional underpinnings. You know the house always has the edge and you know in the long run that edge should defeat you. Thus, the average craps player, even the one who makes the most conservative traditional bets, emotionally expects to lose at the game. Thus, you aren't devastated when you do lose.

How thrilling, however, when in the short-term fluctuations of that game, a hot shooter comes along and you win! Maybe that's why long-time craps players are so exuberant during hot rolls, while the expert blackjack player is not. (Unless he's putting on an act for the benefit of the pit.) Thus, while craps has a negative financial expectation, it has a positive emotional one. You *expect* to lose but *hope* to win. When you lose it is not as devastating, but when you win, you're elated.

Now, all the top blackjack writers have explained the roller-coaster nature of the game, and have cautioned would-be card counters to be aware of the wild fluctuations that can occur in the game. But to be intellectually aware is not the same as being emotionally prepared. This is what experience teaches you. As the ancient Greeks said: "A man must suffer to be wise!" The great blackjack players are experts in counting, variations in strategy, money management—and suffering.

P.C. makes his living playing blackjack and he loves the game, but he has this to say about its emotional impact: "Blackjack should be sponsored by Maalox because you have more *Maalox moments* than you care to think about. No book has ever addressed the emotional pounding you take as a professional player. Maybe it's not something that you can be prepared for, but believe me, it's something you're gonna get."

P.C.'s wife is also a skilled player but she does not do it for a living.

"I couldn't," she says. "Every time I double on an 11 and get an ace, every time I double on a 10 versus a 10 in high counts I get a headache. And when I split aces and get two garbage cards, I think to myself—this is worse than giving birth. Yet, I do love to play the game, but I also need to hold down a job and know my life doesn't depend on the turn of the cards. If I had to play blackjack for a living, it would kill me."

Another female counter is a long-time Atlantic City player.

"I've played the Claridge four-deck, high-stakes game for minimums of $50 or more, and in three years I'm up about what my expectation would be. But my nerves are shot. If I didn't love the game so much—really, the money—I would quit. You put yourself through an emotional wringer every time you play."

The truth is that most of the skilled players I've met have a love-hate relationship with the game. They at once express the emotional beating they consistently take, yet they protest in the end that they love the game and will continue to play it.

Perhaps the best analogy I can use to describe this relationship is that of boxing. The skilled card counter is like a world champion boxer who is in the ring with an opponent who is *almost* his equal. In a long fight, the great fighter will land more punches and hurt his opponent more than his opponent will hurt him. But this fact does not mitigate the pounding the great fighter takes. At the end of the fight, the great fighter is in worse shape than he was at the beginning, despite the fact that he eventually won.

I believe that the same holds true for blackjack. The casino is a tough antagonist that does not give an inch. You have to be aggressive and fearless. You have to be willing to take the inevitable "pounding."

So, if the negative emotional expectation is correct, why do skilled blackjack players bother with the game? First, it is a contest of skill and will, and when you see that in the long run you can win, you have a sense of pride in your accomplishment. This pride is not an emotional high as such, but is rather a quiet confirmation of your worth. Very few people are capable of doing what you are doing—consistently beating the casinos.

The fighter who sits in his hospital bed, bloody, bruised, but victorious, knows that he has been damaged but he also knows that he has won! And, frankly speaking, sometimes winning *is* everything.

Chapter Twenty-Two

Twenty-Two Days of Play: A Personal Blackjack Diary

Day One

I'm on the plane to Vegas as I write this. I can't believe it's been a year since I last visited this greatest of all gaming cities. In that time I've visited many gambling venues, including Mississippi, Connecticut, and Atlantic City. But it's not the same thing. This is the King Kong of gaming venues. The Godzilla of gambling. It used to be that I'd visit Vegas five or six times a year, staying anywhere from a week to a month or more at a clip. No more. My schedule is crammed. That's probably why I feel this great excitement in me as we fly over the Grand Canyon. I can see the Canyon as I look to my left. That means we're maybe 20 minutes from stepping foot on terra Vegas. "One small step for a man, one giant leap for a gambler!" Can't wait to renew the old acquaintances, check out the best games, and get into battle. My heart is racing. No matter how often I've come, no matter how many times I challenge this city, each and every time feels as if it's the first.

***

A.P. and I picked up the rental car, checked into the hotel. We're staying at the Imperial Palace on this trip. It's centrally located and across the street from Caesars. According to my sources, the best games this summer are at Mirage, Treasure Island, Aladdin and downtown at the Golden Nugget. Some good reports have come in about the games at Maxim, Harrah's, Boulder Station and Sam's Town. I'll try them all.

As I was waiting to check in, I checked out the two-deck games at the Imperial Palace. These weren't bad, so—violating a general rule of mine not to play where I stay when I'm on extended and serious gaming trips—I might even try my hand at the Imperial Palace's games, too.

Now the battle begins, but a battle of a different kind. This one is not against the casinos but with myself. You see, I'm anxious to get into the action. The joke is just last week I was in Atlantic City but I can feel that tingle in my belly. However, I'm also tired from a five-and-a-half-hour plane flight. I should get a little something to eat; then I should relax, maybe take a nap. Oh, the tables are tugging at me. I can feel their pull. This is nothing new. I always feel this way when I first arrive in any gaming town—whether I played last week or not. The tables are a siren call that says: "Come to me! I'll give you excitement beyond your wildest dreams."

***

The beautiful A.P. and I leave our bags in the room and go across the street to the Mirage to get lunch. Lunch, then a nap, then dinner, then a walk up and down the Strip to check everything out. Then tonight, I'll call the people I've lined up for interviews for my new book [the book you are now reading] and make arrangements to meet with them during the course of my three weeks here. I'm not playing my first day. Discipline. Self-control. I'll dictate the playing schedule, not the siren call of the tables!

I realize that mine is a somewhat different playing philosophy from other gambling writers who believe that since we have the edge in blackjack, we should put in as much time as we can at the tables and only leave when we're making mistakes or so exhausted we can't see straight. I don't buy that philosophy anymore. When I first started playing blackjack I used to put in those long hours waiting to get into the mythical "long run." I was a winning player, yes, but I never really enjoyed myself. I was too tired to enjoy myself. No matter how much money I make at blackjack, I make much more money with other things. Because of the horrible fact that casinos can bar you, the amount of money I can bet at blackjack is limited (thus the amount I can win is severely limited). I don't want to call attention to myself and be asked to leave. I want to play until I become so old I double over after I win the biggest double down of my life and say, "So long, world, it's been fun." But it's no fun being bleary-eyed and exhausted all the time. So why play endless hours? Seven years ago I quit doing that. I followed the Captain's advice and I cut down. I'm still winning just as much as before but I'm enjoying it more. The beautiful A.P. says that I have developed a sixth sense of when to leave a game and that's why playing less is making me as much. Maybe. Or maybe it's just that when you play endless hours you do make mistakes that cut down your edge only you don't realize it. So maybe that's the reason I'm making as much money as before. I don't know and I truly don't care. I'm not playing my first day. The tables can call all they want. I'm turning a deaf ear.

Day Two

I've figured out my schedule. I want to play for maybe three, four hours a day, conduct interviews for about the same amount of time daily. Playing the tables will give me the fresh "war stories" I need to give a human face to blackjack and the interviews will give me the expert perspectives I need to make the book authoritative.

***

It's now time for battle. I'm going downstairs and I'm going to play a little before breakfast. It's about 6:15 in the morning. A.P. is doing her morning ritual of sit-ups, crunches, and whatever else she does to look the way she looks. I don't do anything for my stomach which assures that I'll continue to look the way I look as well. Thankfully, the Imperial Palace has a health club. Now, we don't have to get up at 5:30 every morning to walk. I can go to the health club at my leisure and walk on the treadmill.

***

I think I made a big mistake this morning playing at the Imperial Palace. I was betting two hands of three units each off the top. Going to up to 12 units on each in a high count and down to one unit bet on only one hand in a very low count. (That's effectively a 24-to-one spread!) I'm now ahead some 20 units after the session. The mistake I made was giving the floorman my name—my *real* name. I realize that he came over because I was betting enough to get me rated as a fairly decent player but come on, what a dope I am, giving my real name! Yes, I'm Frank Scoblete, great gaming author. Oh, yeah, I count cards and I consistently beat the casinos. So can I have a comp? Boy am I some dope. I didn't even know this guy and the Imperial Palace isn't exactly one of these fearless casinos that never sweats good players, and I give him my name. Jeez.

Now, there are pit people who know me, know I write about gambling and know my skill level and don't hassle me when I play. These are truly astute men and women who recognize that I can't hurt them all that badly even if I were to play in their casinos eight hours a day, 365 days a year. My biggest bet, in the highest of counts, is not going make even a blip on the casino tally sheet. Also, when I find a good casino, I write about it and that has to ultimateiy help their bottom line some. So some casino people don't really care if I beat them or not.

Others, though, are paranoid. And you always have to be careful. So here I am at the Imperial Palace giving a floorman, who I never met, my REAL name.

***

This afternoon we played at Treasure Island. I like all of Steve Wynn's casinos. They are all bright, clean and attract a high-class clientele. I have had only two problems with him (notice how I personalize everything?)—I haven't had good luck at his blackjack games (which have always been good games) and once I was asked to leave the Golden Nugget, a cheap move. I've written about this elsewhere. Still, I had good luck this afternoon at Treasure Island and now I'm up some 45 units.

Of course, the bigger the casino, the more levels of bureaucracy. Two maintenance men came over to fix the scanner that reads whether the ace is under the 10 or 10 under the ace machine (I forget what the little device is called, probably a "scanner"). It wasn't broken but someone had put in a request to have it fixed. The dealer kept saying: "It's working fine, it's working fine." But the fix-it men insisted that they had to replace it and this delayed the game, as they found it difficult to remove the old one.

***

Tonight we played at the Aladdin. Now, the Aladdin has a great two-deck game and a great six-deck game since both games cut only 26 cards out of play. Believe it or not it is probably better for a card counter to play the six-deck game because in extremely high counts you can probably pump those bets way up there, as you'll have a positive count for several rounds. But since I play six-deck games in Atlantic City on a regular basis, I prefer to play single and double deck when I can. So I hit the double-deck games. There were only two.

And I ran into my first ploppy of the trip. Tonight we had Mr. and Mrs. Ploppy—a husband and wife team—who were brain damaged, perhaps brain dead. Mr. Ploppy's strategy was to split any pair—against any dealer up card—and to hit any hand of his that was under 17, regardless of what the dealer had, unless the dealer had a 10 showing, then he stayed. He never doubled down. Fine. If that's the way he wants to play, fine. I realize that he can't hurt my overall expectations. This I know intellectually and from all those computer studies. Emotionally sometimes I don't know this and at times bad play does irritate me because I'm only human.

Tonight I just enjoyed the show. Because what a show it was. You see Mr. Ploppy thought of himself as a blackjack expert and Mrs. Ploppy went along with that thinking. Mr. Ploppy also drooled and Mrs. Ploppy was something of a wizened, hunched thing. They weren't all that old but they had horrible skin and teeth. I don't know about you but the physically repulsive have always had a certain fascination for me. These ploppys also wanted everyone to play at the table the way they played and, unfortunately, a guy sat down who had never played before. He soon was taught the ploppy way.

"I'll tell you how to play," said Mr. Ploppy right off the bat when the guy mentioned he had no idea of what he was doing. The dealer rolled her eyes.

"He good," said Mrs. Ploppy. She smiled, showing us her cavities.

"Don't listen to him," Mr. Ploppy said, pointing to me. "He doubles down too much. Never double down because that's a trick. That's a trick. A big trick."

"What's a double down?" said the guy.

"On some hands you might want to double the size of you bet and only take one card," said the dealer.

"Ah ha ha," laughed Mrs. Ploppy for whatever reason.

"I'll only tell you to do what I do," said Mr. Ploppy seriously as a *globule* of spit rolled down his chin.

I noticed that the dealer flinched. I guessed that she was hoping that he wouldn't wipe his chin and then pick up the cards leaving you-know-what on them. He didn't. The spit just fell off onto his shirt, adding to a stain that was already there.

"Now, you see, I have two threes and the dealer has a nine," said Mr. Ploppy. "I split them." So he put the cards on the table and split them. He put an extra five dollars down. "It's good to split," he said and spit. The spit hit the table and stayed in a little ball near where he had split. The dealer winced. The beautiful A.P. whispered in my ear: "I think I'm going to be sick."

The dealer hit Mr. Ploppy's first three with an eight. The lucky guy now had 11. He should double down. He took another hit. Received a 10. Then the dealer hit Mr. Ploppy's other three with a seven. Lucky Mr. Ploppy, he should double down again. This time he hit and got another 10. The dealer turned over her hand and she had a nine under—giving her 18. Ploppy won on both his hands. The gods of chance loved Mr. Ploppy. He should not have split his threes but he did. Then he was rewarded with two excellent double-down hands (it was a positive count at the time too) which he didn't double down on. Had he doubled down, he would have won twice as much. Oh, well.

That night I lost 20 units and Mr. Ploppy and Mrs. Ploppy were winning. At one point in the game Mr. Ploppy said he had to go to the bathroom. He told Mrs. Ploppy to take his place.

"She's got EPS," he said.

"What's that?" asked the guy.

"She has mental powers," said Mr. Ploppy. I surmised he meant to say she had ESP.

"Ah ha ha," laughed Mrs. Ploppy. Then she sat down in her husband's seat. "It's hot, ah ha ha," she laughed. Just at that point the floorman came over and put four new decks into play so the dealer had to pause and do the new deck thing which consisted of mixing the cards and letting the automatic shuffling machine shuffle first one then the other, then one then the other (they use four decks—two and two—when using an automatic shuffler.) Well, Mrs. Ploppy laughed the whole time. Everything was funny and it was downright hilarious when Mr. Ploppy came back and she told him that she hadn't even gotten to use her "EPS" because the decks were being shuffled. Mr. Ploppy laughed and spit and laughed and spit in joy.

And as I cashed in, I wondered if these two had ever had offspring and if so what zoo they were in.

Total for day: +25 units.

Total for trip: +25 units.

Day Three

I didn't play this morning. Slept late. Had a relaxing breakfast, then went to the health spa and worked out.

Late afternoon, I played at the Imperial Palace. I hadn't planned on it but I noticed that one dealer was going particularly deep into the deck. So I sat down. There were two young men at the table; they couldn't have been more than 23 years old. They were doing the Ken Uston thing, and it was noticeable to me and to the pit that they were counting cards. There was only one Ken Uston, just as there is only one you and one me. You have to play within the confines of the person you are. Unfortunately, many people have read Uston's books and try to mimic his style of play and his persona. This is especially true of young men who are looking to prove their manhood in the card-counting arena. They bring a lot of attention on themselves and on the tables where they play. These two guys were obviously counting because they would jump their bets from five dollars to $50. Now, that's a one-to-10 spread. I was using a one-to-24 spread. The reason they were being noticed and I wasn't (hopefully) was because I started with three units on one hand and three units on another hand. I never increased the bet by more than double. So if the count called for an increased bet, I'd go up a max of three units—which is only doubling my initial bet— or, if I had six units, I'd double that to 12 if the count stayed high. If the count went negative, I'd go down a unit on each hand, or two units, and finally, if the count were really low, I'd play one hand of one unit or take an occasional trip to the bathroom. That's one to 24 (or zero to 24 if you count the bathroom trips). That's a big enough spread to beat any double-deck game. But these guys were jumping from five dollars to $50 and soon the pit was watching them. As fortune framed it, they were losing most of those big bets and so they were down a considerable sum. I pity them. Some casinos like to see counters get in a hole and then ask them to leave. It doubles the indignity. Not only are you losing but you are being told to get out because you're too good. I played until I lost several hands and the time felt right to take a break.

***

I had won 10 units at the Imperial Palace and then ambled over to the Mirage to check out their games. With one exception, every double-deck game was either a $50 or $100 minimum. That exception was a $25 table that was packed.

Took the tram to Treasure Island where I promptly lost the 10 units I had won at Imperial Palace. The Treasure Island dealers are still buzzing about the bum who won 1.4 million dollars (see chapter 16). So I got some fascinating information for my 10 units.

***

Tonight we dined at Antonio's at the Rio. If the Rio had good games it would be the number one place in Vegas. It's off the beaten track but well worth a visit. Antonio's is my favorite restaurant in Vegas. Elegant and classy without being pretentious. The chef is an artist.

After dinner we hit the Aladdin again. Mr. and Mrs. Ploppy were not there. Won 30 units.

Total for day: +30 units.

Total for trip: +55 units.

Day Four

Maybe it's me, but I seem to sit at tables with the weirdest people. The guy this morning couldn't even be called a ploppy proper, because even ploppydom requires some semblance of humanity. I was next to a guy who chain-smoked and mumbled in some demonic language. He was tall and skinny with oversized features: big nose, big lips, big ears (filled with reddish sow-like hair) big hands. He was covered in hair. I know this because his clothes had some holes in them and they were buttoned incorrectly, exposing his hairy stomach—which had ashes smeared on it because of all the cigarettes he smoked. Why didn't I leave the table? Because I was winning and winning.

Every time the weird guy got a hand, he would mumble something in that strange tongue, take a deep drag from the cigarette dangling from his lips (he rarely removed it unless it was to stamp it out and light up a new one). The ash would inevitably fall off, onto the table or onto him. Then he would squeeze his cards and look to see what hand he got. It was a ritual. His right hand was bandaged with an ace bandage, the kind you use for sprains, but there was caked blood showing through. He also smelled. But I've smelled worse than him. Vegas can be an olfactory nightmare for someone with a sensitive nose. The bums on the streets come in assorted disgusting scents that I'll leave to your imagination.

I dubbed him "the Exorcist" because I was sure he was not speaking a foreign human language unless the language of hell can be considered that.

At a certain point in the game he started to shake and rock and drag on the cigarette until it was all the way down to the filter in one mighty drag. Then he stood up and dusted himself off (getting the ashes onto me) and left.

That session I won 75 units—a good win. When I was cashing my chips in, I saw the Exorcist playing a slot machine called "Blazing Sevens." The sevens looked like the flames from hell. Fitting.

No afternoon session. A.P. and I went to see a movie after I interviewed some people.

Tonight I won five units at Treasure Island.

Total for day: + 80 units.

Total for trip: + 135 units.

Day Five

Played with K.F. this afternoon and we played at the Aladdin for a couple of hours. I won two units. K.F. is a stickler for blackjack-playing conditions and won't play any game where he can't get at least a two percent edge by his reckoning. I'm not exactly sure what my edge is but K.F. estimates it's somewhere in the one to 1.5 percent range—"probably closer to one percent," he once told me. What's strange is that I seem to win more than my overt edge indicates. A.P. says that's because I never allow myself to take a beating at any one given session. That's not 100 percent accurate. In the past, I have taken some beatings. Whatever the technical reasons for my overall wins in blackjack, I don't really care. Just keep them coming, you gods of fate, and I'll be a happy fella.

Tonight I won again at Aladdin, only this time it was a decent one—60 units. I'm on a hot streak in Vegas. How long will it last? Let it be forever!

Total for day: +62 units.

Total for trip: +197 units.

Day Six

Today was another relaxing, walk-around-after-breakfast, workout day. Didn't get to play until late afternoon. I played head-to-head with a surly dealer at the Imperial Palace. When I gave her a tip, she didn't even acknowledge it. So I stopped tipping. When you deal with the public, in whatever capacity, you have to think of yourself as an actor on a stage and always give the proper performance. A dealer's performance, at the very least, should be pleasant and professional. They don't have to yuck it up or be overly friendly but they shouldn't be rude—even when they have just cause, which often they do. They have to pretend pleasantness, if necessary, because part of their individual and collective incomes ride on their performance with players. This dealer just scowled.

Let me take that actor analogy one step further. That actor gets on stage and no matter what is happening in his personal life, he must play his part on stage as if he has no personal life. Waiters, waitresses, counter people, dealers, teachers, doctors, lawyers—anyone who deals with the public at large—had better develop the skills of an actor or the public will eat them alive. Pretend, pretend, pretend you enjoy what you're doing and like the people you're dealing with. But Ms. Surly stayed the same and I didn't tip and I won 47 more units. I'm hot!

***

Hot like a firecracker! Tonight we hit Treasure Island for 81 units. The Steve Wynn jinx is now officially over. God, it feels so good to be winning! I know I should stay cool and calm, like a professional, but I just can't. It feels so good to be winning! I'm like a fighter who receives a million dollars for the match. When I win, I don't jump up and down in the ring because I was paid a million bucks. I jump up and down because I won! Because I beat the opponent! Today I won 128 units. That gives me a total of 325 units for six days. Not bad at all!

Day Seven

This morning the hot streak went on unabated. We drove over to the Rio for their great breakfast buffet and then drove to Sam's Town to check out the single-deck games. What a bogus game. You can't take insurance! In high counts, and in single deck these occur often, sometimes the difference between winning and losing is the insurance bet. So I skipped the single deck and played double deck with a dealer who gave excellent penetration. Won another 18 units. Now, I'm up 343 units for the trip! Happy days!

***

Boom to bust! Lost 27 units in the blink of an eye at Treasure Island before going over to Caesars Palace for a boxing match. Count got high and I lost just about every hand (at least it felt that way).

The fight was interesting. In the main event, Jorge Paez came into the ring in a wedding dress and proceeded to take a beating before he walloped his opponent in the back of the head (a no-no) sending him crashing to the canvas, whereupon Paez hit the guy when he was down and out. So Paez was disqualified. And the winner was unconscious for 10 minutes. Since Vegas is the wedding capital of the world, I wonder if this was symbolic of marriage? Fights in Vegas tend to bring out the cave dwellers.

Total for day: −9 units.
Total for trip: +316 units.

Day Eight

Nothing good lasts forever and perhaps that's why we talk about heaven because in heaven all the good things do last forever. Now, heaven might be different things to different people. To a blackjack player, heaven is a hot streak that lasts for eternity. It's doubling down in high counts and getting the perfect card ad infinitum.

My streak ended last night with a whimper. Today the bang came. Went to the Aladdin this afternoon and the magic genie creamed me. I lost 114 units because every time the count went up, I went down to defeat.

But I did get to witness some interesting players. There was the Hindu woman who counted and played perfectly. She was all wrapped up in a sari, covered head to foot, but that didn't stop her from getting the money out there. What a terrific disguise! Who would suspect such a conservative, religious-looking woman of counting cards and being a casino killer? She had a relative with her who also played for big money but this woman (who looked just like her) didn't count and tended to be somewhat of a complainer. I asked the card-counting Hindu where she lived and she said "in Los Angeles." (Note: I saw her almost every day from this day on.) She would open her betting at $30 and go up to $100 and sometimes down to $20. A one-to-five spread. She was good.

***

Tonight I decided to take time off from playing, so the beautiful A.P. and I went to Caesars for some Chinese food, then we walked around first Caesars and then the Mirage watching the really high rollers, and then we played the "What-Do-You-Think-That-Person-Does-For-A-Living" game when we saw people betting extraordinary amounts of money.

I'm just like anyone else when confronted with a man or woman who is so rich that he or she can bet what some people make in a month or a year on one hand of blackjack or one spin of a roulette wheel or one throw of the dice. I'm fascinated as to the source of their money. What do they do for a living to be able to bet, oh, $10,000 a hand at blackjack?

Total for day: −114 units.
Total for trip: +202 units.

Day Nine

Hammered! Lost 64 units at the Aladdin this morning. I was sitting next to two middle-aged gay men who were always arguing. They were counters but they couldn't seem to get their act together so they were always disagreeing as to what the count was and how much to bet. The pit ignored them but they were a fascinating study. I swear, at any moment they were going to break up the relationship.

"You always do this to me!" said the one to the other. "We discuss what we're to do and then you change. I can't take living with you any more!"

"You've got to be flexible," said the other to the one, "and go with the flow of the cards."

"We're losing our asses and you're over-betting our bankroll," said the one.

"I earn the money don't I?" said the other.

"Oh, you are cruel! And I do nothing? So what do I do, nothing? I'm the best thing that ever happened to you and don't you forget it."

"Raise your bet to a hundred," said the other.

"No," said the one.

"It's +4," said the other.

"You play your hand, I'll play mine."

"But it's *our* money!" said the other.

"Are you betting this round?" asked the dealer.

"Pass me by," said the one.

"Wait," said the other and he placed $100 in the one's betting circle.

The one snorted and turned his head from the other. And so it went. They argued endlessly while I lost money.

***

The afternoon was no better. I played at Harrah's and couldn't do a thing. Lost 12 units. Harrah's was bright and clean but its "party pit" was just too damn loud. Any noise is louder when you're losing.

Didn't play again tonight. Did a bunch of interviews. A.P. and I had a late dinner and I was tired so we went back to the room, watched some television and went to sleep.

Total for day: −76 units.

Total for trip: +126 units.

Day Ten

Today I decided to play K.F.'s way. K.F. looks for special promotions to take advantage of. This particular one was being given by a travel agency situated in the Sands. You pay a $30 fee and give the casino four hours of action at a minimum of five dollars a hand. At the end of four hours the travel agency gives you your $30 back plus another $40 as a reward. So you are being paid $40 to play four hours of blackjack. Not a bad deal, especially if the game is beatable, which the Sands game marginally was. So I joined.

Now, I usually don't like to play in these things because I don't like to know that I have to play four hours in one day at one casino.

This is based on my temperament and not on the mathematics of the proposition. If you could find something like this promotion to play every day (and in Vegas you often can), then in the course of a year, you would make out fairly well as a lower-level player.

Just for argument's sake, let's say the game is even. In the long run, you would earn that $40 free and clear each and every day for four hours of work. There were also some food comps that went along with the promotion, so you got a free meal at times in the bargain. But my temperament, at least at this stage in my playing career, is not to want to be beholden to any casino for a given amount of time. My secondary fear is giving in my real name, which you have to do since they ask for photo ID. Call me paranoid.

But today I decided to go for the guaranteed $40 and a respite from my losing. Or so I thought. The problem was that even with the $40 gift, I still wound up losing three units in the four hours of play. To top it off, one of the pit people was constantly taking the cards out of the discard rack to show me he knew I was counting (he noticed that I made quite a few successful insurance bets—a sure tip-off that a person is counting). So for much of the four hours I just flat bet $25 and I'd go down to five dollars in a low count. I never raised my bet over that $25. Still, it was a rotten day. What made it even more of a rotten day was that the Sands was not a pleasant place at which to play. I had only two nice dealers in the four hours. That pit bull was a pain. I was almost hoping he'd ask me to leave. There were several drunks as well.

One dealer was especially annoying. She was an older woman (65 if she was a day) who had evidently gotten by in life by doing the "I'm a wittle girl" routine. She had massive breasts and bleached-blonde hair and the worst face-lift you ever saw. You could see the tuck marks under her chin and the stretch line to her ears from the upper and lower portions of her face where the skin was drawn back. A bad face-lift is just a bad face-lift, the luck of the medical draw. But your character is the real you and it was her character that was irritating.

Nothing is more ridiculous than a grown woman doing the little girl routine. I can't stand it in actresses and I hate it in real life. How can you take an adult seriously when she's "just a wittle girl"? But this ancient hag was doing this little girl routine. It must have gone over great in the 1950s when she was young and those enormous breasts were charging their way out of a tight sweater or protruding provocatively from a low-cut evening gown. Now, she just acted and sounded and looked ridiculous. And she was a rotten dealer to boot, always collecting bets the players had won and explaining: "Ew, I made a wittle mistakey!" when the players told her she was taking their winning bets. She should just accept the fact that there's more to life than whatever she thought life was about when she was young and desirable as she bounced through those hot Las Vegas nights in the good old days when Frank Sinatra could remember his lyrics. Those days are gone.

There was one funny guy at the Sands though. He was a real character. After every hand that he won, he'd shout out: "Whoopee!" If he won more than one hand in a row, he'd shout out: "Whoopee! A streak!" So one of the four hours was fun because this guy was fun. Nuts, but fun. Most of the dealers hated him because he was so upbeat.

Something's happening at the Sands. This used to be a high-roller place and now it's a sweat joint. Its day as one of Vegas' main casinos is over. An ancient ruin.

So it was a wasted day with a three-unit loss. Despite the fact that playing these special promotions is a good bet, I'm passing it up from here on in. (K.F. played this every other day during the two months he was in Vegas and came away with a good profit. It is a good bet if you want to give that mandatory four hours.)

Total for day: −3 units.

Total for trip: +123 units.

Day Eleven

Why do the ploppys win? How can the gods of fortune be so fickle as to give the dolts of the world even short-term lightning strikes of luck? Oh, yes, I know, anyone can get lucky in the short run but in the long run . . . blah, blah, blah. I caution people about that myself in all my writings. But we all live in the short run, actually the shortest run, which is called the "here and now." And in the here and now, today, four of the greatest ploppys to walk the earth just kept winning and winning and winning. They were Eveready Battery ploppys and one, a guy at Golden Nugget, was so drunk, I thought he'd fall off his stool or throw up on the table. He did neither. He just played his strategy (which made no sense, not even being internally consistent—sometimes he'd hit his 14 against a 10, sometimes he wouldn't, sometimes he'd double, sometimes he'd just burp) but he always won.

I lost.

At the Mirage two ploppys, a skinny husband and a brutish wife from some Eastern European country, were busy racking up the dough by playing atrociously.

I lost.

At the Aladdin the biggest, meanest-looking ploppy I have ever seen just kept going around the pit and placing bets at random. She won them all. No she wasn't counting. She'd jump into the middle of a low count and double down on a seven against the dealer's anything. And win. She was nasty, too. Just pushing aside people as she played from table to table. If the killing of elephants were legal, she'd be one pachyderm I'd bag.

The day ended with a 95 unit loss. Not a good day at all.

Total for day: −95 units.

Total for trip: +28 units.

Day Twelve

And God said: "Let there be blackjacks all around!" And it rained blackjacks. Today was a good day. The morning started auspiciously enough at the Imperial Palace. I played for 20 minutes and the count went up and I had my 24 units up (12 and 12) and I won hand after hand. Everything went well. I won 44 units, just like that.

After a relaxing breakfast, where I delighted in turning my luck around, the beautiful A.P. and I went over to Treasure Island where we won another 44 units. This took a little longer, a three-hour session, but it feels just as good. What will tonight hold?

***

Gold!

Went to the Aladdin. What a great night! First we had a great table. There was an elderly lady from England who was a joy. One of the great characters I've met. I love spunky, take-it-to-life older folk. This woman had a house in Florida, a house in England and she traveled with the seasons. She visited Las Vegas on a regular basis and she just loved blackjack. She played perfect basic strategy and she'd try to capitalize on her streaks—that is to say, if she were winning a little she would slowly increase her bets. Since she played perfect basic strategy, her overall expectation was about even and, according to her, "I'm a little more up than down" in her blackjack-playing career. She had great stories and she was a marvelous conversationalist.

Also at the table was a guy we dubbed "Mr. Blackjack" because he seemed to get a blackjack once every four hands. We played for three hours at this table and "Mr. Blackjack" just kept getting those blackjacks. He was Vietnamese and every time he got his signature hand, he'd giggle. The rest of the table would applaud. We were simultaneously happy for him and jealous as hell.

There was also a newlywed couple who were quite pleasant. They were also basic-strategy players.

The time flew and when it was all over, I had one of my best days in recent memory—a win of 351 units! It's for nights like these that I recommend playing blackjack. An enjoyable group of people and . . . a BIG, BIG win! A 439-unit day!

Total for trip: + 467 units.

Day Thirteen

At the Imperial Palace we're staying on the 13th floor (unlike many hotels, the Imperial Palace actually has a 13th floor—you don't go from 12 to 14) and this is now the 13th day. First I have to do some interviews and then I'll hit the tables. Will it be a lucky or unlucky 13th day?

***

LUCK IS MY LADY!

The beautiful A.P. and I continue with our winning ways. We're having a terrific run at the Aladdin, which is turning out to be quite a nice place to play, with a pit that doesn't seem to sweat my level of action (which is, admittedly, not a level I would sweat if I ran a casino). And we're having a hot time! This afternoon, we won another 79 units at Aladdin. Then we played for 10 minutes at the Flamingo Hilton with a dealer that dealt deep. We picked up 12 units. Then she was replaced with a dealer who was cutting off half the decks and we left.

Tonight the luck continues! A huge 231-unit win at Mirage and Treasure Island. We left the Mirage up 138 units. We had been up almost 200 units but then things turned. So we took the tram over to Treasure Island where we blitzed them. Got the dealers talking about the bum who won 1.4 million. I'm going to have a great section on this bum who won so much money.

A great day with a 322 unit win. Who's afraid of the number 13? Total for trip: +789.

Day Fourteen

Oh, Dame Fortune, you are shining on me today!
Morning, Imperial Palace: 23 units
Late Morning, Harrah's: +19 units
Afternoon, Aladdin: +35 units
Late Afternoon, Golden Nugget: +7 units
Evening, Treasure Island: +64 units
Evening, Aladdin: +78 units

It was an exhausting, exhilarating day! I put in close to 12 hours of play! It just happened. I had set up appointments to talk to people at these various places. Then I decided to play. The time just goes when you're winning. I'm too tired to even write. Let me add this all up and see where I am. I won 226 units today. Not bad.

Total for trip: +1015 units.

Day Fifteen

This is shaping up as a great trip. After the rocky time, I just keep winning and winning. I keep thinking that's it's possible that I could go home with a 2,000-unit win. That is a substantial win. I really shouldn't fantasize like this because it can turn at any minute. We woke up late and we ate a leisurely breakfast at the Rio. Then we came back to the Imperial Palace and had a long workout. I'm savoring my wins from the last few days and enjoying that glow of success. I'll play tonight. Now it's nap time.

***

Tonight was a glorious night. A huge win at Aladdin. The British woman was there, the card-counting Hindu woman was there, and "Mr. Blackjack" was there. When I came to the table the British woman said: "He's still getting those blackjacks!"

And he was. Maybe he was a psychic and he ordered the cards to be shuffled in a certain pattern so that he'd get blackjacks. Who knows?

I won another 342 units tonight. This is the best streak of luck that I've had in years and years. Usually I scratch out little wins. Twelve to 24-unit wins spread over time can add up. This is essentially one or two big bets. These high double and triple figure wins are something rare. But boy am I enjoying them. It's great to be on Lady Luck's love list. Oh, let it continue!

I can smell a 2,000 unit win for this trip.

Total for trip: +1357 units.

Day Sixteen

The beautiful A.P. and I went over to Caesars for the breakfast buffet. When AP came back with her dish, she was concerned that her eggs were too loose.

"Do you think these are too loose? You know, you can get salmonella."

"I don't know," I said and buried my head in the newspaper.

"I'm worried about salmonella," she said.

"Just go get more and leave the plate," I said from inside the newspaper.

"Waitress!" called out A.P.

The waitress came over. She was an older woman, pleasant but somewhat tired.

"Yes? You want more coffee?" the waitress said.

"I'm concerned that these scrambled eggs are too runny," said A.P.

"Oh," said the waitress, peering at the eggs. "They look all right to me."

"You can get salmonella if eggs aren't cooked properly," said A.P.

"I didn't know that," said the waitress.

"Maybe I should have the chef make me some eggs," said A.P.

"Good idea, honey," said the waitress.

A.P. got up and went over to the chef. I was alone at the table with the waitress.

"I never heard of that," said the waitress.

"Oh, yes," I said. "Yes, you can get salmonella from uncooked or undercooked eggs, as well as from other things."

"Like?" asked the waitress.

"Uh, turtles, you know, turtles that you give kids can have that germ in them."

The waitress then turned to the table next to us. The well-dressed couple had been avidly listening to our conversation.

"Did you know about that?" asked the waitress of the other couple.

"No," said the well-dressed man.

"No," said the well-dressed woman.

Three tables away, a bald man yelled out: "I did!"

"I never knew you could get salmonella from eggs," said the waitress loudly.

"Who said that?" shouted a red-headed woman from across the room.

"This man over here," said the waitress pointing to me.

I nodded and tried to bury myself in the paper.

"Who?" asked the overweight man walking by with a plate filled with scrambled eggs and piled five inches high with bacon.

"Here," pointed the waitress.

"Hi," I said.

"Take a look at these eggs," the overweight man said, showing me his plate.

"You probably have more to worry about with cholesterol than salmonella," I said jokingly.

"You're crazy," shouted the red-headed woman from across the room. "I've been eating eggs all my life and I never got it."

"Uncooked eggs," I mumbled.

"He said 'uncooked eggs,'" shouted the waitress to the red-headed woman across the room.

"He's crazy! I used to eat uncooked eggs in eggnogs! Never got sick!" shouted the red-headed woman from across the room.

"Are you a doctor?' said the well-dressed woman at the table next to me.

"No," I said. "I'm just reading the newspaper."

"He says there's a story in the newspaper," said the waitress.

"Let me read that when you're done!" shouted the red-headed woman from across the room.

Thankfully, after an eternity, someone called the waitress over for a refill of coffee, the waitress moved on and things returned to normal.

A.P. came back with her new eggs (over hard and break the yolks).

"I feel much better," she said. "Better safe than sorry." Then she smiled her radiant smile. "Now, we can relax and enjoy our breakfast."

"Yeah," I said.

"Don't forget!" shouted the red-headed woman from across the room, "I want to read that story."

"Who's she?" asked A.P.

"Some woman who eats eggs," I said.

***

Maybe we should have gotten a tiny dose of salmonella because it would have kept us from the tables. Bad day. Lost 34 units at Sam's Town before dinner at Diamond Lil's. Then went over to the Aladdin where we lost another 23 units. We finished our rotten day at Treasure Island where we lost 7 units. Minus 64 units for today.

Total for trip: +1293 units.

Day Seventeen

Hammered! Lost 111 units at Aladdin. Then won three units at Imperial Palace. Then took a clubbing for 56 units at Mirage.

Bad day. Lost 164 units.

Total for trip: +1129.

Day Eighteen

I'm starting to think about going home. That means I'm starting to figure whether I've got a guaranteed win or if I'm still in danger of losing should the bad streak continue. It's iffy.

Lost another 41 units today in two separate sessions at Mirage.

Total for trip: +1088 units.

Day Nineteen

This is becoming depressing. I win my small bets of one and two units in low counts and lose my high bets of 12 units in high counts. There were a lot of high counts today. Blackjacks for everyone but me.

I'd bust my hand and the dealer would bust and everyone else would have pat hands. I went from casino to casino. I'm on a bad streak, a negative fluctuation in probability as the math boys put it. It feels crummy. Lost 227 units today.

Total for trip: +861 units.

Day Twenty

K.F. asked me this question: "Do you ever get gun-shy when you've been losing? Does your heart pound when those big bets are out? Do you ever think: 'what the hell am I doing to myself?'"

"Yes," I said. "Right now I'm going through it. I'm being hammered and I'm not happy."

I lost 158 units during five different sessions at five casinos.

Total for trip: +703 units.

Day Twenty-One

I have a choice to make. Tomorrow I go home, back to New York. Chances are I won't be in Vegas for a long time, especially if some of the writing projects I'm working on pan out. The best games are here. Single and double deck. I can always find good penetration. When I get back home, I'm stuck with Atlantic City's six deckers. I'll be in Atlantic City three weeks from tomorrow for a gaming festival. All the big writers of gaming books will be there.

Here is my dilemma. Do I quit, right now, today, and go home tomorrow up 703 units? Or do I stay and play these great games figuring that my edge is realized over time? Is my win of 703 units (the proverbial bird in the hand) enough? Or do I want to go after those two birds in the bush?

The mathematics says to play. My fellow gambling writers would (mostly) say to play, because logic says to play whenever you have the advantage. If I lived in Vegas, I wouldn't hesitate to play and play and play and ride out the cold streak. In Vegas I have an edge over the house. But I only have today and tomorrow and then I'm on the red-eye back to New York. That's an extremely short run and in the short run anything can happen. Of course, even if I were to lose that 703 units, it would make little dent on my gambling bankroll. Dilemma.

And what about my psyche?

I like to win. I play to win. I like that feeling of boarding a plane knowing I beat this town. A part of my ego or self worth is tied up in the idea that I can defeat a town that defeats almost everyone else.

"A.P., what am I going to do?"

"Do whatever you want, play or don't play," she said.

"But I want to go home a winner," I said. "I'm on a bad streak."

"Then don't play."

"But I have an edge in these games. Logic says to play."

"Then play," she said.

"You're not helping me," I said.

"All right," she said. "pretend we're on the plane coming here. Now, you look into the future and you see that you won 703 units. You see yourself on the plane going back with 703 units in your pocket. How would you feel?"

"Good."

"You would feel good?"

"Yes, I said that already. I would feel good."

"Now, say you won another 400 units between today and tomorrow. How would you feel?"

"Even better."

"If you were to lose 400 or all 703 units?"

"Worse," I said.

"So there's your choice," she said. "You are guaranteed feeling good. Once again the mighty Scobe [Scobe is my nickname] defeats Las Vegas. Or, you could feel even better. Or, worse. One last thing. In terms of degree—is it a stronger degree feeling good, or feeling better, or feeling worse? Is feeling worse far stronger than feeling better?"

"A.P., you're beautiful."

"You decided?"

"Yes," I said. "The strongest feeling is the feeling of getting on that plane tomorrow night and knowing I won. The 703 units is a decent win. I'll take it."

"There you go," she said.

So that's that. My playing for this trip is over. Today, I'll just do vacation-type things and wrap up some writing business. We'll breakfast and walk and work out and swim. We'll go to a show or a movie. My playing is over.

Total for trip: +703 units.

Day Twenty-Two

I do feel a little pull from the siren call of the tables today. But I have control. I'll take my 703 units and be happy.

***

I'm on the plane now. We're about to taxi onto the runway and fly into the dark night of the desert. I'm a winner. I'm happy. I'm proud that I could resist the tables for two days and take this win home with me. Yes, I could have broken out of the losing streak and come home with more. But had I lost, it would probably be a year before I could get revenge on Vegas. I prefer to spend that year with the glow that comes from once again being one of a small group of people who can come to this town and leave with more than he started.

The plane is up in the air and as it dips I can see the Strip and the lights from all the casinos.

Vegas calls to me.

I answer: "I beat you."

Total for trip: +703 units.

Chapter Twenty-Three
Recommended Books, Magazines and Newsletters

All the books and newsletters that follow are recommended. However, some of the books are a little dated and although they are interesting to read for their insights into the game and the people who play and offer them, their strategies are either outdated or overrated. The simple Hi-Lo count that is offered in this book is all you need to be a proficient card counter and a winning player. I wouldn't bother trying to learn some of the more complicated counting systems featured in some of these recommended books. Many of the older books will try to sell you on multiple-level counts in the mistaken notion that these will *significantly* increase your winnings. They won't. When the authors made those claims, however, they were made in good faith, as the popular wisdom of the times was that the more complicated the count, the better the results. Recent thinking and research tends to show that the marginally better theoretical performance of advanced counting systems is more than offset by the difficulty in actually executing them for prolonged periods in casinos. Even a single mistake in a session would be enough to erase whatever theoretical advantage an advanced count has for a player.

So if you really want to pursue card counting seriously, master the Hi-Lo and follow the strategy indices of those more recent authors whose specialty is this particular count.

Many of these books are not generally available in bookstores, as they do not have a popular appeal. But if you're serious about blackjack and want to continue your reading, most of the books can be obtained from their publishers by direct mail.

Books

Professional Blackjack by Stanford Wong. Pi Yee Press, 7910 Ivanhoe Ave. #34, La Jolla, CA 92037. ($19.95) This is the book for the Hi-Lo count, as it has indices for every possible variation you're ever (un)likely to meet. One of the leading theorists of the game and one of its legendary players, Stanford Wong's book is great for players who really want to dig in. Has complete indices on Las Vegas' Double Exposure game, as well as strategy charts detailing the mathematical expectations for every kind of game. Be prepared for some detailed mathematics but the format of the book is decidedly reader-friendly. Buy the updated version in soft cover. In addition to this particular book, Stanford Wong has a host of other books on blackjack (all interesting and worthwhile reading), including *Blackjack Secrets* (Pi Yee Press). Wong also sells computer software [my computer guy, Dr. James Schneider, used Wong's *Blackjack Count Analyzer* (Pi Yee Press) to back up his own programs' findings and told me it's a great program to have if you're a blackjack computer buff]. Wong also has a newsletter. Write to him at the above address and he'll send you a list of his offerings.

Fundamentals of Blackjack by Carlson R. Chambliss and Thomas Roginski. GBC Press, 630 11th St., Box 4115, Las Vegas, NV 89127. ($12.95) A must-read for the advanced and expert player or the novice who isn't afraid of a little mathematics. It is well-written, lucid, and to the point. Excellent strategies for the various single- and multiple-deck rules and variations. Examines all the major counting systems based on two criteria—playing efficiency and betting efficiency. An excellent reference book for the serious player by two scholars of the game. The two authors have another book, *Playing Blackjack in Atlantic City* (same publisher), which is worth reading although some of the advice is no longer applicable, since the Atlantic City game has changed somewhat over the years. Chambliss and Roginski are researchers first and foremost and their efforts have a somewhat scholarly bent. I used this as one of my first sources of reference into the game. It's another reader-friendly book and highly worthwhile.

Julian's No-Nonsense Guide to Winning Blackjack by John F. Julian. Paone Press, PO Box 610, Lynbrook, NY 11563. ($16.95) I wish Mr. Julian's book had been around when I first started playing because it would have saved me a lot of aggravation. An excellent book for new and intermediate players. Contains information on all the latest games and options, plus Scan and Sprint Strategies for single- and multiple-deck games respectively. What makes the book outstanding for beginners is the wonderful method Mr. Julian lays out for memorizing the single- and multiple-deck basic strategies. In addition, he has tests at the end of each section so you can see how much you have actually learned. At the end of the book is *The Ultimate Blackjack Test*, a 100-question test on all aspects of blackjack. This alone is worth the price of the book.

The Blackjack Formula ($10), *Blackjack for Profit* ($9.95), *Blackbelt in Blackjack* ($12.95), all by Arnold Snyder. RGE Publishing, 414 Santa Clara Ave., Oakland, CA 94610. Three excellent books by one of the great computer blackjack buffs. Snyder has shown quite clearly by his computer simulations which games are beatable and which games are losing propositions for even the most skilled counter. Snyder is a prolific writer with a pleasing style and his columns and articles appear in a host of magazines. Snyder also publishes his own newsletter and is author of *The Over-Under Report*, an 18-page handbook that tackles how to beat this option. Snyder calls himself the "Bishop of Blackjack." Amen.

Blackjack for Blood by Bryce Carlson. CompuStar Press, 1223 Wilshire Blvd., Santa Monica, CA 90403. ($19.95) This is a book by a high-stakes player who pushes an advanced point count system he dubs the

Omega II, which is the same as Richard Canfield's "Master Count" that has been selling for $250. My advice is to stick with the Hi-Lo count. But I highly recommend the book for its colorful description of what it's like to be a BIG player in today's casinos. His sections on casino comportment or how to act like a "gambler" as opposed to an "expert" as well as his advice on how to win over pit bosses, get onto junkets, etc., is needed by those of you who might want to bet big without being bounced from the casino scene. Carlson is a daring player and a good writer. He is a frequent contributor to *Blackjack Forum* and his opinions are always unusual, as they shed light on aspects of the game or of player comportment not covered (or even considered) by other writers.

The Morons of Blackjack and Other Monsters by King Scobe. Paone Press, PO Box 610, Lynbrook, NY 11563. ($16.95) King Scobe is my favorite blackjack author because, well, because he's my alter ego. King Scobe writes about all the things a blackjack player experiences and feels. There's *more* to blackjack than count systems and strategies. This book is all about those *mores*. Deals with what it feels like to be banned; how the casinos discriminate against men and demean women; how morons and moronic play can affect your emotional expectations and your blood pressure. Essays on the New American Religion, the New American Caste System, how NOT to be a card counter. You'll meet your fellow gamblers in profiles that come alive and jump off the pages. A must read, if I do say so myself. Anything Scobe says I subscribe to 100 percent! Of course, I am somewhat prejudiced in this.

Beat the Dealer by Edward O. Thorp. Vintage Books, 201 E. 50th St., New York, NY 10022. ($7.95) You should read this book after you have become proficient in blackjack, since it is seriously outdated. This was the first book to explore the possibility of beating the casinos by counting cards. It's still a fascinatingly good read because you go back in time to the Las Vegas of old and a game that will never be again. Forget about his count systems and enjoy the nostalgia. Thorp was the first seriously recognized threat to the casinos' bottom line and as such he has achieved almost legendary status in the eyes of blackjack writers, players and casino personnel alike. Thorp has other excellent books on gambling.

The World's Greatest Blackjack Book by Lance Humble and Carl Cooper. Doubleday, 666 5th Ave., New York, NY 10103. ($9.95) A guy named *Humble* writes a book that he considers the *greatest!* As pseudo-nyms go I would have preferred Lance *Hubris* for a book so titled but either way the irony is evident and intended. Actually, it's quite a good book and contains an excellent count system called the Hi-Opt which can be used against regular games *and* Face-up or Double Exposure blackjack. It is also a decent count to use for the Over-Under 13 option that is appearing in casinos all over America. Humble and Cooper have some intriguing things to say about casino cheating as well as how not to get barred. Deals with human and technical matters. Humble has a newsletter also, as well as other blackjack books, but this book is his "greatest!"

The Big Player by Ken Uston. Holt, Rinehart and Winston, 383 Madison Ave., New York, NY 10017. ($7.95) *Million Dollar Blackjack* by Ken Uston. Gambling Times, Inc. 16760 Stagg St., #213, Van Nuys, CA 91406. ($14.95) *Ken Uston on Blackjack* by Ken Uston. Lyle Stuart, Inc., Carol Publishing Group, 600 Madison Ave., New York, NY 10022. ($16.95) If you are interested in reading about blackjack not only as a skill and technique but as a human adventure, then read these three books by Ken Uston, the late, great, "King of 21." Read them in the order in which they appear above because they chronicle his life, times, and evolving knowledge of the game. They are terrific reads. One of the greatest "team" players in blackjack history, Uston made a small fortune playing blackjack in Las Vegas and Atlantic City. Unfortunately, because of Uston, casinos have tightened their rules and procedures and made it more difficult for the rest of us to win wagon loads of money. You will not be disappointed by "Kenny," as his friends called him. When you're finished reading about him, go to the casinos and watch how many men try to imitate his playing style and personality. Imitation is the greatest form of flattery. Very few could imitate his skill and writing ability. He lived hard, died young and what a damn shame.

Cheating at Blackjack by Dustin D. Marks. Index Publishing Group, Inc., 3368 Governor Drive, Suite 273, San Diego, CA 92122. ($19.95) Everything you ever wanted to know about cheating at blackjack but you wouldn't want to do it. Criminals of the creative sort (as opposed to street thugs and unimaginative thieves) are a fascinating breed. Fun book but don't try any of this stuff.

Blackjack Your Way to Riches by Richard Albert Canfield. Lyle Stuart, Inc., Carol Publishing Group, 600 Madison Ave., New York, NY 10022. ($9.95) One of the older books. I read this when I first started out. Loved it. Figured I'd abandon my attempt to write the Great American Novel and concentrate on making a few million dollars playing blackjack. I'm back to writing that novel. Nevertheless, this book is a fascinating read, although it does promise more than it can deliver. You'll meet some interesting blackjack players who share their "secrets" and very interesting it is indeed. It's upbeat and positive.

Playing Blackjack as a Business by Lawrence Revere. Lyle Stuart, Inc., Carol Publishing Group, 600 Madison Ave., New York, NY 10022. ($14.95) Another older book by one of the great professional gamblers and . . . con artists? saints? shysters? crooks? gods? of the old Las Vegas of mobsters and beatable blackjack games. Revere (not his real name) was a blackjack legend and was supposedly banned from every casino in Vegas. When it was published, this book was the bible to many players. God is dead and so is Revere. Another nostalgia piece but well worth the effort.

Blackjack: A Professional Reference by Michael Dalton. Spiral Bound. Spur of the Moment Publishing, PO Box 541967, Merritt Island, FL 32954. ($29.95) This book is exactly what it says it is—a reference to everything you ever wanted to know about blackjack but didn't know you wanted to know that much. Presented in dictionary format, it is an A to Z guide covering blackjack systems, strategies, books, authors, techniques, rules, terminology, history, videos, software, publications and more, all fully cross-referenced. A great reference book for the serious player's blackjack library. Dalton also has a blackjack newsletter. Be sure to buy the most recently updated issue.

Blackjack: A Winner's Handbook ($8.95), *Blackjack's Winning Formula* ($8.95) by Jerry Patterson, *Break the Dealer* ($8.95) by Jerry Patterson and Eddie Olsen. Perigee Books, 200 Madison Avenue, New York, NY 10016. All three are good books. Patterson and Olsen challenge the idea of the random shuffle and offer alternative ways of thinking about the game—dealer and player biases in the shoe game, card clumping, etc. All these books heavily plug Patterson's clinics and TARGET system for selecting tables—which is a home study course that is quite costly. Patterson and Olsen are blackjack renegades and have come in for heavy fire for their "new" ideas. However, Olsen has one of the best newsletters and in recent years he seems to have disassociated himself from Patterson.

Turning the Tables on Las Vegas by Ian Anderson. Random House, 201 E. 50th St., New York, NY 10022. ($10) A truly fun book that captures the pleasure and thrill of playing blackjack for high stakes in Las Vegas. The book was written in the mid-1970s as casinos were becoming increasingly more paranoid about skilled players. This is another how-to-behave book as opposed to a how-to-play book. Very few people will be able to mimic Ian Anderson because very few people have his kind of sterling money and sparkling personality. This book is a joy to read. Ian is himself a blackjack legend.

The Theory of Blackjack by Peter A. Griffin. Huntington Press, PO Box 28041, Las Vegas, NV 89126. ($9.95) This is a book for the mathematically inclined. It is scholarly, erudite and thorough. Griffin is a good writer and mixes fun with his formulas. Technical and intelligent. He's a researcher and thinker and, by his own admission, not much of a player. Griffin is refreshing, self-effacing, and sharp, and a welcome relief from the legions of blackjack "experts" who are stale, self-centered, and dull. Still, you wouldn't think the simple act of playing cards could generate so many charts and formulas!

Blackjack Essays by Mason Malmuth. GBC, Box 4115, Las Vegas, NV 89127. ($19.95) Mason Malmuth is an intriguing theorist and he will challenge some of your sacred beliefs if you have been gambling for any length of time. This book will open your eyes to other ways of looking at the game. Buy the updated version of the book, as it's a smooth read.

Getting the Best of It by David Sklansky. Two Plus Two Publications, 3955 South Algonquin Dr. # 268, Las Vegas, NV 89119 ($29.85) Although sections of this book deal with games other than blackjack, Sklansky's insights are worth the hefty price of the book. Another great theorist who knows his way around the casino and can write clearly and cleverly.

Other Books of Interest to Blackjack Players

Bargain City: Booking, Betting, and Beating the New Las Vegas by Anthony Curtis. Huntington Press, 5280 S. Valley View Blvd., Suite B, Las Vegas, NV 89118. ($11.95) This is the book for anyone who wants to thoroughly take advantage of everything that Las Vegas has to offer in the way of freebies and special promotions. Curtis knows whereof he speaks, as he is also the publisher of the newsletter, *The Las Vegas Advisor*, which keeps tabs on, well, the tabs for everything in this spectacular city. In addition to being an excellent writer, Curtis is a marvelous player and is known as one of the best tournament players in the world.

Comp City: A Guide to Free Las Vegas Vacations by Max Rubin. Huntington Press, 5280 S. Valley View Blvd., Suite B, Las Vegas, NV 89118. ($39.95) The be-all and end-all on the subject of comps from the man dubbed as the "comp wizard." It's a fun read and there's something for everyone in its pages. Well-written and worth the price.

Magazines and Newsletters

Chance and Circumstance. Published four times a year by Paone Press, Box 610, Lynbrook, NY 11563; single issue $15; subscription $50 per year; 8½ × 11 format; no advertising. This is the greatest newsletter on the face of the earth. Read this and you're guaranteed to win a million dollars a minute from. . . .Okay, okay, you guessed it. This is *my* newsletter and even if you read it and memorize it, you aren't likely to win anything close to a million, but it was fun dreaming, wasn't it? *Chance and Circumstance* isn't strictly about blackjack, it covers everything I'm interested in and I'm interested in the human condition and in chance and the circumstances where we take these chances.

Blackjack Forum. Published four times a year by RGE Publishing, 414 Santa Clara Ave., Oakland, CA 94610. Covers all aspects of blackjack, from counting to camouflage, as well as side issues in gambling theory and practice. Reviews all the major casinos' games as well as books and software. Also carries a synopsis of other magazines and journals covering the gambling scene. Strong analysis by computer of many arcane and interesting blackjack questions. Name writers in each issue. Edited and inspired by Arnold "Bishop" Snyder who pours his grace on the magazine. Always interesting, well-written, thought provoking, entertaining and informative.

Robert Gates' Blackjack Monthly. Published monthly by Richard Canfield and Associates, PO Box 2830, Escondido, CA 92033. Includes a weekly hot line number. Generally has two or more pieces by Robert Gates that are well-written, challenging and informative. These can be about anything, not just blackjack. Has a thorough monthly update on all the casinos. Gives information on dealers who might be shoddy in their practices, giving the players a little better game.

Eddie Olsen's Blackjack Confidential Magazine. Published eight times a year by Blackjack Confidential Publishing Company, Inc., 513 Salsbury Rd., Cherry Hill, NJ 08034. This magazine is loaded with information and statistics on casino wins, games, strategies. Has general interest pieces and personality profiles as well as several technical or inspirational pieces each issue. Doesn't rate every casino's games but offers the best bets. Has some of the best tournament results as well as information about upcoming tournaments. Also contains book reviews and information about other casino games as well as a show guide of upcoming performances.

Wong's Current Blackjack News. Published monthly, plus special editions as required, by Pi Yee Press, 7910 Ivanhoe Ave. #34, La Jolla, CA 92037. Can be anywhere from one page to several pages. Deals with table conditions everywhere and is always up-to-date. Any new promotions that can help a player are instantly sent in special reports. If you are a serious Nevada player, this newsletter can be a real resource. When you subscribe, you receive the "Instant Update" handbook that contains the rules for every casino in Nevada and Atlantic City. You can also call a hot-line and correspond by phone or fax with the editor, Stanford Wong.

Dalton's Blackjack Review. Published four times a year by Spur of the Moment Publishing, PO Box 541967, Merritt Island, FL 32954. Book and product reviews, limited updates on games, plus several articles of general interest to card counters and basic-strategy players in each issue. Doesn't just focus on Las Vegas and Atlantic City but gives the newly emerging Indian casinos and Mississippi casinos their due.

Chapter Twenty-Four
The Last Word: The Voices of the Blackjack Kingdom

As I did for *Break the One-Armed Bandits!*, I have interviewed many people for *Best Blackjack* and listened to many more as I played the game. I've read and reread all the other experts. Now is the time for them all to speak. These are the voices of the blackjack kingdom from expert to eccentric and in no particular order or rank.

"The difficulty of making money as a card counter is not math, but psychology. Some people are good actors. Some are not. Some are very perceptive of others' attitudes and are capable of manipulating people. Some cannot do this. To make it as a card counter, you must often be sociable and friendly to dealers and pit bosses while simultaneously deceiving them into thinking you're just another dumb gambler."
—Arnold Snyder, *Blackbelt in Blackjack*

"Let me tell you right now, I always put up a tip for the dealer right away. This lets the dealer know I'm on his side. I find I win a lot more when I tip the dealers. The cards just come out right. That's the way it is in a casino. You have to take care of the dealers and they'll take care of you."

—Franklin Marsh, New Jersey, blackjack player

"Learning to play blackjack is like learning to lift weights. Athletes who take up weight training find that their early progress is rapid. That is, the amount of weight they can lift increases significantly right away. However, they later find that more and more work is required to make smaller and smaller gains. Such is the case with blackjack play. The gains from learning basic strategy are substantial, but progressing beyond this stage into the world of card counting and professional-level play requires much more study in return for improvements that come much slower and in proportionately smaller doses."

—Anthony Curtis, *Bargain City*

"I don't discount the role of ESP in playing gambling games. I have had nights where dealers have willed themselves to win. I had a dealer at the President [in Biloxi, Mississippi] that was so happy every time one of the players lost. She was sour but her face would light up when she took our money. She'd sneer when we'd double down. I lost a lot that night. I think she willed herself to win because she hated her job. She probably hated the whole world."

—Byron Sanders, Mississippi, college student, blackjack player

"I've seen it happen with my own eyes. You have everything going your way and then some idiot sits at the table and everything goes the other way. The idiot changes everything. I've seen it happen so many times with my own eyes. I don't remember it happening the other way. I don't ever remember having a rotten day and suddenly some jerk sits down and doubles on a 12, splits 10s, stands on an eight and all of a sudden the dealer starts busting and everyone starts winning. It never happens that way. Yet you writers keep saying it does. It does when hell freezes over or when the Pope's no longer Catholic."

—Martin O'Neil, California, blackjack player

"I am cold-blooded. I play to win. I always practice a few minutes at home before playing to get into a blackjack-playing frame of mind. I will only play under the best playing conditions, and then, for no more than one hour at a single club. I never sit down at a table with more than two other players, and they must be good players. Bad players tend to change everything; mainly they disturb your concentration. If playing conditions are not right, wait and play the next day."

—Lawrence Revere, *Playing Blackjack as a Business*

"I was the losingest blackjack player who ever lived until I started to play basic strategy. Now I just lose a little. I'm too lazy to count cards because I like to drink and talk when I play. I like to socialize. But basic strategy has saved me a lot of money. I can play it when I'm drunk. It's like second nature. I was going to say it's like riding a bicycle but I can't ride a bicycle when I'm drunk. Most of basic strategy is logical. What's not logical I take on faith. The way I figure it, the computers know more than we mortals do. I'll drink to that!"

—Roy Smith, New York, blackjack player

"I like the casinos the way they used to be, where you had to get dressed to enter. You still have to wear a tie in most clubs in Britain but in the colonies—I still call America the colonies, no offense meant, love, because America is my second home—in the colonies, you see people practically stark [naked] and most of the ill-dressed are decidedly not lovely to look at. But I like blackjack too much to give up my trips to Vegas. I used to do volunteer work for old folks—but they were all younger than me! If they played blackjack, they wouldn't be so crotchety."

—Victoria Mattingly, England, blackjack player

"No matter how powerful the [card-counting] system . . . it pales in significance next to our egos. The most difficult aspect of systems play in the casino is that it is almost impossible not to begin using our own 'hunches' and ignore the system. The way to conquer this urge is to handle the judgment playing decisions according to a predetermined plan. How many hands to play, how much to bet, and money-management techniques should all be decided before sitting down. You can even plan when to go to the bathroom!"

—Lance Humble and Carl Cooper,
The World's Greatest Blackjack Book

"The hardest thing I learned to do at a blackjack table was get up when I was losing. You always think the next hand, the next shoe is going to be the one that takes you over the top—especially if you've been losing into high counts. On bad days it's never that way. The next hand is a loser and the next shoe is a loser, too, and it doesn't matter what the count is. Some days it's just not clicking and that's the way it is. You might as well hang it up because it wasn't meant to be. I don't mean this in a superstitious way—as if you were fated to lose. I mean, I guess, don't throw good money after bad. Take the loss and take a hike and live to fight another day."

—Jeffrey Bernstein, California, card counter

"See here. I split everything when a dealer's got a four, five or six. Everything: 10s, fives, eights, sevens, you name it. I think the writers of the books and the casinos are in cahoots together. They pay these guys to write how to play so that the casinos will make the most money. Only suckers read these books. If they really knew how to play blackjack, these writers would be playin' and not writin' about it. They'd all be rich. They ain't because they don't know squat. Look at what they got you doin'—hitting 12 against a [dealer's] two. Everyone knows you always get a 10 when you do that. Hit that 12 and make a side bet that a 10 comes up and you'll win that side bet. These gamblin' writers are idiots. I wouldn't listen to one of them if you paid me."

—George Armano, New York, blackjack player

"There are too many examples in the literature of the well-dressed blackjack player who walks into a casino, plays for a few minutes, varies his bet as appropriate, and leaves $400 or $500 ahead. Unfortunately, things don't work this way. To win at blackjack, one needs not only to count, but to play the hands correctly as well. This includes properly taking advantage of the player options of doubling down, splitting, and insurance. The point is that when these options are executed, the player is putting extra money on the table, and that extra money, along with the bonus payment for holding blackjack, contributes to becoming a winner. . . . But walking into a casino with the plan of playing for 20 minutes and walking away a big winner is totally unrealistic."

—Mason Malmuth, *Blackjack Essays*

"My emotions have run the gamut from the inebriated elation following a big win which induced me to pound out a chorus of celebration on the top of an occupied Reno police car—to the frustrated depths of biting a hole through a card after picking up what seemed my 23rd consecutive stiff hand against a dealer's 10-up card. I've stared at the ceiling in the mockingly named Victory Motel, wondering how in the name of Probability I could be good enough to win $400 in six hours of steady play downtown and bad enough to then lose $100 in each of nine Las Vegas Strip casinos in only three and a half hours that evening."

—Peter A. Griffin, *The Theory of Blackjack*

"Someone told me you can't win on cruise ships. What do they mean by that? I win everywhere. I know how to do it. It isn't like it's that big a secret but for some reason no one seems to follow me. Here's what I do. I sit on the last seat [third base] so I make all the decisions for the whole table. That's how you do it. I base my strategy on whether or not I think the dealer will bust and I base this on looking at the cards that are in play. You just feel these things. I never lose anywhere. I win on cruise ships and in Atlantic City. I haven't been to Vegas yet but I'm planning on it. I don't think I need to read any books on it. They'd just confuse me. Blackjack is easy as pie with blueberry topping and whipped cream."

—Ben Shue, New York, blackjack player (six months)

"Some players are really animals when they play. I once had a player push over the whole blackjack layout and try to attack me. The guy had lost a fortune and he was playing recklessly. He was doubling his bets after all his losses and he hit a streak of maybe 14, 15 hands in a row that he lost. He was getting wiped out. First he started cursing me—as if I had something to do with his bad luck. Then he started threatening me. Then he went for me. We had him arrested for assault. Would you believe that the guy returned the next week, out on bail, and tried to play at my table again? He said to me, quite seriously, that he believed he was due to beat me sooner or later. I hoped he meant at blackjack and not physically. Anyway, the security team asked him to leave. He left."

—Andrea Glenn, Las Vegas, blackjack dealer

"Blackjack . . . is a life-or-death struggle between the skillful card player and the ever vigilant casino surveillance experts. It is a 'game' played for real money and at high stakes, with each side maintaining its own cadre of analysts, strategists, generals and foot soldiers. It is a battle of wits and nerve. Within this context, any manner of strategic assault and devious camouflage is permitted. At its best, this is a gentleman's game. . . . At times like these [the arrest of counters], blackjack is not a game, a sport, a gentlemen's competition—but a *real* war, where the two sides are not 'opponents' but true enemies. . . ."

—Arnold Snyder, *Blackjack Forum*, December 1995

"Few achievements in life are more gratifying or immediately profitable than getting a big play down in a casino. The satisfaction comes from the planning, the teamwork, the precision timing, and, of course, the play itself. Afterwards, the sense of accomplishment and the mutual respect among team members is a feeling no person can ever forget. Of course, it's also rather nice to put a few dollars in your pocket. Let me ask you something. When you are on your deathbed, what will you want to remember about your life? Just *what* is a more satisfying achievement—how much money you made for some fat corporate executive who never knew you existed, or a play you got down in a casino? A play during which the casino never even had an idea it was getting screwed . . . a play when the casino thought you were some lucky stiff on the streak of your life."

—Dustin D. Marks, *Cheating at Blackjack*

"If I had to do it over again, I would never play blackjack. If I had strength of character, I would quit now and never play another hand of blackjack. But I can't do it over and I can't stop. I love the game. I love it the way those golf nuts love golfing. They can't stay off the links, I can't stay away from the blackjack tables. I've lost so much money at this game that the casinos should erect a monument to me."

—Leonard Simmons, Texas, blackjack player

"The game of blackjack is a big bore. Writers say that you get to make choices but really you have to play basic strategy to have a prayer so that all the choices are made already depending on the hand. You could sit a computer down to play for you because there really are no choices to make if you know what you're doing. It's a big bore."

—William Benning, Florida, former blackjack player

"Everything the books say is true. I know so because I do it. I count cards. I vary my bets. I win. I've been winning for 15 years now and it isn't a fluke or just luck. You don't get rich playing blackjack but you sure as hell aren't being taken by the casinos as so many other players are. It took me maybe two months to get good but now it's no problem to play for a few hours. I can count, carry on a conversation. It's not that hard once you get the hang of it. Why anyone would go to a casino and not play a game where they can get an edge is a question I've asked myself a million times. You don't have much of an edge when you count but an edge is an edge. You don't win every time out but you win overall. What more could you want?"

—Terry Reilly, Pennsylvania, card counter

"People come to Las Vegas to forget the burdens of their workaday world, to enjoy a weekend fling, lose themselves in fantasy and, as they say, to let 'er rip. And so they do. I have seen normally rational people blow thousands at the tables in a few frenzied hours, drunk on the crazy magic of the place—only to come crashing back to reality the next day, their faces masks of shock and despair. In the midst of all this insanity, I go about the business of making a living playing 21. I enjoy Las Vegas to the fullest, including top-name shows, the gourmet dining, and the elegant accommodations, but I avoid the traps. I hit and I split. I make money and then I move on."

—Bryce Carlson, *Blackjack for Blood*

"You must be cold and calculating. Steely blue eyes will do. You must have no emotional attachment to that money you throw on the table. It must mean little to you. If you lose it, so what; it's only money. If you cannot afford to lose it, you cannot afford to bet it. In no way is short-run profit guaranteed. You cannot plan on winning the next hand. Lady Luck has a heart of stone. You will be ahead if you play long enough, but only if. The actual play is a hand at a time and you must be emotionally able to handle the losses that will occur regularly. Bet an amount you can live without. You must be able to withstand a one-day loss of 20 times whatever is your big bet, because such a loss will occur occasionally."

—Stanford Wong, *Professional Blackjack*

"The problem with blackjack is that everyone is an expert. Everyone is always offering their opinions on how you should play this hand or how you should bet. They tell you when to double and split. You sit at some tables and people argue with perfect strangers over what to do with this hand or that hand. People you've never seen before in your life start calling you names if you don't play the game the way they expect you to play it. In any other area of life you would see some manners. But at the blackjack table people will call you an idiot for no apparent reason. Usually these people don't even play basic strategy but they still think they're experts. But I wouldn't play any other game."

—Emma Levinson, Massachusetts, blackjack player

"In Las Vegas it seems that everyone has written a book on blackjack. All self-published. I played with one guy, he told me to buy his book. I did. He sold it to me right there at the table. The dealer was laughing. It was barely readable, it was so poorly written. The advice matched the writing. The guy had never heard of basic strategy and his way of counting cards was absurd. Once two guys who thought they were experts had a fierce argument about how much to bet off the top in single-deck games where the casino has no edge. They almost came to blows. Blackjack is filled with characters and they all have books."

—Ralph Davis, Arizona, blackjack player

"I am so bored with being a dealer. It's the same old stuff every day. Here's what you hear when the players come to the table. 'Have you been hot today, Kristen?' Or they'll say, 'I hope you're going to be good to me.' When you ask them how they are, they'll say, 'We'll see after a few hands.' They never just say, 'Okay, how are you?' Or they glare at you and say, 'I'm miserable.' Or they'll start moaning about their losses. During the game, they threaten not to tip you if you don't give them good hands. 'You'll win, Kristen, if I win!' Most of the people who think they have a good sense of humor don't. Everyone thinks you know all the other dealers because you work in the same place. I barely know the other dealers. Players will scold you and say, 'Better tell Louise that she should smile more when the players win.' I don't even know who Louise is! These are just the regular people, mind you. The really obnoxious ones you don't want to know about. And there seem to be millions of those! If people are so miserable when they gamble, why do it? You wouldn't catch me dead playing blackjack. I'm burnt out. I want to find a career where I never see another blackjack player ever again."

—Kristen Clements, Las Vegas, blackjack dealer

"Gamblers everywhere else in the world are suckers. It's Americans who figured out how to play blackjack to win. Who do you think were the forefathers of basic strategy? That's right. And who was the first card-counting revolutionary? Ditto. And the strategist who came up with card-counting teams? Yep. And the foot-controlled blackjack computer? Uh huh. And comp counting? Yours truly—a God-fearin' Texan. 'So,' you ask, 'why do Americans love blackjack so much?' Because it *can be beaten*. Period. Probably not by 99.9% of the people who play it, but by a few, and that's enough to keep the hope alive. Comp wizards love blackjack too, but for another reason. Blackjack is the only mainstream casino game for which the house advantage versus a particular player can not be readily determined. That's because the magnitude of the casino's advantage depends on the skill of the player, and players' skills vary widely. Still, the house assigns the same expected loss to every player, usually somewhere around 2% because that's what the casino wins on average. Bottom line? Once you become a good blackjack player your (comp) gains will be subsidized by the losses of the bad players."

—Max Rubin, *Comp City*

"On the whole, my experiences playing blackjack have been fun. Most of the blackjack players I've encountered have been friendly and rather intelligent. I find that many of them have read the same books as I have. Playing blackjack is a nice way to pass the time. You can't get hurt if you know what you're doing."

—Lily Conrad, age 83, Canada, blackjack player

"Blackjack pits should be divided into smoking and non-smoking pits. Not just smoking and non-smoking tables. I can't think when some chimney is smoking next to me. I once punched a guy who was smoking a cigar and blowing the smoke in my face. He beat me up."

—Joseph G. Donnelly, Georgia, blackjack player

"The real struggle is not between you and the casino. The real struggle is between you and yourself."

—The Captain in *Beat the Craps out of the Casinos: How to Play Craps and Win!*

Glossary

Ace: The highest card in poker, the die with one dot, and another name for a dollar. In blackjack the ace can be valued as either one or 11.

Ace adjustment: The variation in bet size based on the number or proportion of aces remaining to be played.

Ace-five count: A simple counting system where the player keeps track of the aces and fives only.

Ace-jack bonus: Some casinos offer double payment for a blackjack made with a jack of spades and an ace of spades.

Ace poor: A lower than average number of aces remain in the unplayed cards.

Ace rich: The remaining cards have more aces, proportionally, than normal.

Ace side count: Keeping track of the number of aces played separately from your counting system.

Act: The persona adopted by some card counters to give the impression that they are not skilled or expert players.

Action: The amount of money you wager over a given period of time. Used as a basis of judgment for comps.

Action player: A player who bets big and for long periods of time. Sometimes used as a euphemism for stupid player.

Advantage: The percentage edge that a player has over the casino or the casino has over the player.

Advantage player: Used to mean a cheat but now means anyone who can get an edge over the casino.

Agent: A person who works with a cheat.

Anchor man: The player who sits to the right of the dealer and is the last to act on his hand. Sometimes referred to as a *third baseman.*

Automatic shuffling machines: Machines that shuffle the cards for the dealer. They usually speed up the game and allow the casino to cut more cards out of play without the attendant down time of waiting for the dealer to shuffle.

Backliner: A person who places a wager on another player's betting square.

Backlining: Placing a wager on another player's betting square. Sometimes known as piggybacking. Good technique to use when guerrilla Wonging in blackjack.

Back counting: To count cards while not playing. This is the technique used by guerrilla gamblers to only bet when they have the edge.

Back room: Card counters will occasionally refer to the "back room"— which is the place card counters are taken when the casino is trying to discourage or ban their play. Often has hints of violence, as in "I was back roomed!"

Bad Rack: Casinoese for a player who doesn't pay his gambling debts.

Balanced count: A card-counting system where all the numbers ultimately add up to zero. The Hi-Lo that is recommended in this book is a balanced count.

Bankroll: The total amount of money a gambler sets aside to gamble with.

Bar: The banning of an individual from playing in a casino. Used against cheats and expert players alike.

Barber pole: A bet consisting of different colored chips all mixed together. Trick often used by card counters to cover the amount of money they are betting.

Base dealer: A dealer (card mechanic) who deals from the bottom of the deck.

Basic strategy: In blackjack, the best possible play of any given hand based on the dealer's up card and the two cards you possess. Basic strategies have been formulated by computers for all possible player hands versus all dealer up cards in all types of blackjack games.

Beard: Someone who places bets for a cheat.

Beat: To win money from someone by cheating.

Bet blind: To bet without seeing your cards.

Bet sizing: To vary the amount of one's bet based on one's advantage at that moment. The Kelly Criterion is a bet-sizing scheme.

Bet variations: To change the level of betting. This can be done by bet sizing or by some other indicator.

Betting efficiency: The measure of how closely a card-counting system approximates the advantage that the player has in a given situation. The highest efficiency is 100 percent.

Betting handle: The total amount of money a player intends to gamble with during a session or over a period of time.

Betting ratio: The ratio of the highest bet to the lowest bet that a person is making.

Betting spread: The highest bet a person is placing in comparison to the lowest bet that person is placing.

Betting strategy: The scheme a player uses to size his bets.

Bias: The tendency of the game to favor either the dealer or the player for prolonged periods. In retrospect, it is easy to ascertain how a given game was biased. Unfortunately, it is much more difficult to predict biases and most systems that claim to do so in blackjack have not held up.

Big Player: The member of a blackjack team that bets the big money on the high counts.

Black action: A bet made with a black ($100) chip.

Black book: The list of excluded persons that every casino in Vegas contributes to. Contains the names and photos of known cheats and law-abiding card counters alike.

Blackjack: A natural. Composed of a 10-value card and an ace. Usually pays off at three to two.

Blacks: Chips valued at $100.

Blind shuffle: Cheating method where the dealer appears to mix the cards while keeping the deck stacked in a prearranged order.

Blistering a deck: Cheating method where certain cards are blistered with a pin so that they can be identified by the dealer touching them.

Body-time: For purposes of comping, how much time your body is at a table. Some of this time will not be risk-time. Card counters who sit out a few hands in low counts will often get credit for playing time.

Bombing for a blackjack: Scanning technique for determining a better-than-average chance for getting a blackjack.

Bottoms: A cheating method where the dealer deals from the bottom of the deck.

Break: To go over 21 in blackjack. Sometimes referred to as busting.

Break down a bet: Separate chips by various denominations. Used by dealers to accurately pay off bets.

Break the deck: To shuffle the cards before continuing play.

Bridge: A card known to the player that is bent.

Bubble peek: Cheating method where the dealer squeezes the top card of the deck between his index finger and the heel of his hand so as to get a look at its denomination before dealing it.

Burn a card: To bury a card at the beginning or during a blackjack round. Used as a device to prevent card counters from getting an edge.

Bury a card: Place a card in the middle of a deck.

Bust: To go over 21 in blackjack. Same as breaking.

Bustout bet: A side bet that is made after the dealer's second card is shown. If the dealer has a hand between 12 and 16, you can place a bet that the dealer's next card will be a 10-value card. Often pays two to one.

Bust Out Joint: A casino that cheats the players.

Buy-in: Exchanging cash for chips at a table. The original amount of cash exchanged for chips in the beginning of a player's action.

Caddy blackjack: Blackjack game where the deal rotates from player to player. Private games use this and games in venues where the casino is not allowed to bank games.

Cage: The cashiers area of a casino where chips are exchanged for cash.

Camouflage: To play in such a way as not to alert the casino that you can count cards at blackjack. Sometimes this is done by making stupid plays that cost you money.

Candy Store: A casino with an excellent and relatively easily beatable blackjack game.

Capping a bet: Adding more chips to a bet that has already won. Also known as *past posting.*

Capping a deck: Adding cards to the top of the deck after the shuffle.

Card clumping: The tendency of groups of cards to stay together for prolonged periods in shoe games because of insufficient shuffling by the dealer.

Card counting: Keeping track of the cards that have been played in blackjack to determine whether you or the casino has the advantage. The only way to win at blackjack in the long run.

Card dauber: A person who marks the cards for purposes of cheating.

Card mechanic: A skilled manipulator who can control the cards as he or she shuffles. Technique used strictly for cheating.

Casing: Keeping track of the cards that have been played.

Casino advantage: The edge, usually shown as a percentage, that the house has over the player.

Casino host: The person responsible for seeing that high rollers are treated with the dignity and graciousness their wallets merit.

Casino manager: The person responsible for seeing that the games of a given casino are handled properly.

Casino win rate: How much of all the money bet a casino wins at a given game. In blackjack the win rate hovers around 15 percent.

Center field: The center betting position in a blackjack game with seven betting squares.

Chasing losses: Increasing your bets in order to recoup what you've lost. Not a good way to play, unless you're using this as a camouflage technique in high counts that call for increased betting.

Check rack: The tray that holds the chips for a game.

Checks: Another name for chips.

Chinese blackjack: A dealer with a 10 up and a four in the hole. Often when the dealer peeks at his hole card, he will mistake the four for an ace. Named after Chinese players who like to squeeze their cards and often mistake a four for an ace in so doing.

Choppy game: A game where neither the house nor the player has been winning consistently. Opposite of a streak.

Clocking: Keeping track of the results of a particular game.

Clumping: When specific groups of cards stay together through the shuffle. Some experts can follow these groups and know when they are about to appear in the game. If it's a clump of high cards, they will bet bigger than usual. If it's a clump of low cards, they will bet smaller than usual.

Cold table: Any table where you are losing.

Color for color: To pay off a bet with the same denomination chips as wagered.

Color up: To exchange smaller denomination chips for larger denomination chips at a table.

Comp: The "freebies" that casinos give out for certain levels of betting.

Concealed computers: Devices used by some blackjack players to get an advantage over the house. These are now considered cheating methods and some states have imposed heavy jail sentences for their use.

Conversion factor: How the running count is divided or multiplied in order to arrive at the true count. This is based on the number of cards that have been played.

Cooler: A deck or shoe of prearranged cards inserted into the game by cheats.

Counter catcher: The individual hired by a casino to catch card counters. Pejoratively known as the "catcher-dog."

Counter measures: The steps casinos take to protect their games against card counters.

Counting down a deck: Keeping track of the count as the cards are dealt. Some individuals practice counting down a deck at home, believing that speed is important. It isn't. No dealer can deal as fast to players as one person can deal to himself.

Cover: How a card counter disguises the fact that he is counting cards. Sometimes this cover is changing the style of one's decisions or betting so as not to be too predictable, to changing one's appearance so as not to appear too intelligent.

Credit line: The amount of credit a player is allowed by a given casino.

Credit manager: The person in charge of determining casino credit for a player.

Crimp: To bend a card for later identification.

Crossroader: A casino cheat.

Cull: To sort cards out of a deck for later use as a dealer shuffles.

Cut card: The card that indicates the shuffle point in a shoe game.

Cut the deck: To divide the deck before dealing. Usually done by a player.

DAS: Abbreviation for double after splits.

Day shift: The casino work shift that usually runs from 10 am to 6 pm.

Daub: To cheat at cards by placing a small amount of paint or ink on a card for purposes of later identifying it.

Dead table: A table that is manned and ready for action but has no players.

Deal: To give out the cards.

Dealer: The casino employee who staffs the games offered.

Dealer bias: A shoe or deck that favors the dealer.

Dealing seconds: Dealing the second card in the deck until you need the first card to either make a good hand or break a player's hand.

Deck: Fifty-two cards from two through ace in four separate suits: hearts, diamonds, spades and clubs.

Desperado: A gambler who plays foolishly, usually chasing his losses.

Deuces: The twos in cards.

Discard rack: The plastic, upright receptacle for cards that have already been played in shoe games.

Double down: In blackjack, to double the size of your bet and receive only one card. You can also double for less than the initial wager.

Double exposure: Blackjack game where both of the dealer's cards are dealt face up.

Double up system: This is also known as the Martingale family of wagers. Player attempts to get all his previous losses back by increasing (doubling) his previous bet. Can ultimately lead to disastrous losses.

Drop: The casino term for the total amount of money and markers wagered at the tables.

Drop box: Where the money is dropped after a player cashes in. Usually located under the table.

Dummy up: To shut up. Some casino pit people will say to chatty dealers: "Dummy up and deal."

Dumping: A casino table that is losing money to the players.

Early surrender: Rarely-found rule in blackjack that allows players to forfeit half their bet, even if the dealer had a blackjack.

Eating cards: To increase the number of hands you are playing in order to use up the remaining cards in the deck. Usually done in low counts when the deck favors the casino. Player will bet the minimum but spread to several hands. Can also be used as a cheating method by hitting for more cards even after you've gone over 21.

Edge: Having the advantage in a game.

Eighty-six: The same as barring someone from playing in the casino.

Eldest hand: The player to the dealer's immediate left.

Element of ruin: The likelihood that a player (or team) will lose his bankroll. Usually expressed as a percentage figure. If you have a one percent element of ruin, you will lose your bankroll one percent of the time on average.

End play: The play of the hands at the end of a deck or shoe when one's advantage is known.

Even money: A bet that pays off at one to one.

Expectation: The amount, usually expressed in a percent or in dollars, that a player should win or lose over an extended period of time. This is based on the game and the player's skill level.

Exposed card: A card inadvertently shown during the play of a hand.

Eye in the sky: The cameras, usually in bubbles, located throughout the casino that videotape the action.

Face cards: The king, queen and jack. Also known as *picture cards.*

Face down: Games where the first two cards are not exposed to the other players. Player may touch the cards to see them. Most hand-held single- and double-deck games are dealt this way.

Face up: Games where all cards are dealt with their values exposed. Most shoe games are dealt this way. Generally, players may not touch their first two cards in such a game.

False cut: A cut of the cards that leaves them in the same order that they were in before.

Fair game: A game where neither the house nor the player has an edge. A game that pays off all bets based on the true odds of that wager.

Favorable deck: A deck whose remaining cards favors the player. Also known as *positive* deck.

First base: The seat at the table immediately to the dealer's left.

First basing: Attempting to see the dealer's hole card when he checks for a blackjack.

Five-card Charlie: Bonus paid for a hand that totals 21 or less than 21 made with five cards.

Five-card surrender: This rule is found in some foreign casinos. A player who has five cards totaling less than 21 may surrender his hand.

Five count: In blackjack, keeping track of the fives only. In craps, the method used by the Captain to avoid horrendous rolls of the dice [see my book *Beat the Craps Out of the Casinos: How to Play Craps and Win!* (Bonus Books)].

Flashing: To show a card to a player. Dealers can flash their hole cards and, in hand-held games, players can flash their first two cards to the other players.

Flat bet: Any player who bets the same amount hand after hand.

Floorman: Individual responsible for supervising several tables in a pit.

Fluctuation in probability: A mathematical term that means good or bad luck, or good or bad streaks, depending on whether the fluctuation is in your favor or not.

Front loader: A blackjack dealer who unknowingly shows his hole card as he places it under the up card.

Front money: Money previously deposited with the cage and used by the player to draw markers against.

Fun book: Coupon book used by casinos to encourage play. Can be used to get an advantage at certain games. Also, contains discounts for drinks, food, etc.

Gaffed: Any gaming device that has been rigged.

Gambling stake: Amount of money reserved for gambling. Same as *bankroll*.

George: A good tipper.

Glim: A small, concealed mirror used to cheat at cards.

Going south: Putting chips in one's pocket so that the casino can't get a good estimate of how much you've won.

Grand Martingale: A wagering system where you double your bets and add one extra unit after a lose. Extremely dangerous betting practice.

Graveyard shift: The 2 am to 10 am working shift in a casino.

Greens: Chips valued at $25.

Griffin Investigations: A detective agency used by Las Vegas casinos to keep track of known cheats. Unfortunately, some card counters are also in this agency's *black book* even though they aren't criminals.

Grifter: A scam artist.

Grind: Derogatory term for low roller. A small-money player. A blackjack player who tries to eek out small wins to make a living.

Grind down: The casino winning all of a player's money due to the advantage it has on bets. Blackjack players try to do this to the casinos.

Grind joint: A casino that caters to low rollers.

Grind system: Any system that attempts to win small amounts frequently against the casinos.

Guerrilla gambling: The combination of smart play and hit-and-run tactics to beat the casinos at their own games.

H-17: Abbreviation for a game where the dealers hit their soft 17s.

Hand: A player's cards in a card game.

Hand-held game: A blackjack game, usually single- and double-deck, dealt from the hand and not from a shoe.

Hand mucking: A casino dealer who palms and then substitutes cards into a game at the appropriate time.

Hard hand: A blackjack hand that cannot use the ace as an 11.

Head-to-head: To play against the dealer with no other player in the game. Sometimes referred to as *face-to-face*, or *heads up*.

Heat: Surveillance by the casino of a suspected card counter. Or pressure put on a card counter to leave before being banned. Also, known as *steam*.

High card: A jack, queen, king or ace.

High-Low: A different spelling for the counting system Hi-Lo in blackjack.

High-low pickup: A cheating method at blackjack when the dealer picks up the cards in high-low alternating order.

High roller: A player who plays for large stakes.

Hit: To receive another card on your hand in blackjack.

Hit and run: Using guerrilla gambling techniques.

Hold: The actual amount that the casinos take from their games.

Holdout shoe: A shoe that has been tampered with to allow the dealer to deal seconds.

Hole card: The second card dealt to the dealer in blackjack, that is face down. Any face-down card.

Hole-card play: Any method used to get a glimpse of the dealer's hole card and to make strategy decisions according to this information.

Hot: A player who has been winning.

Hot and cold system: Another name for the streak method of betting.

Hot table: A table where the players have been winning.

House edge: The mathematical edge that the casino has on a given bet.

House person: A dealer who is unusually concerned with the casino's profits. A dealer who enjoys watching the players lose. A dealer who identifies with the casino.

Hustler: A gambling cheat or a dealer who attempts to get players to tip him.

Index: The count necessary to deviate from basic strategy. The value of a card.

Insurance: A side wager at blackjack, for up to half the original wager, that the dealer has a blackjack when he has an ace showing.

Irregularity: A departure from the standard procedures at a given game.

Jackpot: A grand payout, either on a machine or at a table game.

Joint bankroll: Two or more players combining their bankrolls so as to wager against a larger bank.

Joker: A wild card that can usually be used as a substitute for any card in the deck. Usually resembles a court jester. On occasion as a promotional gimmick, jokers will be added to blackjack. This is usually good for the players if none of the other rules are altered.

Junket: A trip arranged, organized and subsidized by a casino to bring gamblers to play at the games.

Junket master: The person in charge of a junket.

Kelly Criterion: A betting system utilizing the knowledge of a player's advantage at any given point in the game. The player bets the proportion of his bankroll that represents his advantage.

Key-card concept: The idea that at certain times in certain games one or two denominations are more important than even the count. For example, no matter how high the count, if there are no more aces in the deck, there will be no blackjacks.

Kibitzer: An individual who is not playing at a given game but is giving unwanted advice.

Laydown: A bet. Also, someone who quits in the middle of a game.

Layout: The design imprinted with the various bets at a given game.

Level one system: Any card-counting system that uses $+1$ or -1 as the value of the cards that are counted.

Levels: Honest gaming equipment and personnel. As in: "This game is on the level."

Locationing: The ability to memorize a group of cards so that when one of the group appears the player knows which cards will follow.

Long run: The concept that a player could play so often that probability would tend to even out. That is, you would start to see the total appearance of numbers approximating what probability theory predicts. A long-run player is one who plays a lot!

Lose all to natural: A rule found in Europe and some other areas that stipulates that should the dealer have a natural, all bets—including double downs and splits—are lost. Horrible rule.

Mark: An individual who has been or is going to be cheated. A sucker.

Marked cards: Cards that have been physically altered in subtle ways so that either a cheating dealer and/or a cheating player can read them when they are face down.

Marker: The check a player fills out before receiving casino credit at a table. A promissory note or I.O.U.

Martingale system of wagering: Doubling one's bet after a loss in an attempt to make back all your losses and a small win. Extremely dangerous.

Match play: A casino promotion where players are given special chips that they can bet. They are paid off in regular casino chips on a win.

Maximum bet: The highest bet allowed at a given table.

Mechanic: Anyone who can manipulate the cards.

Mimic the dealer: A playing strategy where the player imitates the dealer who plays by the house rules. The house has approximately a 5.5 percent advantage over this type of player.

Minimum bet: The smallest bet allowed at a given table.

Mirroring: Using any shiny object to get a peek at the dealer's hole card.

Money at risk: Money that has been wagered and can be lost.

Money management: The methods a player uses to conserve his bankroll from ruin.

Money plays: The call that alerts the dealer and the pit that you are betting cash and not chips.

Mucker: Anyone who uses sleight-of-hand techniques to cheat at cards or other games.

Multiparameter count: A card-counting technique where you keep a separate count of the cards that count as zero in your normal card-counting system.

Multiple-deck game: Blackjack played with more than one deck which gives the house more of an advantage over the player. Also, any shoe game with more than one deck.

Multiple hands: To play more than one hand at blackjack.

Nail: To catch someone cheating. "We nailed him."

Natural: A blackjack, an ace and a 10-value card.

Negative count: A count that favors the casino.

Negative progression: Any system of wagering where you increase bets after a loss.

Nickel: A five-dollar chip—usually red.

Nut: The total amount of money needed to run a casino or the total amount of money an individual needs to succeed at what he is doing.

Odds: The likelihood of a given event happening.

Off the top: The first hand from after the shuffle.

On the square: A game that is honest.

Opposition betting: Betting against the count. Used by card trackers and clump players.

Over-Under 13: Side bet with a very heavy house edge that the next hand's first two cards will total either over 13 or under 13. Dealer wins all 13s.

Paddle: The tool used to push the money into the drop box.

Paint: A picture card. When a player says, "Paint me," he is asking for a picture card.

Painter: A name for an individual who cheats at cards by daubing them with a small amount of paint. Also known as a *Picasso*.

Palm: To conceal money or chips in one's hand.

Parlay: To double one's bet after a win.

Past posting: Placing a winning wager *after* a decision has been reached. Usually done by capping a bet.

Pat hand: Any hand in a card game that does not require getting additional cards.

P.C.: The house edge expressed as a percentage.

Peeking: A dealer checking to see what the hole card is when he has an ace or 10 on top.

Penetration: How deeply a dealer deals into a deck or a shoe at blackjack. This is a key variable in assessing the beatability of a blackjack game.

Penny ante: A game played for small stakes.

Pinching: Illegally removing chips from one's bet after an unfavorable decision.

Pit: An area consisting of a number of gaming tables.

Pit boss: The individual in charge of a pit.

Playing efficiency: The measure which indicates how closely a card-counting system responds to changes in playing strategy and deck composition. Systems without side counts can approach a maximum efficiency of 70 percent.

Ploppy: The very worst kind of player. Plays his or her own strategy and is not adverse to sharing his or her "secrets"—for free!

Plus-minus system: Another name for the Hi-Lo system or High-Low system of card counting. Cards are given a +1 or a −1 value.

Positive count: A count that favors the player.

Power of the pen (or pencil): The ability to issue hotel comps to players on the part of some casino executives.

Preferential shuffling: Shuffling the cards when the remaining deck favors the players and dealing the cards when the remaining deck favors the house. Devastating method used by some casinos to "cheat" players.

Premium players: A casino term meaning big bettors or players with big credit lines.

Press: To increase the amount wagered, usually by doubling it, after a win.

Producer: Casino term for a player who losses often and for large sums. This individual is a producer of profits for the casino.

Prop: Another name for *shill.* A person employed by a casino to play a game to generate action. Most often used in baccarat and poker.

Proportional betting: To bet a proportion of your money based on your advantage or some other betting scheme.

Proposition bet: Any bet that is a longshot and carries a heavy house edge. Usually side bets at blackjack are prop bets and should be avoided.

Push: Casinoese for tie.

Quarters: Chips valued at $25. Also known as *greens.*

Random shuffle: To intermix the cards in such a manner that no intentional clumping takes place. In any random shuffle there will be streaks of low and high cards but these will not be predictable. A new deck requires seven shuffles for the cards to be intermixed randomly.

Rank count: A card-counting system that only keeps track of one or a couple of card values.

Rating: Evaluating a player's play for the purpose of comps.

Rating card: The card used for rating a player.

Reds: Casino chips worth five dollars.

RFB: Complimentary room, food and beverage.

Rich deck: A deck that has many 10-value cards remaining to be played.

Riffle: Splitting the deck in two and shuffling both sections into each other.

Riot act: Being told by a casino in no uncertain terms that your play is not wanted and that, if you return, you will be arrested. This is being "read the riot act."

Ruin: Losing your bankroll. The probability of losing every penny of your bankroll. See *element of ruin.*

Rule card: The card that shows the rules for a given game.

Running count: In blackjack, the raw count that has not been divided (or multiplied) by the number of decks remaining.

Rush: A quick winning streak.

S-17: Abbreviation for dealer standing on all 17s.

Scanning: The quick perusal of the cards that have been played for the purposes of determining advantage.

Scam: Any scheme to defraud a casino or player.

Scared money: Money a player can't afford to lose. Also known as *perspiration pennies.*

Scratch: In hand-held games, the player's brushing of the cards along the felt to indicate that he wants a hit.

Seconds: A cheating method where the second card and not the top card is dealt. The top card is saved to either make a hand or break a hand.

Session: A given period of play at a casino. Usually terminated at a pre-determined time, or at a certain level of wins or losses.

Shift boss: The individual in charge of the casino during a given work shift.

Shill: An individual employed by the casino to play games that are being underplayed.

Shoe: The box that holds the decks for a card game.

Short deck: To remove certain cards from the deck or shoe to increase one's chances of winning. The casino would want to remove large cards; the players would want to remove small cards.

Short run: The limited amount of time during any given session when probability theory will seemingly be skewered by streaks or fluctuations.

Short shoe: A blackjack shoe that has had cards advantageous to the players removed.

Shuffle check: Some casinos require a floorman to check the shuffle before the dealer puts the cards in the shoe. This check is to insure that the cards are thoroughly mixed so shuffle trackers are thwarted.

Shuffle point: The number of cards or decks a dealer deals out before he breaks the deck or shoe and shuffles.

Shuffle tracking: Watching as the cards are being shuffled to memorize and later locate groups of cards.

Shuffle up: Technique used to thwart card counters. Dealer will shuffle after every deal or when a player enters a game and bets big money.

Side bet: A second bet, in addition to the normal bet, on a proposition at a table game. For example, insurance and Over-Under 13.

Side count: To keep a separate count of cards other than those in your basic counting system. Generally, counting systems that value the ace as zero will keep a separate count for them.

Single-deck blackjack: The best game in the casino if the rules are liberal.

Slug: A group of cards that have been prearranged in a given order and inserted into a deck. Any group of cards inserted whole into a deck. Also, a piece of rounded metal inserted into a slot machine that mimics a coin.

Snapper: An archaic term for a blackjack. A *red snapper* is a blackjack composed of two red cards. Also a term for a dealer who audibly snaps the card being dealt. This sometimes indicates that a dealer is dealing seconds.

Soft hand: A hand at blackjack where the ace can be used as either 11 or one.

Soft players: Unskilled players who are easy to beat.

Split: To make two hands from a pair at blackjack.

Spook: A player who gets the dealer's hole card in blackjack and relays that information to his accomplices.

Spooking: The process of discovering the dealer's hole card at blackjack by another player—who is usually at another table—and then relaying that information to the player who is playing against the dealer.

Spread: The difference between the minimum and maximum bets a player makes. Also, the total number of hands a player plays during a round.

Squares: A game or player that is honest. "This game is on the square."

Stacked deck: A deck that has been prearranged.

Stand: To keep the cards you have. Not to draw any more cards.

Steaming: A player who is visibly upset and is playing recklessly at a table. Sometimes used as a camouflage technique in order to get big bets out.

Stiff: In blackjack, a total of 12 through 16. Also, not to tip a cocktail server.

Strip: Las Vegas Boulevard. Three miles of casinos.

Strip shuffle: Dealer pulls a group of cards off the top, inverting the order of the groups.

Sub: A secret pocket in a dealer uniform where he deposits chips he's stealing.

Surrender: A blackjack option where the player may give up half his bet. Player loses full bet if the dealer has a blackjack, however. Sometimes known as *late surrender.*

Sweat: Casinos who are upset by players winning are said to "sweat" out their games. Also, a player who is losing and is worried.

Swing shift: The shift that runs from 6 pm to 2 am.

Table games: Any game in a casino that is played at a table.

Table-hopping: Moving from table to table in a casino. Utilizing guerrilla techniques.

Take down: To recall a wager before a decision.

Take the edge: Giving yourself an edge at a game—usually by cheating. Card counters have an edge without cheating.

Tapped out: To lose one's entire bankroll.

TARGET: A method to find hot tables.

Team play: Anywhere from two to several to dozens of players working together to beat the casinos.

Tell: An unconscious signal that a dealer gives when peeking for a blackjack. Also any unconscious signal that allows you to know what a player has.

Third base: The position to the dealer's right at blackjack. Player acts on his hand last.

Toke: A tip to a casino employee.

Toke hustler: A dealer who tries to get the players to tip him.

Tom: Casinoese for a poor tipper.

Topping the deck: Palming cards.

Tough out: The Captain's term for a skilled player who doesn't beat himself. See my books about the Captain.

Tournaments: Blackjack games where the players compete not just against the dealer but against other players for cash and prizes.

True count: The adjusted count that reflects the count per remaining decks.

True odds: The actual probability of an event happening.

Tubes: Where the chips are kept in the chip rack.

Turn-over dealing: Cheating method where the dealer turns over the cards that have just been played and redeals them.

Twenty-one: Another name for blackjack.

Unbalanced count: A card-counting system where all the values do not add up to zero.

Underground joint: An illegal casino.

Unfavorable deck: A deck or shoe in blackjack that favors the casino.

Unit: The minimum bet a player makes is considered one unit. A player whose minimum bid is five dollars and a player whose minimum is $100 are both betting *one unit.*

Up card: Any card that is dealt face up.

Vic: A sucker. Short for victim.

Vig or vigorish: The casino tax on a bet. Also known as *juice.*

Virgin principle: The superstition that a beginner will have luck. Also known as *beginner's luck.*

Wager: Another term for a bet.

Warp: A bent card. Often in hand-held games where new decks are not routinely put into play, certain cards (10s and aces) will become bent.

Wash: One bet cancels out another bet. Also, the process of mixing fresh cards together on the top of the table without lifting them.

Wild card: A card that can be used for any other card in a game.

Win rate: How much a player will win based upon his counting system. Often expressed as dollars per hands played.

Wired: Poker term that is sometimes used in blackjack to indicate a strong hand such as a 20.

Wongers: Players who practice Wonging.

Wonging: Hit-and-run style of playing in high counts only. Named after blackjack author, Stanford Wong. Requires that a player back count and jump into a game when the conditions are favorable.

Zero: A loser.

Index